P9-DOA-558

GRAND DESIGNS

The Impact of Corporate Strategies on Workers, Unions, and Communities

Charles Craypo and Bruce Nissen, Editors

ILR Press
Ithaca, New York

Library of Congress Cataloging-in-Publication Data

Grand designs: the impact of corporate strategies on workers, unions, and communities / Charles Craypo and Bruce Nissen, editors.
p. cm.
Includes bibliographical references and index.
ISBN 0-87546-309-6 (acid-free paper) — ISBN 0-87546-310-X (pbk)
1. Trade-unions—United States. 2. Industrial relations—United States. 3. Labor—United States. 4. Unemployment—United States. 5. Plant shutdowns—United States. 6. Business relocation—United States. 7. Corporate reorganizations—United States. 8. United States—Economic conditions—1981– 9. Industry and state—United States. 10. Public relations—Trade-unions—United States.
I. Craypo, Charles, 1936– . II. Nissen, Bruce, 1948– .
HD6508.G73 1993
331'.0973—dc20 93-13434

Copies may be ordered through bookstores or directly from

ILR Press
School of Industrial and Labor Relations
Cornell University
Ithaca, NY 14853-3901

Printed on acid-free paper in the United States of America

5 4 3 2

For Jack, Carrie, and Susan—with love.
—Charles Craypo

To my family—Karen, Jared, and Leif—and my friend Lynn Feekin.
—Bruce Nissen

Contents

Tables

Acknowledgments

SOCIAL SCIENCE CASE STUDIES require lengthy periods of organization and gestation. A large number of persons in addition to the authors become involved in the process: the practitioners themselves, various observers, and, of course, colleagues and students. Thus by the time this volume was ready for publication, the list of advisers, benefactors, and facilitators had grown far too long to be enumerated here. It does not, however, diminish our gratitude for those who assisted us in this project.

We both benefited from sabbatical leaves from our respective universities during the preparation of this volume. Especially helpful to Charles Craypo were Notre Dame labor economists Teresa Ghilarducci and Ned Lorenz, whose perceptions and suggestions inspired portions of the analysis, and Frank Wilkinson, whose model of productive systems was instrumental in the conception and organization of the project. Charles Craypo is also indebted to Robert F. Harbrant, Eleanor Kennelly, Stuart Weisberg, and Harold A. Forman for identifying and making available documents and secondary sources on meatpacking.

Bruce Nissen wishes to acknowledge the assistance he received from the staff of the Calumet Project for Industrial Jobs, especially the director, Lynn Feekin.

The contributors are indebted to Erica Fox, whose editorial expertise made the final manuscript more precise, lucid, and focused than it might have been without her, and to Juli Tate, who transcribed seemingly endless changes and revisions in the manuscript. Her skill, patience, and good humor throughout the process are appreciated. Finally, we want to thank Fran Benson and Patty Peltekos, director and managing editor of ILR Press, for sharing our belief that industrial decline in the Midwest is a story worth telling and for their competence and care in seeing the project through to completion.

GRAND DESIGNS

Chapter 1
INTRODUCTION

Charles Craypo and Bruce Nissen

THE YEARS BETWEEN World War II and the mid-1970s have been called the Golden Age of the American economy insofar as it grew faster, accumulated more productive capital, achieved greater gains in productivity, and generated higher living standards than in any other period in recent history (Glyn et al. 1990). Continued real economic growth gave way, however, to long-term decline in goods-producing industries and economic stagflation in the 1970s. Recession in the early 1980s was followed by low rates of real growth and productivity during the rest of the decade and another business downturn in the early 1990s. Real earnings fell for individual workers, and families managed to maintain their living standards only by sending more members into the work force and working longer hours.[1] Many new jobs paid low wages and offered little hope of training and advancement. More Americans were in poverty or were underemployed than before, and overall income distribution shifted in favor of the rich (Harrison and Bluestone 1988; Mishel and Frankel 1991). Internationally, the United States fell far behind its major industrial rivals, Japan and Germany.[2]

The 1980s and early 1990s was also a period of growing trade deficits, unstable dollar exchange rates, rising consumer and federal government debt, widening income and wealth disparities, and rapid increases in the proportion of low-paying service jobs. Union workers and their communities were especially hard hit by these trends. Unions experienced sharp declines not only in membership and bargaining power but also in political influence, public acceptance, and social importance (Kochan, Katz, and McKersie 1986; Marshall 1987; Goldfield 1987; Moody 1988; Nissen 1990b; Craypo 1992). Communities that had been dependent on particular manufacturing industries experienced plant phasedowns and shutdowns as American industry shifted production to alternative plants and locations that promised lower labor costs and more favorable business environments (Cumbler 1989; Nader and Taylor 1986; Perrucci et al. 1988; Nash 1989). *Rustbelt* and *deindustrialized* became apt descriptions of factory towns in eastern and Great Lakes states.

Goods-producing jobs were in decline everywhere in the nation but especially in such midwestern factory towns as Gary, Indiana, Flint, Michigan, and Youngstown, Ohio. During the first half of the 1980s the Midwest fell behind the rest of the country in net job growth; employment rose about 7 percent elsewhere but declined in the Midwest (Markusen and Carlson 1989). With the collapse of the real estate market in the Northeast and other parts of the country, however, the Midwest experienced a period of relative prosperity in the late 1980s and weathered the 1990–91 recession better than other regions.

The downward trend in manufacturing employment nevertheless continues. In the Great Lakes region of the Midwest, the number of jobs in goods-producing sectors (manufacturing, mining, and construction) fell 2.5 percent in 1991, compared with 4.3 percent nationally. Illinois, for example, reported a net loss of 221 manufacturing plants and firms in 1991.[3] Meanwhile, union membership as a ratio of the eligible work force continues to fall. By the early 1990s it was estimated at 16 percent.

One explanation for the decline of union jobs and the ability of unions to organize new members is that negotiated labor costs and restrictive work practices have driven up production costs and product prices and have made unionized firms uncompetitive against domestic (often nonunion) rivals and foreign (often low-wage) producers, and high union wages have prompted employers to resist unionization of their labor forces with every means at their disposal and almost regardless of cost. These explanations are based on orthodox economic theory, case studies, and plausible empirical interpretations of studies that show statistical correlations between unionization and negotiated wage increases on the one hand and declines in the number of production workers on the other (Linneman and Wachter 1986; Northrup 1989; Freeman 1986; Hilke and Nelson 1987; Hirsch 1991).

The conventional explanation implies that wage differentials between union and nonunion plants have been central to the competitive problems of American industry and that the elimination of these differentials would have had enough of an impact on costs and prices to make a difference competitively. As G. N. Hatsopoulos, P. R. Krugman, and L. H. Summers (1988) argue, these are dubious propositions. Moreover, the argument that unions essentially brought about their own decline is not supported by disaggregated industry data on imports, including autos and steel, two industries in which the antiunion argument might appear convincing on the surface (Karier 1992).

In the industrial relations literature, the most prominent explanation for union decline is the "strategic choices" model developed at the Massachusetts Institute of Technology (Kochan, Katz, and McKersie 1986). According to this perspective, an older "New Deal industrial relations system" based on Keynesian economic analysis and the legal protection of the Wagner Act actively promoted unionism and adversarial collective bargaining. For their part, unions practiced job-control unionism, which left business decisions to management and concentrated on legal contracts and contract administration. Now the old system is being superseded by a human resources model, which is primarily nonunion, emphasizes flexible work rules and job classifications, and introduces worker participation in direct production processes. In the face of this more flexible and productive system, it is argued, unions must embrace new forms of labor-management cooperation and participation if they and their employers are to survive and prosper. The old industrial relations system and job-control unionism are dysfunctional in the modern industrial environment.

Alternative explanations for union and community decline have been put forward. One approach argues that large firms in basic manufacturing industries and conglomerate corporations systematically relocated plants and equipment from unionized, high "social wage" (wages and benefits plus public services) locations to nonunion, low-cost southern, southwestern, and overseas sites. These movements "deindustrialized" both the Midwest and some manufacturing centers in other parts of the country, such as New York (Bluestone and Harrison 1982; Markusen 1985). A second alternative interpretation posits that decentralized organization and bargaining structures, once a source of union power, now offer large firms the opportunity to play local unions against international unions and unions against communities, based on the power of individual employers to grant or withhold jobs (Clark 1989; Nader and Taylor 1986). A third interpretation is that large corporations are hegemonic in their relations with communities and local labor unions because these corporations have historically controlled social, political, and economic trends, and union power in the post–World War II period was atypical (Nash 1989; Cumbler 1989).

A fourth explanation is that much of America's manufacturing decline is the result of unwise corporate administrative and operating decisions concerning managerial leadership, products, and production processes (Hayes and Abernathy 1980; Magaziner and Reich 1982). A fifth, and final, explanation is that unions and collective bargaining have had little or no adverse impact on American economic competitiveness and could be positive factors in American economic revitalization if U.S. employers would abandon their traditional animus toward organized labor and accept unions as equal and legitimate institutions in the productive system (Mishel and Voos 1992).

Underlying some of these interpretations is the thesis that American unions historically have been shaped by external forces and events rather than been instrumental in shaping them. According to this view, unions are therefore unable to mount effective counterstrategies and initiatives in response to their current decline. In other words, organized labor is reactive rather than proactive (Brody 1971; Filipelli 1990).

To assess the comparative relevance and accuracy of either conventional or alternative explanations of union and manufacturing decline in American communities, it is essential to examine specific cases. Aggregate numbers and abstract theories call attention to the problem but do not explain how industrial decline actually occurs in specific locations and workplaces. Plant closings, production phasedowns and relocations, labor-management disputes over jobs and the terms of employment, economic development programs, and job wars among cities and states were decisive factors in the structural transition from the Golden Age of the postwar years to the declining standards of the 1980s and 1990s. To gain deeper insight into these trends, it is necessary to describe and analyze them in the context of detailed case studies. Without such case studies, the inferences drawn from the masses of data may miss critical factors that are embedded in structures, institutions, and practices. This book describes and analyzes several case studies of industrial decline in the Midwest in an attempt to provide such a context.

The case studies in this book do not represent a sample of experiences involving manufacturing firms, local unions, and communities. Instead, the firms were involved in disputes and confrontations that received local and sometimes national attention, and the empirical data and contextual information necessary to examine these disputes were available. The cases therefore do not typify the labor and community relationships of all manufacturing firms during the time period covered. They illustrate, however, how evolutionary changes in U.S. industrial systems and environments enable, and perhaps even encourage, large corporations to transform labor relations and corporate-community relationships unilaterally. They do not reveal what most corporations are doing but what most corporations are capable of doing in the context of a changed environment. They chronicle the events and outcomes that occurred in individual plants and communities and the actions of specific local unions, managers, and governments. Taken together, they describe what is generally acknowledged to be the effective dismantling of much of the nation's postwar productive structure and industrial relations systems.

Most of the events and outcomes described in these cases could not have happened in basic American manufacturing before, say, the mid-1970s. These cases show how the events happened and suggest some of the reasons they occurred. They enable us to identify structural and behavioral patterns that point to some of the deeper, more fundamental trends shaping American industry. Case studies do not replace alternative investigative methods; they complement them. Their advantage over purely theoretical and quantitative studies is that they enable us to gain detailed understanding of an occurrence or set of occurrences. Theoretical formulations and aggregate data findings thus can be tested against actual events. One case finding that contradicts a deductive generalization should be enough to suspend judgment or at least call for a revision or expansion of the explanatory framework. Case studies alone cannot provide reliable generalizations, but combined with additional, wider evidence, they can provide a more accurate understanding of trends. Case studies strengthen our ability to understand complexity because they rely on few assumptions. They also address situations as wholes and enable us to assess conjunctions of variables (particularly in comparative case study research), rather than requiring us to assume that variables operate in isolation, which is necessary in much quantitative research. Case studies thus provide a closer analytical look than is possible with purely statistical methods based on correlations of quantifiable data or highly deductive models. Such proximity to the subject matter is crucial to the adequate development and testing of general theories (Ragin 1987; Wilber and Harrison 1978; Diesing 1971).

Employers, especially those who years ago may have reluctantly accepted industrial unions and collective bargaining, now are encouraged to adopt "union-free" labor policies or to force unions to make contract concessions. The objective, in either case, is to lower direct labor costs and remove institutional restrictions on management control over production processes. This is true whether the firm's strategy is to gain a competitive edge over existing firms through "low wages" or to meet competitive threats from aggressive rivals.

At the same time, manufacturing communities suffering job losses and shrinking revenues as a result of capital flight have been encouraged to adopt a "good business climate" approach to local and regional economic growth. This approach emphasizes, almost exclusively, the importance of government subsidies to manufacturers as a way of creating and retaining jobs. It also requires local officials and economic development agencies to lower the social wage and to support businesses in disputes with labor organizations and community activists over job issues. Northern factory towns have thus adopted development strategies similar to those that southern states and cities used against them earlier (Goodman 1979; Crouch 1986; Russo 1986; Glickman and Woodward 1989).

The case studies in this book describe and explain the inability of midwestern workers and communities to sustain good jobs and high living standards in the face of corporate mobility and diversity. They describe and analyze the challenges confronting workers involved in plant closings, industrial strikes, and government-subsidized plant relocations that occurred between the mid-1970s and the early 1990s. These cases show how corporations unilaterally changed the post–World War II industrial system, with the result that unions and communities from the 1970s until the mid-1980s were almost totally ineffective against corporate threats to deny jobs and payrolls on terms other than those dictated by the corporation. By the late 1980s, however, local labor and government began resisting, and in the early 1990s they could point to some isolated gains. The final case study in this book describes how community-based coalitions made such gains in the Calumet steel region of Gary and East Chicago, Indiana.

During the Golden Age, businesses, unions, and local communities developed national manufacturing networks that were consistent with the public policies, technology, and industrial organization systems of that era. Each established its own "grand design" to ensure its current and future interest in the productive system; each had a large stake in economic stability and prosperity.[4] These grand designs were functional and successful in the short run because they served the immediate interests of everyone involved. They enabled firms to adjust price and output at profitable levels, workers to share in the steady increases in output and productivity through collective bargaining, and communities to grow and prosper side by side with their corporate partners. Although the firms differed in detail by locale and in the items manufactured, they shared certain important features.

At the core were absentee-owned and -managed factories and regional service centers. These operated as local units of large firms in oligopolized product markets. They were unionized and subject to the terms and conditions of employment negotiated in company and industrywide bargaining units. Outside the core were locally owned secondary supply and service firms doing business at the discretion of the core companies. These firms also had to observe the prevailing labor standards of a unionized community. A unique form of industrial stability emerged in which unions and communities generally accepted the market objectives, legitimacy, and ultimate operating authority of employers, and firms did not engage in actions that seriously damaged local unions and communities. Differences were resolved through existing institutions and processes, that is, government decision making and collective bargaining.

By the late 1970s, however, the postwar grand designs were starting to collapse. Product market stability, negotiated labor standards, and manufacturing-based community growth broke down. Corporate acceptance of unions and collective bargaining could no longer be taken for granted, and in many instances it had been displaced by aggressive union-avoidance strategies. In defense of their actions, individual firms typically cited intensified competition in their product markets. Secure, profitable product markets, which provided the basis for expanding production and subsequent economies of scale and continued prosperity, in many cases had disappeared or were being threatened by foreign and domestic competition based on superior product design and quality, more efficient production techniques (technology), and lower labor costs. In some instances the new corporate strategies enabled companies to take advantage of changing industrial environments to capture market shares from declining old-line firms in oligopolized markets. In other instances the strategies were designed to get the firms out of threatened product markets as cheaply as possible. In still others the corporation responded by improving its products and production methods or paying lower labor costs or with some combination of the two strategies.

These strategies invariably put firms in an adversarial relationship with unions and communities that might stand in the way of the firms' achieving the objectives of their new strategies. Unions and communities also were viewed as potential sources of funds in the form of contract concessions and business incentives to help finance corporate and production reorganization. Thus, as is evident in the cases studied, employers invariably took aggressive steps to alter their postwar relations with vulnerable unions and communities. Some demanded wage reductions and erosion of working conditions as well as tax exemptions and direct operating subsidies in exchange for indefinite commitments and vague promises to keep plants open, although in practice such commitments were only temporary at best. Others asked for nothing and simply shut down operations and relocated elsewhere. Either way, the effect was to replace the postwar system of industrial interdependency and negotiation with one of economic domination and ultimatum.

The case studies in this volume are arranged roughly in the order in which the events occurred, from the mid-1970s through 1991. Union-management relations and business-community relations evolved from one stage to another during these years. In the first stage, between 1975 and 1985, employers took advantage of the opportunities provided by changing industrial, social, political, and legal environments. Employers that could not or would not relocate production operations elsewhere developed new tactics and weapons to defeat unions at the bargaining table and in strikes. Many employers that could relocate profitably did so, or at least threatened to do so to extract contract concessions from once-powerful local unions. In this way traditional labor standards and conditions were eroded, long-standing manufacturing operations were terminated, and operations were transferred to low-wage, low-tax, and unregulated business environments, at minimal cost and inconvenience to the firms.

Employers also actively enlisted the support of state and municipal governments. Many asked for and received financial subsidies either to stay in particular locations or to move to new ones. In addition, they exploited workers' desire for manufacturing jobs, both in the industrial communities that were losing them and in those that had never had them. They found it relatively easy, for example, to convince states and communities to adopt a low social wage posture or to persuade them to side with business when local activists and unions opposed corporate acquisitions and relocations, when employers demanded local union contract concessions, and when other disputes broke out over the competing rights and interests of those having a stake in existing manufacturing operations.

In the second part of this era, during 1986–91, some unions and communities began to resist these initiatives with limited success. Employers still held the balance of power, however, and as a result they were able to sustain the adverse trends started in the 1970s. By now unions and communities had some experience with and understanding of the changes occurring in postwar labor relations and their relative bargaining power. They also had seen the effects of employer mobility and the constant threat of industrial relocation and were becoming familiar with the uncertain link between public subsidies for business and long-term job creation and retention. Some unions were more sophisticated in their responses to business threats and demands, although not necessarily more successful in resisting them. Corporations continued to control these situations because they had the power to grant or deny industrial jobs, payrolls, and tax revenues to workers and communities (see, for example, Nader and Taylor 1986; chap. 1), but at least labor and government were more aware of the possibility that these situations would arise and therefore better able to participate and respond to them.

The first four cases in this book are from the 1975–85 period. The first is Charles Jeszeck's account of how the major domestic rubber companies relocated tire production from aging plants in Akron, Ohio, to newer plants in the South and Southwest. Jeszeck describes how radial tire production in foreign-owned plants made Akron workers and factories expendable. Any U.S. company that intended to survive as a domestic tire producer either had to retrofit unionized Akron plants to produce radials or had to operate elsewhere on a nonunion basis or under subunion labor standards. He explains why the traditional militancy of the Akron unions and the somewhat paternalistic relations between the tire makers and the city were not enough to save union jobs and community standards.

The Akron companies waited too long before recognizing and accommodating to the global trend toward radial tires.[5] Competitive radial tire production demanded levels of labor and technical experience and know-how that they did not possess. The companies may therefore have concluded that they did not have the time and resources to acquire such capability. As a result, all except Goodyear (which had little choice in the matter) sold and liquidated their tire-making capacity, often to foreign producers, and expanded vertically into auto- and tire-care services and diversified into unrelated businesses. In the process, all of them (including Goodyear) abandoned their Akron plants, usually after having gotten contract concessions from the unions there. Foreign firms did not enjoy their competitive advantage because of union wage premiums, however. It is true that Michelin operated nonunion in South Carolina, but, as Jeszeck shows, when Bridgestone (Japanese) acquired a closed Firestone plant it restored some of the wages the local union previously had given to Firestone in a vain attempt to keep the plant open; Bridgestone also upgraded the plant's health and safety program and later acted as the pattern setter in tire industry contract negotiations (BNA 1991).

Adrienne Birecree describes how Clinton Corn Products Company, a major subsidiary of the food processor and distributor Standard Brands, Inc., defeated and eventually decertified a historically strong local union at its Clinton Corn plant in Clinton, Iowa, during 1979–80. As part of its approach, Standard Brands successfully used replacement workers to break a strike, thereby becoming one of the first employers to do so. Birecree shows why Standard Brands came to regard the plant as part of a larger strategy to shift emphasis from industrial to consumer-branded products. The effect was to change the status of the Clinton facility from a key profit center in the parent company's operations to a short-run "cash cow" for its overall reorganization program. She also explains why the local union so misjudged the situation that it undertook a strike that could end only in defeat and possible decertification.

Standard Brands created much of its own product market difficulties by licensing rival firms to manufacture a patented corn sweetener that had been the leading source of profits for its Clinton subsidiary. The industry overcapacity that resulted, combined with changing government policies on sugar prices, made it difficult for Clinton Corn to meet Standard Brands' target rate of profit and prompted the latter to use what profits could still be squeezed out of the subsidiary to help finance expansion of the parent company into such consumer-branded products as hard liquor.

The third case study from this time period, by David Ranney, analyzes the widely publicized shutdown of Wisconsin Steel Company (WSC) in Chicago. International Harvester (IH) sold WSC to a small, highly leveraged conglomerate in a transaction that enabled IH to escape paying its pension obligations when the mill closed in 1980. Ranney describes why the independent union that represented the Wisconsin Steel workers was internally divided and therefore unable to respond to events leading up to the closing.

International Harvester failed to modernize or find alternative product lines for its Wisconsin Steel subsidiary after the latter was no longer a useful supplier within the vertically integrated structure of IH. Harvester also was under pressure in its major product lines—heavy trucks, construction equipment, and farm machines—and therefore eager to rid itself of WSC. No buyers appeared, however, and IH could not close the mill because it was obligated to pay WSC workers $85 million in vested pensions and other monies in the event of a shutdown. "So Harvester tried to close the mill indirectly," writes the labor lawyer who spent the next seven years trying to get IH to make good on its obligations:

> It transferred title to (Envirodyne) a dummy corporation. Then, when this corporate shell went bankrupt, Harvester could say, "Too bad, they're not our pensions now." . . . Harvester had dumped all the pension liabilities but kept control of all the assets. It could keep running the mill as if it still owned it. . . .
>
> The deal was so mean, so vile, that even the investment bankers gagged. Lehman Brothers, the investment banking firm handling the sale, went to Harvester and objected on simple moral grounds. . . .

> Harvester kept the mill going for a decent interval (two years). Then, on March 28, 1980, with no warning to the workers, Harvester pulled the plug. It foreclosed on the mortgages, and the mill went down the drain. In minutes, WSC was in bankruptcy (Geoghegan 1991:85–86).

The final case study from 1975–85 is by Keith Knauss and Michael Matuszak, participant observers in the events they describe. It involves Ingersoll-Rand's (I-R) shutdown of a heavy bearings plant in South Bend, Indiana. As they explain, the shutdown was part of a plan to relocate and consolidate the operations of I-R's Torrington subsidiary from northern (union) to southern (nonunion) plants. The entire global bearings manufacturing industry was being consolidated and automated as a result of increased competition from Japanese producers and technological advances that enabled major companies such as SKF of Sweden, the world's largest bearings manufacturer, to build factories in which steel came in at one end and finished bearings came out the other in a continuous, on-line production process. The results were global overcapacity, plant closings, and job losses. During the five years after 1972 during which SKF rationalized its bearings operation worldwide, twenty thousand jobs were eliminated in the industry (Grayson 1985; chap. 3). Thus, the question for I-R/Torrington, the second largest domestic producer behind Timkin and the sixth largest in the world, was not whether to modernize its manufacturing operations but how to do so: by renovating existing facilities in the Midwest and Northeast or by constructing new plants in the South and using different work forces.

In the early 1960s, Torrington revealed a corporate strategy of relocating plants from high-wage, high-tax locations to states offering "competitive labor costs, realistic government regulations, prudence in tax structures [and] cooperative attitudes in the community and among its leaders" (*Torrington Register,* May 31, 1961). This policy was, if anything, intensified after Ingersoll-Rand acquired Torrington and included the relocation of its South Bend bearings operation to South Carolina. In the process, Torrington's management led everyone to believe that the northern plant could be saved through hard work and cooperation, although internal company documents intercepted by workers and made available to local union officials revealed that the decision to relocate had already been made.

Nevertheless, neither elected union officers nor city officials were prepared to challenge the company before or after the closing, apparently in the belief that doing so would alienate Torrington and other businesses and reduce the prospects of workers, union, and community either retaining existing jobs with Torrington or attracting new manufacturing. Moreover, Torrington was able to persuade union workers to implement a new "cell-manufacturing" production process before it closed the plant and transferred the cell machinery and know-how to South Carolina.

The remaining cases occurred in the second half of the 1980s and early 1990s. In the first chapter on this time period, David Fasenfest reviews and analyzes business incentives. These include various financial subsidies made by federal, state, and city governments to manufacturers to create or retain jobs in Detroit (General Motors), Chicago (Milton Bradley/Playskool), and Duluth, Minnesota (Triangle Corporation/Diamond Tool). In each instance communities had to respond quickly and positively to employer demands and ultimatums for tax concessions and other incentives without reciprocal corporate commitments regarding production and job performance in their communities and in the absence of sufficient information regarding corporate financial need. Detroit did get a new General Motors plant but far behind schedule, with far fewer jobs than originally expected, with no long-term guarantees, and at considerable financial cost to the city and destruction of suburban Hamtramck, where the plant was located. Chicago and Duluth eventually had to go to court to recover funds after Milton Bradley and the Triangle Corporation relocated production elsewhere in violation of the terms of their government subsidies.

From these cases Fasenfest concludes that communities need to develop and advance strategies that serve their own interests and their own needs rather than just those of the companies in an attempt to provide them with a satisfactory business climate. Such strategies should include safeguards regarding public monies, specific project costs and benefits to the community, and mechanisms to monitor firm performance and, if necessary, sanctions against unsatisfactory or bad-faith performance.

The next case study is by Bruce Nissen. He analyzes the role of strategic corporate acquisitions and divestitures in the decline and eventual closing of the Blaw-Knox steel foundry in East Chicago, Indiana, and the efforts of a community coalition to keep it operating under new ownership and after economic conversion from military production. He describes how White Consolidated (WCI) acquired this once-thriving steel machine shop and foundry and eventually turned it into a cash cow in WCI's cost-benefit calculations and why the coalition rescue effort ultimately failed.

Just as Standard Brands and Harvester seized the opportunities that the corporate merger and acquisition environment offered them, so did White Consolidated. And just as Standard Brands did with Clinton Corn Products, White Consolidated used its Blaw-Knox subsidiary as a source of funds to help finance internal expansion from industrial production to consumer-branded products. When it began a massive restructuring of the company, White used a formula that matched existing market shares against projected sales growth and profit performance for each product division, an operating principle that dominated executive decisions in conglomerate companies during the 1970s (Bluestone and Harrison 1982:149–60). In 1981, long after Blaw-Knox's machine shop had ceased to be profitable in the declining steel industry, White Consolidated, like Harvester did with Wisconsin Steel, sold the still-profitable foundry to a smaller group of investors. But the new owners put nothing into the mill; they simply took out the final bit of return on existing military orders (tank turrets for the Pentagon) before shutting it down.

Gene Daniels describes the events surrounding a federal government subsidy that American Crane improperly used to relocate production of industrial cranes by its Amhoist division from St. Paul, Minnesota, to Wilmington, North Carolina. This followed an unsuccessful corporate acquisition and diversification program in response to declining domestic markets for its industrial cranes. Congressional intervention forced the company to repay the federal relocation subsidy. American Crane later fell into bankruptcy and sold Amhoist to a Canadian firm that closed the Wilmington plant. Using this case as a prototype for industrial relocation generally during the 1980s, Daniels examines the interaction of three common industrial experiences: corporate reorganization strategies in response to intensified competition in traditional product lines; the failure of unions to recognize and respond to events leading to plant closings and relocations; and loss of community control over local economic development.

In the early 1980s Amhoist found itself in a dwindling, increasingly competitive market for industrial cranes. It tried to survive by relocating to the South with government financial support and using nonunion labor, rather than by sharing an industrial strategy with the union based on participation and cooperation and inviting the St. Paul community to assist it in keeping the local plant open. Amhoist escaped the union and the community but had to give back some of the relocation subsidy and, more important, continued to lose ground in the market. In making the move south, it had replaced skilled, experienced labor with untried, inexperienced workers in a production process that required considerable human skill and judgment. Both St. Paul and Wilmington lost in the end because Amhoist went into bankruptcy and sold its crane division to a firm that relocated production out of Wilmington.

Charles Craypo describes how an experienced and informed local union reversed what appeared to be a failing job action in response to a lockout of union workers at Iowa Beef Processors' (IBP) Dakota City, Nebraska, flagship plant. Union success in this instance prevented possible decertification of the local. With the lockout strike well under way, the union got Congress to investigate and confirm union charges that IBP was keeping improper health and safety records. Organized labor also built a union-community coalition that helped sustain the strike until revelations by Congress prompted IBP to settle the strike and negotiate a comprehensive plant safety program.

The IBP case represents those situations in which new companies use low labor costs, among other things, to take away dominant market shares from traditional producers, in this instance old-line beef packers such as Swift and Wilson. IBP did not respond to foreign or nonunion competition by cutting wages and reducing labor standards. Rather, IBP was the competition, and low labor costs were an important weapon in its assault on established employers and union labor. Altogether IBP adopted three major cost-saving practices: it located processing plants near western cattle ranges and feeding lots; it reduced whole carcasses to packaged beef cuts ready for direct shipment; and it operated either nonunion or unionized but low-wage plants. Where it did negotiate with unions, it successfully avoided meeting industry standards and settlement patterns. IBP was so successful in driving out the traditional packers and making record profits in the industry that it encouraged large, vertically integrated processors such as Excel and ConAgra to enter the industry and compete against IBP on its own terms.

Bruce Nissen concludes the case studies with a description of the successful efforts of the Calumet Project, a community-based coalition in the Calumet region of northwest Indiana. Among the Calumet Project's accomplishments during 1990–91, following its failure to convert the Blaw-Knox foundry, were the following: it persuaded LaSalle Steel to cancel tentative plans to relocate two core production operations from its unionized plant in Hammond, Indiana, to a presumably nonunion site 110 miles south in Frankfort, Indiana; and it succeeded in getting a city ordinance passed in Hammond in 1990 requiring extensive disclosure by firms receiving tax abatements in connection with the city's economic development program and an Indiana state law (passed later that year) requiring cities to rescind tax abatements when firms fail to meet their commitments regarding the creation of jobs. Further, it got an ordinance passed in Gary, Indiana, the following year requiring proof of need by firms asking for tax abatements, subsequent creation of "good" jobs in terms of pay and benefits, and stronger recovery measures in the event of unsatisfactory performance.

These gains are indeed impressive when compared with the uniform failures of unions and communities in the cases that occurred during the first half of the 1980s. Moreover, these gains are clearly superior to the partial victories won by unions and communities in the second half of the decade when, for example, no employer was persuaded or required to reverse a decision to relocate production as LaSalle Steel was.

The difference, Nissen concludes, is that the Calumet Project operated on the assumption that labor and the community have to work together because their interests are mutual concerning both issues that traditionally are considered union-related and those generally considered to be community-related. Nonetheless, he cautions against concluding on the basis of a small number of isolated victories that the environment has changed in favor of labor and communities and against corporate hegemony. Coalitions will have a difficult time achieving even limited objectives if market forces are so overwhelming that they leave firms no choice but to follow through with concession and relocation threats; firms have complete mobility and in no way are dependent on local resources, opinion makers, and power brokers; and the coalitions are unable to overcome division within and between unions and communities. Under these conditions, he says, "corporate interests will inevitably prevail in any clash with labor and community interests."

These cases identify several themes and patterns at work in the dismantling of the successful postwar grand designs of unions and manufacturing communities. Although these events occurred in the Midwest, the trends they reveal are national in scope. Deindustrialization and union decline affected every region of the nation during the 1970s and 1980s, and every state and city found itself in competition for jobs with other states and communities. What makes these cases especially instructive and poignant is that the Midwest symbolized American industrial might and apotheosized the ability of democratic institutions such as trade unions and local governments to provide high living standards to working-class families in the market economy. These stories also reveal the power dynamics underlying the transformations taking place in the 1970s and 1980s. In the process they challenge conventional views on the causes of industrial decline and of union and community relations with corporations. In the final chapter we analyze these themes and patterns and draw policy and organizational conclusions from them.

Chapter 2
Decline of Tire Manufacturing in Akron

Charles Jeszeck

AFTER 1970 MAJOR DOMESTIC manufacturing firms responded to foreign competition by retreating into strategic market segments, diversifying into other product lines, transferring production to lower-cost plants, or using some combination of these strategies. As a result, historic manufacturing centers such as Akron, Ohio, were deindustrialized and now provide sites for corporate offices and technical facilities while manufacturing occurs in southern states or overseas.

Known as America's rubber city, Akron once produced nearly two-thirds of the nation's tires and more than half its nontire rubber goods. Today it produces very little of either, and, as table 2.1 shows, employment in tires and rubber products dropped from thirty-seven thousand in 1950 to thirty-

Table 2.1. Five-year annual average employment levels of Akron tire companies, 1950–86 (in thousands of production workers)

Years	Goodrich	Firestone	Goodyear	GenCorp	Mohawk	Total	1950–55
1950–55	10.40	9.60	14.00	2.00	.70	36.70	100%
1956–60	7.60	7.10	12.60	2.00	.60	29.90	82
1961–65	5.70	5.80	9.20	2.00	.60	23.30	64
1966–70	4.70	5.00	8.70	1.90	.60	20.90	57
1971–75	2.90	3.70	6.80	1.50	.40	15.30	42
1976–80	2.20	2.20	4.00	1.60	.30[a]	10.20	28
1981–85	1.70	0.50	2.60	0.60[b]	–	5.40	15
1986	0.9	0.25	2.30	0.20	–	3.60	10

Sources: Figures from 1950–84 calculated from data obtained from URW Research Department, November 1984. Later figures estimated from the *Akron Beacon Journal*, selected articles, April–June 1985 and April, May, July, and October 1986.

[a]Plant closed in 1978.

[b]Plant closed in 1983; 200 workers remained employed in mixing operations to GenCorp's off-the-road tire plant in Bryan, Ohio.

six hundred in 1986. Most of the jobs in rubber products were gone by 1970, most of those in tires by the early 1980s. The last passenger-car tire to come out of Akron was built in 1977, the last truck tire in 1981, and the last aircraft tire in 1988.

This chapter describes and analyzes the exodus of Akron's tire production and the responses made by managers, workers, and the union. I begin by describing the decline of Akron tire production during 1930–87. I then discuss the responses of domestic tire companies to foreign sales and production in the United States and the impact of these responses on jobs, unions, and collective bargaining in Akron. Finally, I analyze the Akron experience as it relates to the interaction between corporate strategies in response to changing product markets and the current inability of organized labor to maintain high labor standards in basic U.S. industries.

Decline of Akron Tire Production, 1930–87

Most of Akron's tire companies started on the East Coast at the turn of the century as manufacturers of bicycle and carriage tires. They moved west to avoid the industry giant, the U.S. Rubber Company (later Uniroyal). The rapid growth of the automobile industry in the Great Lakes states in the teens, together with U.S. Rubber's reluctance to produce auto tires, encouraged the Akron companies to manufacture tires, and by the 1920s they were the dominant firms. Although they built some branch plants in California, the Akron firms concentrated production in Akron, and by 1930 the city accounted for nearly two-thirds of all tires produced in the United States (table 2.2).

New plant construction in the South and West during the 1930s reduced Akron's proportion of total tire production. The companies did not, however, close plants or lay off workers in Akron as a result.[1] Overall tire output accelerated in World War II, of course, and plants in both Akron and other places were expanded. In addition, seven new ones were built outside Akron to meet military needs. Expansions and new construction naturally slowed after the war, but the proportion of jobs in Akron continued to decline as companies shifted certain (labor-intensive) passenger tire production to non-Akron plants and concentrated (skill-intensive) bus and truck tires in Akron.

Of the six dominant tire companies in Akron after 1930, three made both tires and rubber products and three only tires. But because tires accounted for more employees and larger sales revenues than other rubber product lines, tire production is the focus of this chapter.[2]

Akron's tire companies were founded and historically were operated by

Table 2.2. Regional distribution of U.S. tire production, 1926–87 (in percent)

Year	Akron	Ohio[a]	South[b]	Other regions
1926	60	70	5	25
1930	65	75	5	20
1937	56	65	5	30
1945	30	–	–	–
1947	33	–	20	–
1968	13	16	31	53
1976	8	13	40	47
1979	2	6	56	38
1982	1	3	67	30
1983	0.1	3	72	25
1984	0.1	3	73	24
1985	0	2	67	31
1987[c]	0	3	76	21

Sources: Jeszeck 1982: 32 for years 1926–79; years 1982–85 are calculated from *Modern Tire Dealer Annual Facts Directory,* January issues for selected years; June 1987 calculated from *Modern Tire Dealer Annual Facts Directory,* January 1987 figures.

[a]Includes Akron.

[b]Includes Alabama, Arkansas, Florida, Kentucky, Louisiana, Mississippi, North and South Carolina, Georgia, Tennessee, Texas, Oklahoma, and Virginia.

[c]June 1987.

individuals and families that generally maintained a paternalistic yet loyal relationship with the city and its workers. The last such family disappeared from the industry in 1985, and none of the outsiders who succeeded it has maintained these traditions.

Goodyear—long the industry leader—was the city's largest employer with five factories and more than nineteen thousand production workers in 1944. Its two largest plants made passenger and commercial tires, whereas the others turned out products such as brake pads and fuel cells. Local 2 of the United Rubber Workers (URW) represented workers at all five plants. Firestone, with a greater emphasis on tire production, employed twelve thousand workers in 1946, all represented by URW Local 7. B. F. Goodrich's truck and passenger tire production was smaller than that of either Goodyear or Firestone, but it made the widest variety of nontire products—from rubber bands to surgical supplies. At its peak during World War II, URW Local 5 represented nearly eleven thousand Goodrich workers in Akron. Smaller than the three major firms, GenCorp produced mainly truck tires; its sixteen hundred to two thousand hourly workers were represented by Local 9. Seiberling, which made mostly passenger tires, was an even smaller producer than GenCorp. Acquired by Firestone in 1965, it employed eight hundred workers.[3] Mohawk, the smallest Akron tire company, produced mostly truck tires and employed about seven hundred workers represented by URW Local 6.

Despite expanding industry sales, Akron tire production remained constant during most of the 1960s because the industry built all of its fourteen new plants in other locations, eight in the South. Tire output declined absolutely in Akron between 1967 and 1979, however, when seventeen more plants were built elsewhere, this time all but one in the South.

Until the late 1960s the URW was able to organize southern tire plants, but after that it had a much more difficult time doing so in all but a few instances. Had it been able to organize more effectively in the South, the employment impact on Akron may have been less severe and the direct labor cost differentials between northern and southern plants of the same companies would have been smaller than they were. Instead, as new southern plants came on line, old Akron plants disappeared, in some instances despite local union concessions (table 2.3). By 1980 southern plants accounted for 75 percent of the industry's passenger and truck tire production (table 2.2); by 1983 Akron had lost all of its passenger and truck tire operations and a few years later all but a fraction of its airplane tire production.

CAUSES OF PLANT DISPERSION, 1930–60

Several conditions explain the initial dispersion of production from Akron, but important among them are the town's labor militancy and the industry's historical antipathy to unionization (e.g., Galbraith 1981:112–14). Management has always been vulnerable to sporadic work stoppages because tire building is a highly sequential process. Thus, as early as the 1920s, the threat of spontaneous job actions by unorganized workers encouraged tire companies to adopt relatively high-paying piece-rate systems. Further, as the nation's tire manufacturing center, Akron logically became the focal point for union organizing efforts in the 1930s, even though its tire companies paid the highest wages in the industry. Shop tensions over work speedups and incentive wage payments eventually exploded into a wave of sitdown strikes (Jeszeck 1982:46–53; Roberts 1944:79–192, 318–58).

In an industry known in labor relations circles for its high incidence of wildcat stoppages, Akron workers used the tactic most often and effectively (Kuhn 1961). They negotiated to replace tight incentive rates with looser (better-paying) ones and established limits on production rates and other work standards (Roberts 1944). But centralized bargaining structures and settlement patterns began to dominate industry labor relations, making Akron standards the norm across the industry and reducing differentials

Table 2.3. Employment and product decline of Akron tire-manufacturing facilities, 1975–82

Firm	Plants closed	Workers affected (est.)	Production operations	Comments
Goodyear	2	2,675	Mostly passenger and truck bias tires: transferred and terminated	Closings used to get URW concessions elsewhere; transfers were to new and existing plants.
Firestone	2	2,800	Mostly passenger bias tires: terminated	Some concessions made; others rejected in the absence of job guarantees.
Goodrich	1	1,400	Mostly radial passenger and nonpassenger tire products: transferred and terminated	Concessions made before all job losses.
GenCorp	1	1,600	Bias truck tires: terminated	Replacement plant promised in return for concessions but plant was not built.
Mohawk	1	320	Bias truck tires: transferred and terminated	Concessions followed by increased productivity before closing.
Seiberling (Firestone)	1	1,000	Bias passenger and truck tires: terminated	Firm won a long strike and then closed the plant.

Sources: Jeszeck 1982, 1986. Other data obtained from URW Research Department, Akron, November 1984.

between it and other locations. As a result of the increased standardization, plant labor relations stabilized in Akron, although it still had better-paying piece rates, higher pay for "down" time, and tighter union restrictions on production processes than other plants, as well as the largest number of craft job classifications, the tightest intraplant wage compression, and the strongest layoff and transfer provisions in the industry (Jeszeck 1982).

When Goodyear supervisors needed some employees to work overtime, for example, local work rules prevented them from arbitrarily choosing from among line workers and instead required them to canvass workers to find out who was both willing and eligible to work the extra hours. Akron workers also typically had "rights" to their machines, meaning that they could not be assigned to work on other jobs when their machines were inoperative or idled. For example, if union workers at GenCorp and Goodrich could not be assigned to their regular machines, they had to be sent home with pay rather than transferred to departments that were shorthanded. And at Goodyear vendors could not make deliveries to the plant but had to let bargaining unit members unload the delivery trucks at their regular pay rates.

Nor could the company make immediate repairs on machines that broke down during the night (third) shift. Instead, workers on the morning shift had to make the repairs. This practice could be traced to the 1940s, when few union members wanted to work the graveyard shift but at the same time the local did not want the firm to hire additional workers who might later compete for day-shift jobs (Jeszeck 1982:170–71).

Finally, Mohawk's practice was to give priority to unskilled production employees instead of skilled workers employed in other crafts when admitting workers into training programs for skilled maintenance jobs. This resulted in longer down times for repairs and higher labor costs. Production workers, of course, had to be paid while their machines were being repaired.

By the 1970s, therefore, management claimed the Akron plants were 10 to 30 percent less productive than other plants outside Akron using the same equipment to build the same tires (table 2.4). To management, the problem in Akron was not high wages but high unit labor costs caused by the restrictive work rules.

Foreign Competition and Domestic Industry Responses

In fact, labor costs were not the primary reason for the decline of domestic tire making in Akron. By 1960, product market developments were more important in plant dispersion. Strong and steady growth in tire demand encouraged firms to increase production capacity during the 1960s and 1970s.

Table 2.4. Productivity levels in Akron versus non-Akron facilities, 1975–78

Plants	Differential
Akron, Los Angeles, and Gadsden (1978). Unionized identical Goodyear bias passenger tire plants using identical machinery.	−20 to −30%
Akron and Danville, Va. (1975). Unionized Goodyear bias truck tire plants.	−18%
Akron and Gadsden (1977). Unionized Goodyear bias passenger tire plants using identical machinery.	−10%
Akron and Union City, Tenn. (1975). Unionized identical Goodyear radial passenger tire plants.	−18%
Akron, Pottstown, Penn., and Los Angeles (1978). Unionized truck tire plants.	−20 to −25%

Sources: Jeszeck 1982 and data from URW Research Department, Akron, December 1980.

Subsequent waves of plant closings were mainly the result of market and technology trends sweeping the industry.

The advent of the radial tire was the key change during this time. Radials were superior to conventional bias-ply tires in both fuel efficiency and product life, but they were virtually unknown in the United States before the mid-1960s. Most American companies made radials in their European plants and produced small batches of them in the United States. But it was much more difficult to manufacture radials successfully for big American cars. Nevertheless, Michelin, the French producer, began exporting large numbers of radials for U.S. retail distribution by Sears; and soon after it began selling them directly to Ford Motor Company as factory tires for Lincoln cars. Michelin thereby gained valuable experience in making large-sized radials. Eventually it had enough of the U.S. market to construct several nonunion radial tire export plants in Nova Scotia, Canada. Then, in 1975, it built three nonunion plants in South Carolina, and in 1989, it acquired Uniroyal-Goodrich for $1.5 billion, which made Michelin the largest tire producer in the United States and the second largest in the world.

Bridgestone, Continental, Pirelli, and other foreign tire firms followed Michelin's lead and began exporting radials to the United States. During the period from 1967 to 1973, non-U.S. companies captured nearly 14 percent of the domestic market, although only Michelin had production operations in this country until the 1980s. In 1983, Bridgestone (Japanese) acquired Firestone's unionized truck tire plant in Nashville to supply Nissan's U.S.

truck and auto plants. Later, in 1988, Bridgestone purchased all of Firestone's domestic tire operations. Another Japanese producer, Sumitomo, purchased Dunlop's (British) two U.S. plants in 1985. Additional forays into U.S. tire manufacturing included the 1987 sale of GenCorp's tire division to Continental Tire (German), a firm that has taken considerable interest in U.S. market growth, and the purchase by Italian-based Pirelli of Armtek's tire plants—formerly Armstrong Tire and Rubber (*Wall Street Journal,* April 25, 1988, 13). Thus, by 1987, more than 20 percent of U.S. tire capacity was foreign-owned and, with additional Bridgestone, Pirelli, and Michelin acquisitions in 1988–89, almost 50 percent by the end of the decade (based on data from the *Wall Street Journal,* Sept. 25, 1989, A3).

CAUSES OF DOMESTIC DECLINE

Why did U.S. tire companies lose their global lead in production technology and control of the huge domestic market? Much of the answer involves a decision by U.S. companies in the late 1960s to postpone radial tire production, thereby creating a void in domestic tire production and inviting overseas firms to fill it with exports and output from their U.S. plants. American firms responded slowly and reluctantly. Most eventually increased radial production somewhat in a belated effort to catch up with the foreigners. They also either gradually or abruptly gave up their competitive response, diversifying into other, presumably more profitable lines of business and abandoning most or all of their traditional tire markets. The result was a wave of plant closings preliminary to firms leaving the tire industry or, in Goodyear's case, to reducing bias-ply tire capacity preparatory to expanding radial production.

As would be expected, the closings enhanced the bargaining power of ailing domestic firms with their local unions. In most instances, subsequent union concessions improved company earnings before the closings or reductions, although the companies did not intend to use the concessions to save threatened jobs and plants. Perhaps the concessions simply helped finance the expansion of nontire rubber operations and corporate diversification.

The most frequent company response was to diversify out of tires and into other businesses. Tire manufacturing had always been a low-profit industry in its return on equity. Global competition reduced profits even more after the 1960s. Many U.S. firms therefore initially retreated into tire market niches in which they were strong and then diversified operations elsewhere. By 1989, Goodyear was the only major U.S. tire maker still involved primarily in tire production. Cooper and several other small companies had survived precisely because they were traditional niche producers.

Firestone, traditionally the industry runner-up to Goodyear, illustrates this diversification strategy. Once a full-line tire maker, in the 1980s it steadily abandoned its various tire markets, as shown in table 2.5 (*Modern Tire Dealer*, Jan. 1986, 38–39, and Jan. 1987, 22). After concluding that research and development costs in radial truck tires were too high to warrant continued production, Firestone stopped making them and instead began marketing those made by Bridgestone. It also sold its chemical, auto parts, and other manufacturing divisions in order to concentrate on retail automotive and tire-care service businesses. Although Firestone made small investments in foreign radial tire capacity during the 1980s, under a new CEO it eventually closed nine tire plants in the United States and moved its corporate headquarters from Akron to Chicago (*Business Week*, Sept. 7, 1987, 68). Then, in 1988, in what was described as the largest sale of U.S. corporate assets to a foreign buyer to date, Firestone sold its worldwide tire operations to Bridgestone for $2.6 billion. Within three years Bridgestone had invested a reported $1.4 billion in Firestone's former manufacturing facilities (*New York Times*, Aug. 1, 1991, C4).

GenCorp, the industry's fourth largest producer, acquired businesses in a variety of nonmanufacturing industries; by 1986, less than half its sales were

Table 2.5. Corporate diversification of U.S. tire firms, 1970–88

Firm	Full-line manufacturing	Overseas operations	Diversified operations	Foreign acquisition	Abandoned tire operations
Firestone	Yes	Yes	Yes	Yes (Bridgestone)	Yes
GenCorp	Yes	Yes	Yes	Yes (Continental)	Yes
Goodrich	Yes	Yes	Yes	Yes (Michelin)	Yes[a]
Goodyear	Yes	Yes	Yes	No	No
Uniroyal	Yes	Yes	Yes	Yes (Michelin)	Yes[a]

Sources: Jeszeck 1982; 312. World Tire Markets, *Predicasts*, April 1984; U.S. Tire Industry, *Dean Witter Industrial Analysis Consumer Group*, September 1984; *Business Week*, March 22, 1985, and April 18, 1986; U.S. Securities and Exchange Commission, corporate 10-K filings, selected years.

[a]Goodrich spun off its tire division, which was then merged with Uniroyal's tire operations and later acquired by Michelin.

from tires. It tried but failed to become the industry's low-cost tire producer by, among other measures, taking major strikes to reduce labor costs; and in 1987, it sold its tire operations to Continental.

B. F. Goodrich, once a full-line tire producer, abandoned its original passenger and most of its truck tire lines, concentrated on selected U.S. market niches for replacement passenger tires, and diversified into nontire manufacturing industries. Industry analysts expected Goodrich to get out of tire production altogether when competition among domestic firms intensified in the mid-1980s. Instead, it entered into a joint venture with Uniroyal in which they combined their tire operations to form a third company, which Michelin later acquired. Goodrich then reorganized as a nonoperating holding company (U.S. Securities and Exchange Commission 1986).

GROWTH AND RELOCATION OF U.S. RADIAL PRODUCTION

U.S. firms saw that radials were capturing domestic markets in the 1960s, but few were ready to commit the financial resources necessary to convert to radial production. Some even refused to believe that radials would ever dominate. As late as 1973, for example, Goodyear's CEO predicted that "radials would remain a third choice [behind bias-ply and bias-belted tires] of American motorists for years to come" (*Forbes,* April 15, 1973, 55). But U.S. firms had other reasons for not manufacturing radials: they were reluctant to produce tires that required 25 to 35 percent more labor hours to make than did bias plys; they had no experience building the technically demanding radials required on large U.S. vehicles; and probably they feared losing the market for their original tires if they shifted to radials.

Goodyear and the others therefore rejected the new product altogether, although as early as 1967 Goodrich had gone to the Big Three U.S. auto companies with an offer to produce radials for them as original equipment. The automakers stayed with bias-ply tires, however, because the rougher ride from radials meant they would have to adjust their suspension systems and, besides, Goodrich would be the only major supplier. Thus, faced with only the small market for radial replacements, Goodrich, like the other domestic producers, concentrated on bias-ply tires.[4] The result was that the American tire makers that did go into radial production made only small numbers of them.

Nevertheless, growing sales of fuel-efficient autos and the 1973–74 oil embargo forced U.S. auto companies and the public to switch to radials faster than the industry anticipated. Radials' share of the market nearly tripled, from 14 to 38 percent, during 1973–75. But even then U.S. firms did not keep up with the market because insufficient production capacity and operating problems slowed output and contributed to a nagging inability to produce high-quality radials. Foreign firms gladly made up the difference in supply and thereby permanently captured a significant domestic market share. Thus, after U.S. tire sales dropped sharply in the late 1970s, domestic producers more or less abandoned any attempt to regain their traditional market position.

Only Goodyear survives as a major U.S.-owned tire producer. And, ironically, that may be only because it sold most of its nontire subsidiaries in 1985 to ward off a hostile takeover attempt by British corporate raider Sir James Goldsmith. The company had no choice but to become a tire company again. Goodyear officials therefore invested in tire production even as some market segments remained weak.

Cooper Tire is the only other significant U.S.-owned producer, but it cannot be considered a "major" manufacturer. It operated three plants, two of them in the South, and then recently purchased an Albany, Georgia, facility that Firestone closed during the early 1980s. A profitable company, Cooper makes passenger radials for the replacement market, especially in the Southeast, and industrial rubber products, mainly automotive parts, which it sells to all nine of the Japanese auto transplants in this country (*Wall Street Journal,* May 18, 1990, B3). Tiny Mohawk Tire, by contrast, also remains committed to tire manufacturing, but its existence depends on volume contracts to supply radial passenger tires to large retailers such as Sears.

Radial tire manufacturing required new capital equipment and more skilled labor than bias-ply tire production, although the basic stages of radial production are essentially the same. Overall, more hours of labor are needed, and builders have to use precision and quality control in making radial tires. In some ways, therefore, radial production is more vulnerable to worker unrest. In any event, when domestic companies expanded radial production they did so in new plants in the South and Southwest, where they could get new work forces and operate union-free. As we shall see, they opened new plants instead of modernizing existing Akron plants and negotiating competitive pay and work standards with unions in return for job security.

The growing demand for radials also made other tires and tire plants obsolete. Radials were more durable and longer-lasting than bias-ply tires, which reduced the overall demand for replacement tires and encouraged U.S. producers to close still more traditional plants in the late 1970s and early 1980s. Total industry shipments in 1985 were lower than those in 1972, and U.S. capacity declined by more than 21 percent between 1979 and

1987. Imports and foreign-owned domestic production nevertheless continued to grow (table 2.6). This intensified traditional cut-throat pricing practices and put added pressure on companies to reduce costs, especially of labor, in order to maintain profit margins in the labor-intensive radial tire plants.

Impact of Industry Strategy on Akron Unions, 1945–85

Hourly employment in Akron's tire industry declined steadily after World War II, but changes in labor relations occurred in three distinct stages, in 1945–65, 1966–76, and 1977–85.

Limited Concessions amid Pattern Bargaining, 1945–65

Stable labor relations and uniform wage and benefit levels prevailed during 1945–65 in each of the industry's Big Five companies—Goodyear, Firestone, Uniroyal, Goodrich, and GenCorp. After the corporations and the URW ratified a national agreement, each plant negotiated a local supplemental agreement to address more specific issues such as work rules. Companies never asked for contract concessions at the national level and seldom did in local negotiations. In response to such requests, the Akron locals occasionally made concessions in work rules in the face of declining employment.

Table 2.6. Imports as a percentage of total U.S. tire sales and as a percentage of foreign-owned U.S. capacity, 1968–87

Year	Percentage of total U.S. shipments	Percentage of U.S. capacity foreign-owned	Total U.S. capacity per day (in 1,000s)
1968	3.7	1.6	911
1975	7.5	3.0	1,016
1977	10.0	5.0	1,018
1978	9.4	5.6	1,015
1979	8.4	6.3	984
1981	11.3	9.9	905
1982	9.7	11.4	853
1984	10.5	11.3	807
1986	17.6	10.6	775
1987	14.0 (est.)	21.3 (est.)	780 (est.)

Sources: 1968 capacity data calculated from *Rubber World*, January 1969; other capacity data calculated from *Modern Tire Dealer Annual Facts Directory*, selected January issues; 1968–80 import data from Jeszeck 1982; later years from *Modern Tire Dealer Annual Facts Directory*, selected January issues.

Akron's tire unions lost more than fifteen thousand jobs during 1950–68, but the companies seldom offered to guarantee specific jobs or to make sizable plant investments in return for union givebacks. Goodyear was the exception.[5] Three times between 1960 and 1965 it approached Local 2 with offers of new investments and stable employment in Akron in return for work-rule changes. Most of the requests involved minor changes affecting small numbers of hourly workers, but two changes were very significant: the abolition of the six-hour day and modification of plantwide seniority.[6] In each instance Goodyear made the promised investments, including limited expenditures in radial tire production. Once, however, it invested even though the local refused to agree to the company's most important concession demands. This suggests that the company considered these investments to be profitable even without the work-rule changes.

LOCAL CONCESSION BARGAINING, 1966–76

The 1966–76 period was a turning point in corporate labor relations policies. Concession demands were more numerous and more frequent, although they continued to focus on work rules rather than money issues. Local unions accepted them only to save jobs and after considerable community and media pressure to do so. As table 2.7 shows, however, such concessions seldom saved targeted jobs. This is because union jobs depended mainly on which strategy particular firms followed in response to structural changes in the industry.

In 1968, Local 2 actually initiated concession bargaining with Goodyear to keep certain production work in Akron. It learned the company planned to transfer eighty tire mold jobs to Indiana and inquired about what it would take to prevent the transfers. This led to negotiations in which Goodyear agreed to build a new mold plant in Akron if the local accepted extensive changes in the production process.[7] Union members approved the changes and Goodyear built the plant in Akron, despite isolated efforts by workers to sabotage the plan on the shop floor, thus saving the existing jobs and creating two hundred more. Unlike the situation later, the companies did not test union strength on these issues in the late 1960s, and, as a result, the locals remained confident in their ability to negotiate future job-saving pacts.

Akron tire production continued to decline, but each time a plant was closed or a product line discontinued the affected local seemed surprised and unprepared.[8] During 1970–72, Goodrich, Firestone, Goodyear, and Mohawk approached Akron locals with concession proposals. Union responses varied, but whether or not they made concessions bore no consistent relationship to the eventual job losses or company investments (table 2.7).

In 1971, Goodyear demanded comprehensive work-rule changes in an effort to undo a history of local negotiations and shop-floor agreements. These changes were necessary, according to Goodyear, to assure "the maximum chance for continued [passenger tire and reclaimed rubber] operations in Akron" (memorandum, Goodyear to Local 2, June 1, 1971). Seven of the demands would save $7.2 million in labor costs, it said, and six others an additional $2.4 million (table 2.8). Despite strong urging from Goodyear and the local media, as well as public awareness of and intense interest in parallel negotiations going on at both Firestone and Goodrich, the Goodyear workers rejected the company's demands. Whether or not they believed that Akron's plants actually were in jeopardy, they believed these standards were critical to local working conditions and established job security and therefore not to be surrendered without certain commitments and guarantees in return. Goodyear was unable to make such commitments at that junction, for the company refused to link its demands to job security.

Goodyear nevertheless asked for specific concessions in 1972 that it said it

Table 2.7. Summary of Akron local union concession agreements, 1960–85

Year	Goodyear	Firestone	GenCorp	Goodrich	Mohawk
1960	Y(I)				
1964	Y(I)				
1965				Y(S)	
1966	Y(I)				
1968	Y(I)				
1970					Y(G)(I)
1971	N(G)(S)	N(G)(D)			
1972	Y(G)(S)	Y(G)(C)		Y(G)(C)(D)	
1973	NY(G)(S)				Y(G)(I)
1974	Y(C)(S)				
1977	Y(G)(C)	Y(G)(C)			
1978	N(G)(C)				NY(G)(C)
1979	Y(S)		Y(D)		
1981	Y(I)	Y(C)			
1982				Y(S)(C)	
1983	Y(I)Y(S)	N(S)			
1985		Y(S)		Y(G)(S)(C) N(G)(S)(D)	

Sources: Jeszeck 1982; *Akron Beacon Journal,* selected articles, 1985–87, and contracts and information obtained from the URW Research Department files, Akron, December 1980 and November 1984.

Y = union accepts concessions; N = union rejects concessions; (I) = investments; (D) = no investment; (S) = jobs saved; (C) = jobs lost; (G) = no employer guarantee.

Table 2.8. Valuation of bargaining concession demands made by Goodyear to maintain passenger tire competitiveness, 1971–73

Items	Money value (in $1,000s)	Ratio of total savings (in percent)
Primary		
Restricted jobs	167	1.7
Consolidated craft	700	7.3
Modified workweek, vacations, and operator classifications	666	6.9
Reduced crew size	650	6.8
Modified piece-rate review	34	0.4
Modified work crew	200	2.1
Subtotal	2,417	25.2
Secondary		
Intensified work	5,000	52.0
Tightened piece rate	1,580	16.4
Made labor more flexible	163	1.7
Nullified arbitration decisions	112	1.2
Removed restrictions on use of apprentices	177	1.8
Reduced job rights	43	0.4
Shifted work from craft to production labor	139	1.4
Subtotal	7,213	74.8
Total value of concession demands	9,631	100.0

Source: URW Research Department files, Akron, December 1980 and November 1984.

needed to prevent a shutdown of the mold plant. This time the threat was more immediate and plausible, so Local 2 agreed to changes in vacation scheduling and seniority.

During local contract negotiations the following year, Goodyear once again asked for the concessions in passenger tires that it had demanded in 1971, and once again it refused to guarantee that the plant would stay open if the union complied. Local 2 responded by granting some givebacks and rejecting others. Goodyear claimed that the union agreed to save just $.03 per hour instead of the $.72 an hour it said it needed and was asking for. The union was not giving enough to save the Akron passenger tire plant in the long run, company officials warned. Goodyear meanwhile began phasing down its truck tire operations—without asking for union concessions there—and later closed the plant, displacing about thirteen hundred workers. Despite the lack of consistency between union concessions and job retentions so far, Local 2 later accepted piece-rate reductions in certain nontire operations.

Firestone said it would consider building a new radial truck tire plant if Akron Local 7 accepted several contract concessions. These included work-rule changes and adoption of a five-day, forty-hour workweek, the elimination of piece work, and lower base wages for the "tirebuilder" job classification.[9] The company offered a bonus plan to compensate for the wage cut, provided, first, the union agreed to unilateral company determination of required work effort and, second, labor productivity improved.

Firestone implied that eventually the same terms would have to be adopted in its other Akron lines. Union officials wanted the radial plant built in Akron but did not want the proposed production standards to become general guidelines. They also feared that the proposed wage cuts would provide a wedge for comparable reductions outside Akron and that, despite company reassurances to the contrary, jobs would be lost following adoption of the forty-hour week. Nonetheless, the lure of a new plant and intense media coverage of Firestone's offer encouraged union leaders to recommend rank-and-file acceptance, although they believed the members would not go along with the proposal unless Firestone guaranteed that the new plant would be located in Akron. Company officials refused to make such a guarantee on the grounds that there was the risk of "a continuing decline of work under prevailing conditions," meaning that the market was not firm enough for them to build another plant (memorandum, Firestone to Local 7, June 8, 1971). Local union leadership therefore recommended against the proposal, and Firestone workers voted unanimously to reject the demands. Firestone subsequently built its radial truck tire plant near Nashville. Firestone sold the plant to Bridgestone in 1983 when it got out of the heavy-truck tire market.

Local 7 agreed to concession bargaining again in 1972 when Firestone announced it might have to close its Akron truck and passenger tire plants. In a ratification vote obviously affected by the earlier loss of the truck tire plant and mounting community pressure to stop Akron's economic decline, members of the local approved a four-point concession package by a two-to-one margin. It included conversion to the forty-hour week, elimination of contractual limits on production, and reductions in pay rates when machines were not in operation. This occurred even though Firestone made no job guarantees in return.

During the next six months, the local lost five hundred nontire jobs and over the next five years more than one thousand altogether. Members turned out the incumbent local officers in the next election, and no further concession talks occurred until 1977.

About the same time, Goodrich embarked on a labor-cost reduction program called HEYMAC (Help Make Akron Competitive), consisting of twelve specific givebacks, the most important of which was a reduction in incentive earnings by retiming pay rates for piece work. Goodrich accompanied the in-plant talks with a public relations campaign aimed at pressuring the union into accepting the changes as a way of preserving jobs in Akron. Local 7's earlier rejection of Firestone's concession demands intensified community pressure on Local 5 to "do something" for the city. Goodrich refused to guarantee investments or jobs in return for the concessions but it did promise "to expand radial passenger tire production in Akron to offset some of the anticipated reductions in other lines of tires" (memorandum, Goodrich to Local 5, April 7, 1972).

After nine months of bargaining, the parties agreed on five specific concessions, including the retiming of all piece rates over a three-year period. Urged by the leadership to support the agreement, members approved it four to one.[10] Again, workers would be disappointed in the results: over the next eighteen months Goodrich continued to invest in plants outside Akron, transferred and eliminated eleven hundred jobs, and failed to substitute radial tire production for discontinued work. Eventually the company terminated passenger tire production in Akron altogether.

Union concessions did produce job security for the membership in one instance. Local 6 gave Mohawk minor concessions in 1970 and three years later agreed to retime piece rates; the firm reciprocated with major capital investments in the Akron plant, including the introduction of radial tire production. Company officials later acknowledged that productivity rose sharply after the agreement, but the end of the Mohawk story would not be a happy one for union workers.

MORE CONCESSIONS AND PLANT CLOSINGS, 1977–85

By 1976, Akron workers and local unions no longer believed concessions would guarantee jobs and capital investment. Continued declines in employment and frequent demands by management for givebacks without guarantees of security had poisoned relations between the companies and the locals. Furthermore, continued increases in the number of imported radial tires and growth in domestic production by foreign firms and the inability of domestic firms to cap labor costs during the 1976 round of national contract negotiations combined to accelerate the pace at which domestic companies were restructuring production and scrambling for market positions. During 1976–

84, twenty-six tire plants were closed in the United States. Meanwhile, unions in the rest of the industry were making concessions.

Local 2 had resisted major givebacks at Goodyear's passenger tire plant, but in 1977 the company threatened to close the facility entirely if it did not get what it wanted in concession bargaining. Convinced this was the case, the union accepted many of the demands it had resisted in 1971, although still without assurance that Goodyear would keep the plant open.

Union fears seemed to be confirmed when productivity improved but the company laid off five hundred workers anyway. Even so, the local made additional concessions aimed at saving passenger tires, only to see the plant close three months later, marking the end of passenger tire production in Akron by Goodyear. Thus, when management then demanded concessions at Goodyear's latex operations but refused to make job guarantees in return, workers rejected the request. Goodyear closed the plant shortly afterward and relocated production to Houston.

What followed was a series of special concessionary bargains in which Goodyear demanded combinations of givebacks applicable to specific product lines. These included wage cuts, the elimination of work rules, reductions in cost-of-living adjustments (COLA), and work schedule changes, sometimes in return for specified job guarantees and sometimes without them. Each time Local 2 accepted some or all of the demands. The problem for the union was that major concessions made to save jobs in one plant or operation were offset shortly afterward by nonnegotiable losses elsewhere. For example, massive givebacks persuaded the company to construct a new air-spring plant in Akron, involving more than two hundred jobs, but later that year Goodyear closed its industrial products plant in Akron without any negotiations, displacing eleven hundred workers.

In 1983, Goodyear again approached the union. It guaranteed three hundred jobs and $14 million in investments in its Akron metal products division in return for continuous shift operations and the elimination of Sunday premium pay. The union accepted. The parties then agreed to change seniority rights in the Akron racing-car tire department in return for 250 jobs. As a result of these adjustments, by the late 1980s Local 2 membership had stabilized at about twenty-one hundred, compared with more than nineteen thousand in 1944.

As table 2.7 shows, Local 2 accepted concession demands on ten out of thirteen occasions during 1960–83. It did so in the absence of any clear causal link between concessions and jobs and despite Goodyear's refusal to guarantee jobs in the passenger tire plant in return for concessions. The key union rejection occurred in 1971. After that Goodyear systematically relocated tire production even in the face of repeated union givebacks.

The results of concession bargaining at Goodrich were no more encouraging for the union than those at Firestone and Goodyear. Yet, after having displaced eleven hundred workers following union acceptance of its HEYMAC program, Goodrich made no new concession demands, and in 1980 it even invested $25 million in its Akron plants—mostly the airplane tire operations—emphasizing that there were "no strings attached." Local 5, under new leadership, actively resisted implementation of HEYMAC through shop-floor "renegotiation" of piece rates and work rules and in various arbitration proceedings, and in 1979 the union claimed to have avoided or eliminated most HEYMAC provisions. Changes in company policy were important in this reversal. Further cutbacks in tire capacity did not hurt the Akron plant because it no longer made passenger and truck tires, only the less vulnerable airplane and farm tires. Goodrich also had expanded its nontire operations, some of which were based in Akron.

Moreover, Goodrich had adopted a less aggressive labor relations policy following a 141-day strike in 1976. It did not relocate large numbers of jobs out of Akron, but in 1982 it asked for another round of concessions, which the union approved. The company claimed to have lost $14 million in Akron in two years and therefore wanted to suspend COLA payments and cut wages and possibly cut them again later if local operations continued to lose money.[11] In return, Goodrich vowed to retain two-thirds of its existing production in Akron for at least three years. The specified product lines were continued, but nearly nine hundred workers received layoff slips as other product lines were terminated. Once again the local officers who had negotiated the concessions were defeated for reelection (*Akron Beacon Journal*, Oct. 14, 1983, A1).

Goodrich made its final concession demands in 1985. It informed the local that about 40 percent of its Akron production jobs definitely would be lost permanently but that the remainder might be saved if labor agreed to consolidate all craft classifications and make layoff and recall rights of individual workers contingent on job skills rather than seniority. Goodrich did not make any job guarantees, but it did agree to restore COLA payments. Local negotiators accepted the terms and recommended rank-and-file ratification before completion of national contract bargaining. The concessions were ratified nine to one.

Later that year the new master contract was negotiated, and contrary to the terms of the earlier concession contract, it included a wage increase for

Local 5 members. When Goodrich became aware of this, it proposed that members of Local 5 vote against the negotiated master agreement, in the hope that it would be defeated and the company and the union could reach a new settlement without a wage increase for the Akron plant. Company negotiators claimed that otherwise the plant would be uncompetitive and perhaps have to be closed.

Despite pressure from Goodrich, the international union, and some other locals, Local 5 voted to accept the national contract with its wage increase. Goodrich eliminated six hundred jobs in Akron as it had threatened to do, but they were in industrial rubber products rather than in airplane tires, and although it later closed two tire plants, neither was in Akron. Local 5 thus had called the company's bluff to close the Akron plant and had won—but only temporarily. Three years later Goodrich built another airplane tire plant in North Carolina and closed its Akron operations (U.S. Securities and Exchange Commission 1986; *Wall Street Journal*, Sept. 25, 1989, A7).

During 1972–76, Firestone eliminated thirteen hundred jobs in Akron in radial tires, nonradial truck and passenger tires, and mechanical products. The company approached the local again in 1977 with concessions to save its nonradial truck tire plant. The local agreed, but the plant was closed anyway in 1980, two years after the shutdown of Firestone's passenger tire plant in Akron, for a combined loss of seventeen hundred jobs, more than half of the previous membership of the local.

In 1981, the local accepted wage cuts and other givebacks to save the remaining jobs, although without company guarantees. This failed, however, and over the next eighteen months Firestone eliminated all production jobs in Akron.

During 1983–85, the remaining 235 maintenance and service workers initially rejected but later accepted wage reductions, elimination of their COLA, and a two-tired pay system in hopes of preserving the remaining jobs. Firestone nevertheless announced plans to relocate its headquarters out of Akron, a move that Bridgestone initially reversed but later carried out when it acquired Firestone's tire business. Thus, by the end of the 1980s, Local 7 had fewer than 250 members (all nonproduction employees), compared with 12,000 in 1946.

GenCorp made no formal concession demands of Local 9 until 1979, although it had indicated to the union as early as 1973 that continued tire production in Akron would require substantial changes in plant operations and had informally discussed operations with officers of the local during 1974–77.[12] Eventually the union accepted concessions, including most of the givebacks being negotiated by the other URW locals. GenCorp promised to build a replacement radial truck tire plant in Akron if the agreement proved effective after two years and "if market conditions warranted." The union also insisted that if the new plant was not built in Akron that GenCorp had to return the money workers were giving up in wage cuts. This demand doubtless reflected rank-and-file skepticism about the effectiveness of labor concessions in light of the experiences to date of other Akron locals.[13] Company officials wanted the two-year trial period because they thought it would take that long to eliminate wasteful "traditional" work practices.

Although both sides later agreed that the experiment was successful and that labor productivity increased, the new plant was never built. GenCorp said it could not proceed because of overcapacity in radial truck tire production and instead closed existing truck tire plants in Akron and Waco, Texas. As required under the concession agreement, Akron workers were compensated for the wage reductions. GenCorp then negotiated the Akron concessions at its three remaining unionized tire plants in the United States and Canada.

The cost of converting to radial production and the prospect of a shrinking market forced smaller companies such as Mansfield out of the industry by the late 1970s. Mohawk initially tried to cooperate with its union by establishing a joint labor-management committee to review work rules and suggest improvements in plant layout. It complemented these changes with new investments, which increased productivity by 25 percent (Jeszeck 1982). Then, in 1973, it told the union it would be necessary to retime incentive rates to justify further investment in the plant. The union complied and again the investments were made. The company later claimed productivity rose 200 to 300 percent as a result.

Things changed for the worse in 1977, however, when Mohawk took a long strike in Akron over pension improvements that matched those in the industry pattern agreement. Mohawk then came back in 1978 with new concession demands. This time it specifically threatened to shut down the plant if it did not get significant financial and contractual changes. Union members accepted the company's key demands but refused others. Again productivity improved following the agreement, and the company installed some new machines. Nevertheless, soon after that Mohawk closed the plant after giving workers only nine days' notice and refusing to negotiate the decision.

Analysis

By the mid-1980s, URW locals in Akron were nearly defunct. Despite major union concessions on wages, work rules, work intensity, and work schedules, the industry had closed seven Akron plants and cut production jobs by 80 percent since 1980. Concessions had helped neither the workers and their union nor the community. The relatively few jobs created by Goodyear following the URW's concessions, for example, were dwarfed by job losses in the company's other Akron plants. Phasedown of tire production continued in Akron whether or not the locals made concessions. Bargaining stalemates were common as Akron managers asked skeptical employees for increasingly heavy concessions without offering job security in return.

Although the experiences of the locals vary, the demise of Akron's tire industry is characterized by several themes. First, concession bargaining occurred because the companies failed to develop new product lines and production processes and as a result had to change corporate structures and long-term strategies concerning products and processes, not because union wages and work rules priced domestic tires out of the market or resulted in poor product quality. Bridgestone, for example, took a very different approach to labor relations in the U.S. plants it acquired from Firestone, which had closed the plants shortly after obtaining wage and other concessions of $3.66 to $7.00 an hour from local unions (Rubin 1988:33). Bridgestone closed one of these plants and returned some of the givebacks to union workers in the other two, while pledging to invest heavily in upgrading the plants and making them competitive (*Business Week*, Feb. 27, 1989, 78–79).[14] More recently, Bridgestone initiated labor-management cooperation programs in these plants.

Radial tires became dominant in both the original equipment and replacement tire markets at a time when Akron had virtually no radial production. Its bias-ply tires were fast becoming an industry anachronism—from 32 percent of original equipment sales and 62 percent of replacement sales in 1977 to less than 0.5 percent and 41 percent respectively in 1981. By 1986, radials had all of the original equipment market and 83 percent of replacement sales. The truck tire market converted to radials even faster than the passenger-car market, mainly because of the market's greater size standardization and because foreign producers were quick to enter the market with radials when Firestone and Uniroyal dropped out of most segments of the truck tire market. Given these trends, it was impossible for local unions to save jobs through contract concessions unless the companies made firm commitments to locate radial tire production in Akron, which none agreed to do. Three of them—Goodrich, Firestone, and General—expressed hope that concessions would bring radial tire manufacturing to Akron, but in no instance did this happen.

Second, during the 1970s, industry efforts to convince the community of Akron that concessions were necessary to secure the city's economic future put considerable pressure on local unions to concede to demands in the public interest. High unemployment, recent job losses in tires, and "public scrutiny" of the Firestone local's earlier rejection of wage reductions that the company claimed were essential for it to construct a new plant in Akron doubtless contributed to union acceptance of concessions in 1972. Similar pressures prompted Goodrich Local 5 to accept the ill-fated HEYMAC program and URW locals at Goodyear and Mohawk to make concessions. As the companies continued to close plants and product lines despite additional concessions, local media reports shifted the onus from union labor to mutual responsibility and the need for cooperation between the parties.

The final blow to whatever optimism remained at the Akron plants was the collapse of the 1979 GenCorp agreement, which initially had been hailed as a model for actions by other companies and locals to reverse the city's shrinking industrial base. Yet even as public cynicism grew and industry credibility diminished, community anger and frustration never were directed at the firms. Like the displaced Flint auto workers in Michael Moore's film *Roger and Me,* displaced Akron tire workers and their community internalized anger and blame rather than directing it elsewhere.

Third, the companies effectively whipsawed Akron and non-Akron URW locals against one another in the concession process. This could not be done, however, until plant shutdowns in Akron in the late 1970s had a sufficient demonstration effect. Industrywide concession agreements in the 1980s clearly encouraged rubber locals everywhere to subordinate their traditional wage solidarity and negotiate separate terms and conditions out of fear that they would lose existing jobs and future investments. Concessions by non-Akron unions were no more reliable in this regard, however, than concessions in Akron (Jeszeck 1986).

The primary concern of the international URW has been to maintain the integrity of national pattern agreements by permitting independent concessions at the plant level. This preoccupation with the master agreement despite increasing concessions by its locals is a similar strategy to the one used by U.S. auto unions during the 1980s. Recently URW locals have questioned this policy as they find it increasingly difficult to hold the line against the spread of concessions among plants of the same company. As a result, in the 1988 rubber industry contract talks, a majority of the Goodyear locals rejected the pattern settlement negotiated between the international and the company because it permitted plant-level concession agreements on issues that previously had required approval of a majority of the members in the firm's other plants. Under the company's new proposal, which Goodyear later abandoned, only the international executive board would have had to approve such givebacks.

Fourth, it is clear that even massive concessions would not have saved the Akron plants. At Firestone, for example, additional concessions by the local did not prevent the shutdown of eleven plants nationwide before the company's exit from the industry. Other Akron locals negotiated extensive work-rule modifications but failed to save their plants. Union givebacks at Mohawk, Goodyear, and GenCorp resulted in sizable increases in productivity but did not prevent the plants from being swamped by what the industry called unfavorable "macro" trends—sliding consumer demand and the shift to radials—regardless of whether or not the firms were acting in good faith. At most, the concessions kept the plants going longer than they would have without them.

A more cynical interpretation of the drive for union concessions is that the companies wanted to increase productivity and "burn out" obsolete, nonradial manufacturing equipment before closing the plants. Under this scenario they had no intention of using the Akron plants as long-term suppliers but simply wanted to generate as much operating revenue from them as possible and perhaps use the concession settlements they got from the Akron locals as a wedge to whipsaw the non-Akron locals into accepting lower labor standards in their new and modernized plants. The objective in this case was to reduce the total cost of converting from bias-ply to radial tire production.

Thus, in either the "good-faith" or the cynical scenario, union concessions would not have saved tire production in Akron. Moreover, typical concession demands during these years clearly were insufficient to finance a new plant even partially. Goodyear, for example, costed out the six major concession demands it made for 1971–76 at $2.4 million per year (table 2.8). At the time it and other tire companies were spending between $75 and $100 million to build or expand a single facility: thirty to forty times the value of its concession demands.

Fifth, despite the different concession strategies among firms and the variations in union responses, the fate of the Akron plants was the same—

job losses and closings. For example, even though Goodyear, more than the others, was committed to being a tire manufacturer, it used union concessions to reduce the costs of operating new plants elsewhere (Jeszeck 1986) and won significant concessions from locals around the country in exchange for concrete offers to make investments.

Although most of its tire plants are organized, Goodyear has one major tire plant that remains nonunion, and it has threatened repeatedly to shift work into this plant and to construct additional such plants if URW locals do not agree to concessions. It steadfastly declined to transfer work to Akron after 1976, however, even though the local there accepted nearly every concession demand made. Instead, it negotiated a concession agreement with its Gadsden, Alabama, local that year to build a new radial passenger tire plant; the plant in Akron was given no such option. Indeed, an industrial relations official of the company later said anonymously that Goodyear "would never build tires in Akron again" because of union work rules and worker attitudes.[15]

In retrospect, Goodyear's concurrent demands for concessions at the Akron passenger tire plant and the shutdown of its Akron truck tire plant were more consistent with an overall conversion strategy than with an effort to keep jobs in Akron. It had built a modern radial truck tire plant in Virginia and subsequently tripled its capacity, which made the Akron plant's bias-ply capacity superfluous; a few years later it closed the Akron facility without offering to negotiate concessions. But Goodyear was also slow to build new radial passenger tire plants outside Akron and therefore needed to continue production in Akron in those lines until it had alternative sources elsewhere, with or without union concessions.

The union at Firestone alternated between resisting and accepting concessions. It rejected them in 1971, even though members were told givebacks might lead to construction of an Akron truck tire plant; then it accepted concessions in 1972 and again in 1977, although job losses and plant closings continued anyway. Having learned from these experiences, the local resisted further concessions in 1979 and Firestone terminated the last of its Akron tire production. Thus, Goodyear made a commitment to (non-Akron) tire production and Firestone left the industry entirely, but union acceptance of concessions in the first instance and avoidance in the second made no difference; each suffered job loss.

Finally, a review of the concessions made by the Akron locals during this time shows that employers preferred work-rule changes to wage reductions. Only after several rounds of work-rule concessions did Firestone, for example, ask for hourly wage cuts. Industrial relations officers from the major Akron firms were unanimous in attaching greater significance to work rules than to wages as deterrents to continued tire production in Akron (Jeszeck 1982). This pattern also appears in concession bargaining outside Akron in the 1980s. Not until the locals in those plants had made generous work-rule concessions were they also forced to make wage givebacks. Often the companies got the same concessions from locals at the non-Akron plants that they had gotten earlier from the Akron unions, having told the Akron workers that if they did not get them they would have to shut down facilities in Akron or transfer the work to the new plants. In some instances the companies took strikes at the non-Akron plants before getting the givebacks (Jeszeck 1986).

Seven-day continuous operation, which alone can result in increases in production of up to 40 percent and which gives management tighter operating control and optimal use of expensive capital equipment, was the most frequent concession made in these negotiations. Such increases in production flexibility and per-unit output are crucial in the tire industry because of its history of cyclical markets and recent stagnant or declining sales in the face of production overcapacity. The result is that both the union and the nonunion segments of the industry currently operate seven-day continuous scheduling.

The Akron tire industry has gone south and will not return. It is a victim of structural changes in domestic and global tire production, mismanagement, and conflict between management and the Akron locals. The last factor was a contributing but not a determining one. Union militancy and strikes at the point of production were made ineffective by obsolete plants, corporate operating mobility, and a declining domestic tire industry. The contract concessions that followed these changes did not and could not save Akron's tire operations. Only timely and proficient radial production could have done that. That probably would have occurred on a plant-by-plant basis, however, rather than in an integrated production region like Akron, whether or not the Akron locals met every concession demand. Domestic firms clearly dismissed Akron as a potential site for substantial investment in radial tire production regardless of what the locals did or did not do. This was despite the experience and skill of the Akron work force, which was "unionized" and historically militant. Because investment and location decisions were beyond the range of union bargaining rights, organized labor in Akron was reduced to a single choice in its response to deindustrialization—capitulate or resist in an adversarial relationship. Either way it had to lose.

The decline of union labor in Akron illustrates the limitations of the existing collective bargaining framework in dealing with domestic industrial restructuring. Like its steel and auto counterparts, what remains of the domestic tire industry probably will survive, although perhaps after even further reductions in capacity. The URW too will be smaller and weaker in its traditional industry jurisdiction and less able to represent the interests of tire workers. Barring renewed union ability to resist, the adoption of worker-oriented economic policies in the United States, or the development of joint labor-management efforts to maintain domestic employment without sacrificing income and job standards, the hard times visited upon tire workers and their union will continue.

America's manufacturing woes in the 1980s often were blamed on workers and unions. The explicit—more often implicit—criticism was that if they had not eroded employer competitiveness through high wages and restrictive work rules, unions would not have lost members when companies were forced to close plants and move production. This interpretation is not true of the tire industry, even though tire production processes gave organized workers considerable control over production and hence the power to negotiate high wages and protective work rules on the shop floor. The flight of tire production from Akron can be explained, instead, mainly by developments that were outside the purview of workers and their unions: corporate shortsightedness, complacency, and slowness to react to new competitive forces in the industry. Popular accounts of Akron's decline notwithstanding, unauthorized work stoppages and restrictive work rules did not destroy the city's tire industry, and concession agreements by Akron local unions did not and could not have saved the industry locally.

Chapter 3
STRIKE AND DECERTIFICATION AT CLINTON CORN PRODUCTS

Adrienne M. Birecree

IN AUGUST 1979, 750 members of Local 6 of the American Federation of Grain Millers (AFGM) struck the Clinton Corn Processing Company (CCPC), a subsidiary of Standard Brands, Inc. (SBI), in Clinton, Iowa. Based on previous labor relations experiences and outcomes at SBI-CCPC, the strikers expected that after a peaceful, reasonably brief strike a compromise settlement would be negotiated containing most of their important demands and they would be back on the job. Instead, management substituted supervisors and local replacement workers for the strikers and pursued an aggressive bargaining strategy, including significant economic concessions and language changes. These concessions, if accepted, would have abolished negotiated work standards and rendered the union powerless as a bargaining agent. In June 1980, after ten months of continued production by the struck plant and unproductive contract negotiations, Local 6 was decertified and the dispute ended.

The Clinton case demonstrates three important trends in labor and industrial relations beginning in 1979. First, the strike was one of the first in which an employer successfully used replacement workers in a relatively large bargaining unit with a history of bargaining power. Second, it shows how a firm's product market initiatives and responses can affect its labor relations policies and practices and how a local union can ignore and misunderstand corporate reorganizations and transitions and as a result become caught unaware and unprepared in the labor-management confrontation that follows. Third, and finally, it shows how the changing industrial environment makes unions, union workers, and communities vulnerable to new, long-term employer strategies involving shifting products and production processes.

It was useful for SBI-CCPC to weaken (or eliminate) the local union as part of a larger strategy to reorganize product lines and production operations from industrial ingredients to consumer-branded products. Although the union posed no threat to the company's authority and capacity to change product lines, it could interfere with the conversion schedule as long as it was the certified bargaining agent for affected workers in Clinton. Further, as long as it had a binding labor contract, it could impose considerable financial costs and penalties during a plant shutdown in Clinton. SBI therefore declined to inform the union or its members of the impending reorganization. To share this information would have constrained its ability to reorganize unilaterally and profitably. Unaware of the plans to reorganize and of Clinton's altered status in SBI's new production priorities, Local 6 went about its labor relations business as if nothing had happened; as a result, it and the members made crucial mistakes leading up to its defeat in the strike and subsequent decertification.

This study considers the structural and institutional factors surrounding the Clinton conflict. In the first part, I trace the development of Standard Brands and its Clinton Corn subsidiary and the economic and political forces that encouraged SBI to reorganize its product lines and confront the Clinton local union. Next, I describe the history of labor relations at Clinton and chronicle the events leading up to and during the 1979 strike. Finally, I analyze the impact of SBI's strategies on Local 6 and the collective bargaining process. The purpose is to show how environmental conditions shaped events and why the labor relations environment in particular made it unlikely if not impossible for Local 6 to respond knowledgeably and constructively in a situation it neither created nor was able to affect.

Standard Brands and Clinton Corn Products

The Parent Corporation

Standard Brands was a diversified food processor and distributor. It was formed in 1929 by the merger of the Fleischman Company, the Royal Baking Powder Company, and the E. W. Gillett Company, Ltd. (Moskowitz, Katz, and Levering 1980:77). Corporate policy into the 1960s revolved around three objectives: (1) organizational growth through diversified mergers and acquisitions; (2) market expansion through increased production capacity in industrial products and heavy advertising and promotional expenditures in certain consumer-branded products; and (3) profitability through price leadership practices in product lines it dominated.

In practice, however, SBI's growth and profits depended mainly on company performance in its line of industrial food ingredients, particularly corn derivatives. Indeed, in the early 1970s, industry analysts characterized SBI as a "staid, musty, old-fashioned" company whose managers were not really interested in rapid expansion and accelerated earnings through product innovation and novel marketing strategies (*Advertising Age,* Feb. 14, 1977, 1). For whatever reasons, in 1975, SBI's directors voted to retire the firm's long-time CEO, after years of hearing internal complaints about his alleged authoritarian management style, and to replace him with F. Ross Johnson, a seasoned General Electric (GE) executive (*New York Times,* May 7, 1980, D2). This change in top management resulted in new directions for SBI in its performance goals, corporate structure, and product market strategy.

Assisted by several GE executives he had brought with him, including a new vice president for human relations, Johnson set out to revamp SBI along GE lines in planning, financial control, and product innovation (*Business Week,* May 16, 1977, 41). He streamlined operations into separate consumer products and food ingredients divisions and introduced "zero-based planning" as a way of targeting SBI's profitable, high-growth markets (*Advertising Age,* Feb. 14, 1977, 14; *Business Week,* Feb. 6, 1978, 91; *International Management,* Feb. 1979, 38–41). Under the new system each existing product line was treated as a new business and its operating efficiency evaluated annually on the basis of defined corporate goals.[1]

In the process, each product line was classified in one of three strategic categories: (1) "invest-grow," to designate products with superior growth and profit potential; (2) "selective support," to designate those with good short-term prospects but uncertain futures; and (3) "divest," to designate those with poor performance outlooks. Based on these identifications, corporate headquarters would divert internal resources from divisions in the latter two categories into its "invest-grow" properties.

In practice, this strategy meant liquidating the "divest" divisions after extracting as much earnings as possible from them in the short run, that is, by "milking" them as "cash cows." According to a 1979 report in the industry trade journal, SBI management had for some time been ferreting out "divest" operations and maximizing their earnings before liquidating them to finance alternative expansion projects (*International Management,* Feb. 1979, 38).[2] The new management thereby scrapped the old growth through acquisition strategy in favor of internal expansion through industrial reorganization and restructuring. The following year *Business Week* (Feb. 18, 1980, 142) identified SBI's industrial-ingredients foods, including corn syrup, which was a mature product line subject to cyclical performance, as an area for elimination. Consumer products was said to be slated for expansion.

CCPC manufactured a natural sweetener called high-fructose corn syrup (HFCS) for industrial food processors. Households use refined cane and beet sugars; industrial food processors use either cane, beet, or corn sweeteners. As use by industrial producers of sweetened foods outpaced domestic use, overall demand shifted from cane and beet to corn sweeteners. Food processors thus purchased 28 percent of all natural sweeteners in 1929 and 60 percent in 1968 (*Food Processing*, Dec. 1974, 34–36). Strong demand pushed up world sugar prices in the 1970s and encouraged industrial users to find natural substitutes. Corn sweetener, comparable to but much cheaper than refined sugar, was the ideal substitute, and HFCS was the best corn sweetener on the market (Knoke and Albrecht 1970).

HFCS was a bonanza for SBI. In the early 1960s, it obtained exclusive licensing from Japanese producers to manufacture HFCS in the United States, and by the end of the decade SBI was still the sole domestic producer. Demand for HFCS continued strong and, combined with the licensing restriction, inflated both prices and profits for SBI (*Business Week*, Feb. 11, 1980, 90). Nevertheless, in the early 1970s, SBI sold licensing rights for HFCS to other producers of domestic sweeteners (perhaps to finance investments in unrelated SBI divisions), and within a few years new plants were producing HFCS. The increase in supply did not appear to dampen the price of HFCS, however, and it was predicted that the overall demand for corn sweetener products would increase three times faster than that for refined sugar. The existing producers, including SBI, were thus encouraged to expand HFCS capacity even more (*Barron's*, Dec. 1, 1975, 70–71). As a result of this widespread expansion, SBI ranked fifth rather than first in corn syrup sales in 1979 (Corporate Data Exchange 1980:40).

At least five variables affect the prices of industrial sweeteners: (1) current supply and demand conditions, (2) historical dominance by a few large producers, (3) economies of scale from mass-production methods, (4) large capital investments and lengthy lead times for new plant construction, and, equally important, (5) government regulation of refined sugar prices. The 1948 Sugar Act first linked sugar prices to changes in the overall consumer price index; this had the effect of setting price floors and guidelines throughout the industry (Knoke and Albrecht 1970). HFCS producers, for example, consistently set prices at 5 to 15 percent of sugar prices, a range that assured them acceptable rates of return on investment (*Barron's*, Dec. 1, 1975, 71).

The regulatory law was repealed in 1974, however, and within a year the prices of both sugar and HFCS had plummeted. This occurred just as the production of HFCS was increasing. Low prices for refined sugar increased demand and undercut the sales of HFCS, leaving HFCS producers, including SBI, saddled with idle facilities and depressed returns on investment. Conditions did not improve markedly until 1979, two years after Congress reinstated the Sugar Act (*Financial World,* Dec. 1, 1978, 30; *Barron's,* Feb. 11, 1980, 4–5).

THE SUBSIDIARY

SBI acquired Clinton Foods in 1956 and renamed it the Clinton Corn Processing Company. CCPC's plant and equipment were continually expanded until it became SBI's largest and most profitable food ingredient line (U.S. Securities and Exchange Commission 1979:5; *Moody's Industrial Manual* 1979:4060–61).

Sales and profits of HFCS in the 1960s helped offset unfavorable market developments threatening SBI's overall performance. By 1974, a record year for CCPC, SBI had expanded the Clinton plant's HFCS capacity by 40 percent. That year, CCPC accounted for 15 percent of SBI's sales and nearly half its profits (*Business Week,* Feb. 11, 1980, 142). SBI planned to have a second HFCS plant in operation by 1977 in Montezuma, New York. CCPC also was a major factor in SBI's ability to double shareholder earnings during 1966–75 (*Milling and Baking News,* Feb. 5, 1974; *Forbes,* Sept. 1, 1976, 59). In late 1975, however, sugar prices, which had been rising in response to booming demand, fell abruptly. CCPC's profits fell along with them.

The situation did not improve until 1977, when Congress again enacted price supports. This time, however, CCPC did not become even marginally profitable until 1979 (*Wall Street Journal,* Nov. 8, 1979, 35). SBI meanwhile publicly blamed its poor overall performance on the "low level of profitability at Clinton, a situation present for the past two and one half years" (*SBI Annual Report* 1978). Indeed, by 1979, food ingredients accounted for only 21 percent of sales and 9 percent of operating income, a direct consequence of the establishment of new firms and overcapacity in the industry. For the first time, according to SBI's annual report for 1979 (p. 33), CCPC's operating performance was below the industry average. This development surely would have made CCPC a candidate for divestiture under SBI's divisional ratings system in the unlikely event that it had not already been so designated.

Because most of its new consumer product lines were not yet profitable, SBI's overall profit performance depended on continued production of HFCS in the short run. CCPC thus became a cash cow four years into the new corporate program to phase out industrial ingredients and expand consumer-branded products.[3] By then, corporate attention was riveted on a major new product line: several brand-name liquors SBI had acquired from the American Distilling Company as the centerpiece of an ambitious initiative by the parent company in that industry (*Wall Street Journal*, Nov. 20, 1979, 8). Soon the business press reported that CEO Ross Johnson expected "major financial assistance from the very operation [CCPC] that so tightly handicapped his first attempt [to diversify] the Standard Brands $500 million-a-year corn milling business." He was quoted to the effect that in 1980 the Clinton operation would "throw off more cash than it" consumed (*Business Week*, Feb. 18, 1980, 144).

Labor Relations and the Strike at Clinton Corn

In 1939, the Grain Millers International Union at CCPC formed an independent local and affiliated directly with the American Federation of Labor (AFL) as a federal local union and with the National Council of Grain Processors as a negotiating unit (Fink 1977:134). Later the AFL chartered the National Council as a separate international union, the American Federation of Grain Millers (AFGM), and the Clinton unit became Local 6 of the AFGM. At its peak, the local represented some 1,200 Clinton workers, but by 1979 the bargaining unit had declined to 750.

The AFGM, a relatively small international union of about thirty-five thousand members in the 1970s, devoted much of its resources to servicing locals that were too small to afford full-time business agents. The rest of its efforts went mainly into negotiating master contracts in the highly centralized cereal industry. The corn syrup locals were big enough to finance their own representatives and therefore were not very dependent on or accountable to the international (telephone interview, Lloyd Frielinger, vice president, central district, AFGM, Des Moines, Feb. 3, 1983).

Local 6 was among the strongest and most militant in an industry known for aggressive local labor unions. It maintained internal solidarity and good relations with the Clinton community. Local 6 negotiating committees and executive boards also imposed tight control over international union relations with the company. It financed a full-time business agent, devised its own bargaining demands, and carried out its own negotiating strategy. International officers and representatives sat in on negotiations, but the local was not accountable to them and consistently negotiated contracts above industry averages and patterns. As a result, its wages were among the highest in the industry and often the object of imitative pattern bargaining by other unions in the Clinton area.[4] Its CCPC contracts in the 1970s included especially strong language to protect seniority principles during layoffs and recalls and to prohibit management from subcontracting work normally done by members of the bargaining unit (interview, Gene Judge, business agent, Carpenter's Union, Clinton, Sept. 25, 1981; interview, William Wentzel, executive board member, Local 6, AFGM, Clinton, Sept. 22, 1981; interview, Mike Krajnevich, business agent, Local 6, AFGM, Clinton, Sept. 26, 1981, and telephone interview, April 13, 1982).

In the decade following World War II, the parties negotiated one-year agreements, sometimes after brief walkouts by Local 6 (Krajnevich interview, 1982). After 1956, however, the various corn syrup locals in the AFGM formed a multiemployer, multiplant negotiating group called the Inter-Union Wet Corn Milling Council. The purpose was to coordinate union demands and settlement patterns across the industry.

Eventually the council succeeded in negotiating reasonably coordinated contract expiration dates among the various corn-processing plants, normally for two-year periods. This enabled them to maximize their potential strike threat and bargaining power (Frielinger interview). During each round of industry bargaining, individual locals would try to exceed the terms and conditions that had been agreed on as acceptable to all the locals and that were considered "the strikable minimum" for individual locals. As the expiration dates became more concentrated, locals that failed to meet or surpass the minimum simply delayed settling (and even worked without contracts) until other locals negotiated at or above the minimum. At that point the stragglers were inclined to strike until they got the pattern or something close to it.

Local 6 often set the pattern in these bargaining rounds. It negotiated two such pattern contracts during the early 1960s and after that sometimes even tried to surpass settlements already accepted by the Corn Milling Council and other locals. (Table 3.1 summarizes CCPC–Local 6 negotiations during 1966–76.) Local 6 won an eleven-day strike in 1966 and conducted successful eight-week and two-week strikes in 1968 and 1970 against company demands that, if accepted, would have reversed the union's earlier contract gains (*Clinton Herald*, June 10, 1980). After the 1980 decertification of Local 6, an AFGM vice president recalled that an atmosphere of "confrontation not negotiation" began to pervade the bargaining table at CCPC in the late 1960s (Frielinger interview). As a result, the local started using wildcat strikes as a tactical weapon at the point of production, in part because

Table 3.1. Summary of CCPC–Local 6 contract negotiations, 1966–76

Bargaining round	Dispute	Issues	Settlement terms
1966	11-day strike	–	–
1968	8-week strike	Mandatory overtime	Company withdrew demand
1970	2-week strike	Pension benefit increase for retirees (nonmandatory bargaining item)	Company doubled benefit levels
1972	Early contract settlement		Parties settled along federal wage guidelines
1974	None	COLA	Industry pattern settlement
1975	Wildcat strike	Disciplinary discharge case	Court ordered union back to work; negotiating and executive board members fired; 130 local union members fired and rehired with loss of seniority; union ordered to pay CCPC $186,835 in lost profits
1976	2-week lockout; 4½ months without contract; 2-week strike	Company refused to follow industry pattern; insurance plan and discipline language also controversial	Company accepted industry pattern

members of the local soon found that the company did not retaliate individually against those involved.

CCPC accepted industry settlement patterns without any resistance in 1972 and 1974. This soothed plant labor relations in Clinton and may have led the workers to believe that CCPC had abandoned all opposition to pattern bargaining and reconciled itself to having a strong union represent its production workers. If so, the workers were misjudging the situation. CCPC was not satisfied with the status quo and indeed was taking steps to change it.

CCPC's management provided the first evidence that it was determined either to weaken or remove the union when it circulated antiunion, anti–collective bargaining literature during a company-sponsored training program for foremen. The materials alleged that unions and collective bargaining were responsible for inefficient production because they inflated operating costs, imposed expensive and intrusive grievance procedures, and instigated periodic production stoppages. CCPC was disadvantaged competitively, they said, because doing business under union contracts meant "running a business with a union business agent looking over our shoulder and in effect having veto power over management's decisions" (Goodfellow 1968:56).

Union-management conflict and confrontation were inevitable. By 1975, a local union officer later recalled (Wentzel interview), CCPC was delaying settlement of formal union grievances, especially those involving nagging health and safety issues, and had intensified irregular and inconvenient work scheduling. Grievances accumulated, and increasingly the local resorted to lengthy (and expensive) arbitration to resolve them (*AFL-CIO News*, Oct. 16, 1976, 1).

Members of the local then called a wildcat strike. A union member had been fired for concealing a small lightbulb in his lunch box as he left the plant and the workers responded by walking off the job in violation of their contract. The strike lasted for two days and ended when the strikers returned under the impression that management had agreed not to retaliate against individual participants in the strike. This was an incorrect assumption. CCPC informed the union it was considering disciplinary action against selected strikers on the basis of a recent court decision that allowed employers to enjoin illegal stoppages and sue unions to recover any operating losses suffered by the owners as a result.

Before the incident was over, forty-five union members had been discharged. This included all but one member of Local 6's executive board and its negotiating committee and several experienced shop-floor stewards. At least 130 other workers were fired and then rehired without seniority (Krajnevich interview, 1981). Management defended the firings as a "normal reaction characterizing any company with any power at all that found itself in those same circumstances" (telephone interview, George Gleason, director, labor relations, SBI, Jan. 25, 1983).[5] By this time CCPC had also changed the name of its labor relations and personnel department to human resources department, thus eliminating the specific reference to union relations, and it had integrated in-plant labor planning and training into corporate finance (*Business Week*, Feb. 26, 1979, 116).

These actions and changes reflected a more openly aggressive policy toward the Clinton union. In 1976, management adamantly refused to follow the industry settlement pattern. When Local 6 rejected CCPC's last contract offer but agreed to continue working without a new contract, the company locked out the workers and tried to maintain operations using supervisors and other non–bargaining unit employees. It called the workers back after two weeks, however, because it could not get sufficient output without them (*AFL-CIO News*, Oct. 16, 1976, 1; *Clinton Herald*, June 10, 1980).

Bargaining continued but ended in stalemate. Once again union members walked off the job, this time in the middle of January 1977, which put the unattended plant in danger of serious mechanical damage because of the freezing weather. The strikers stayed out a week before negotiations resumed and the company accepted the industry pattern. In return, Local 6 agreed to participate with CCPC in a joint human relations committee made up of production workers and company foremen. Relations continued to be tense, however, as the company increased mandatory overtime and denied personal leave requests in order to meet production needs without hiring additional workers (Wentzel interview).

Also in early 1977, an arbitrator decided the 1975 disciplinary cases. He chided the company for imposing severe penalties but nevertheless upheld all but one of the firings and ordered the union to compensate CCPC by paying $200,000 for the wildcat action (Krajnevich interview, 1981). Meanwhile, unsettled grievances continued to accumulate pending additional arbitration. This situation not only aggravated the strained labor relations but also jeopardized Local 6's financial condition.[6]

The new human relations committee conducted an employee attitude survey and released the results a few months before the 1979 contract negotiations started. Findings showed that workers were relatively satisfied with wages and benefits but not with working conditions, especially plant sanitation, job safety, worker training, and equipment maintenance (poor conditions in these areas are often noticeable in plants slated for shutdown). Young workers complained about the inconveniences of shift work and mandatory overtime and indicated they wanted more discretion over vacation schedules and personal leave. The loudest complaint, however, involved the deteriorating union-management relationship and its effect on worker morale and the overall atmosphere in the plant. Workers were convinced that management was aware of the growing seriousness of this problem but chose not to respond (Birecree 1984, appendix II).

During initial contract talks in 1979 CCPC demanded language changes involving worker discipline, seniority rights, and grievance procedures. It offered a wage and benefits package below the federal pay guidelines that had been implemented by the Carter administration and wanted to eliminate or at least cap the cost-of-living clause. In support of its demands, the company pointed to the government's regulation of sugar prices, the Soviets' influence on corn prices worldwide, and the increased competition in the industrial ingredients market. Management claimed it had to improve productivity and reduce direct labor costs to be competitive.

Union negotiators rejected the demands, saying they would punish workers unfairly, restrict union representation in the plant, and generate additional disciplinary actions and arbitration cases. Indeed, the union still wanted to renegotiate the discharge cases from the 1975 wildcat strike. CCPC officials refused because, a company officer said later (Gleason interview, 1983), they were convinced that a show of leniency would encourage more illegal strikes.

CCPC presented its "final" offer a week before the contract expired. It contained essentially the same wage and benefits package and also reduced the COLA benefit formula and modified the arbitration procedure in ways that threatened to make it even more costly to the union. The company mailed a copy of its offer to each member of the bargaining unit, a practice that is historically associated with GE-style Boulwareism but that was unprecedented at CCPC. Then, as it had always done in the past, the company closed the plant for several hours a few days before the contract expired to enable union members to meet and vote on the final offer.

At the meeting, to which the local media were invited, union leaders advised members to reject the company's proposal and instead authorize a twelve-day strike to protest CCPC's bargaining tactics. They later justified the action on the grounds that they were convinced the company was trying to undermine membership confidence in the union (Krajnevich interview, 1981; Frielinger interview).[7] Union members duly rejected the offer and approved the protest strike. Angered by Local 6's tactics, the management of CCPC refused to modify its offer unilaterally but did agree to meet with the union once more before the contract expired to avert a strike.

As a result, in a final bargaining session two days before the scheduled walkout, CCPC added $.20 per hour to its earlier offer, but, contrary to union demands, all the money was to be for across-the-board wage increases over three years rather than for time-paid-not-worked benefits, such as vacations and personal leave days. Nevertheless, the following day the union negotiating committee notified CCPC that it would recommend executive board approval and rank-and-file ratification of the company's last-minute offer with only minor adjustments. Management was pleased but warned that if union members failed to report to work as scheduled it would withdraw the settlement offer.

When the union negotiating committee met with the members of the local's executive board, the latter expressed dissatisfaction with the offer but, after heated discussion, gave their approval. Local 6's business agent immediately informed CCPC of the outcome, which seemed to settle the dispute.

Matters took an unexpected turn during the early-morning hours before the scheduled membership vote. Members of the bargaining committee and of the board who believed that the company was bluffing and would improve the package if the union struck called for a second vote and narrowly reversed the committee's previous decision to ratify the offer.

Local union officials did not inform CCPC of the change, however, and at the membership meeting later that morning the board advised the rank and file to vote against the offer and begin the twelve-day protest strike.[8] The members supported the recommendation and rejected the offer by a three-to-one margin, mainly because management had refused to allocate the additional money for benefits instead of wages. This action officially put the local on strike (Krajnevich interview, 1981; Gleason interview).

Managers at CCPC considered the union's failure to notify them of the second executive board meeting unprofessional, unethical, and unforgivable. Meanwhile, for the first time in the history of Local 6–CCPC labor relations (and two years before President Ronald Reagan permanently replaced striking air traffic controllers), the company placed an ad in the local paper for replacement workers in the event of a strike and began hiring workers the day the strike started (*Clinton Herald*, Aug. 1, 1979). CCPC paid $3.00 to $4.00 more in hourly compensation than other area employers and had no difficulty filling the jobs with local workers. CCPC told the replacements that the law protected their right to work during the strike and assured them their jobs would be permanent.

A week later the company withdrew its final offer and replaced it with one that, if accepted, would have given CCPC the right to discipline the strikers without arbitrating the cases and to retain the replacement workers instead of recalling union members. In effect, Local 6 was being asked to agree to the terms of its own demise. CCPC publicly warned the union it would never get a better offer. Nevertheless, the members of the negotiating committee rejected the offer overwhelmingly (Concerned Citizens 1983).

The strike continued for a month without further talks or signs of compromise. Then, in early September 1979, the company demanded additional union concessions. It wanted to eliminate most skilled trades job classifications under the contract, cluster production jobs into composite classifications, and contract out at least one-quarter of the work formerly done by the members of the bargaining unit. These changes would save the company $5 to $6 million and were necessary, company negotiators said, to compensate CCPC for the losses it had incurred because of the strike (*Clinton Herald*, Oct. 1, 1979). By this logic, the longer the strike lasted, the more the union would have to give up. The union refused to accept the additional concessions and insisted that the striking workers be given employment preference over the replacements when the strike was settled.

The union was stopped cold, however, when CCPC announced that the future of the Clinton plant depended entirely on the city's willingness to protect the safety and job rights of the replacement workers. Indeed, the company suggested that the plant might be closed in any event. The prospect of losing their largest employer (1,350 jobs) brought community officials into the dispute, generally—and perhaps understandably—in support of CCPC's position. In addition to the $25 million in annual payroll, CCPC had paid $1,171,000 in taxes to the city for schools and services during the preceding year. In the face of a recent decline in industrial expansion, city leaders felt they could not afford to offend the company.

Community support can be a powerful determinant in the outcome of a labor-management dispute. In this case the strike divided the community and resulted in diminished support for the bargaining demands of the union workers. Some community groups abandoned the union after acts of property violence were attributed to strikers; others did so after the National Labor Relations Board (NLRB) found the local guilty of unfair labor practices for having insisted before the strike that CCPC bargain over nonmandatory items (*Clinton Herald*, March 6, 1980). Some groups refused to pass judgment on either side and tried to pressure the parties to resolve their differences. The mayor of Clinton, for example, attempted to contact plant officials and SBI executives in New York and urge them to settle the dispute in the interests of the community (interview, Dwayne Walters, mayor, Clinton, Sept. 25, 1981). Still others sympathized with labor throughout the dispute. Local religious organizations and a group called Concerned Citizens offered the most support. The Clinton Catholic Workers and another parish group from nearby Camanche, Iowa, organized demonstrations and pro-strike teach-ins aimed at influencing public opinion (Concerned Citizens 1983). And, during Local 6's subsequent decertification election, an interreligious task force affiliated with the National Federation of Priests Council prepared a detailed report on the strike in an attempt to win support for an equitable resolution (*Clinton Herald,* May 21, 1980).[9]

As the negotiations continued CCPC demanded still more concessions (e.g., loss of severance pay and pensions for union members, who the company said it would not allow back into the plant because of their strike activities). After five months on strike, local union officials had no idea what it would take to get their members back to work. They therefore asked management for a complete list of the company's terms and conditions for a settlement. CCPC responded with a twelve-point proposal containing all of the company's poststrike demands and its prestrike economic package and language changes (table 3.2, Jan. 9, 1980). CCPC's labor relations director later characterized these measures as those companies normally require to ensure control and efficiency following a lengthy stoppage (Gleason interview), but the strikers again rejected them decisively. CCPC then broke off negotiations on the grounds that the local had no intention of resolving the strike.

A final attempt to settle the dispute occurred a few weeks later in a meeting between SBI officials and national union officers from the AFGM and the AFL-CIO. SBI had agreed to talks at that level provided the AFGM promised to put Local 6 under administrative trusteeship. This was not necessary because local officers approved of the top-level negotiations (*Clinton Herald,* March 8, 1980). These talks continued until the parties agreed to a federal mediator's proposed settlement in April 1980, eight months after the stoppage began.

The five-year agreement included the union's original concessions, company changes in the seniority system, a procedure for recalling the strikers based on their individual qualifications rather than their seniority, and the discharge of several union activists. With 80 percent of the eligible members casting ballots,[10] the proposal was defeated ten to one, whereupon SBI announced it would make no further offers. The director of labor relations later explained that national bargaining had failed because the union insisted that the replacement workers be discharged after the strike (Gleason interview). This was impossible, from the company's perspective, because these were loyal workers who had been promised permanent employment.[11]

As these negotiations were under way, an independent attorney filed a decertification petition on behalf of the "hundreds" of disgruntled strikers he said had crossed the picket line to go back to work and now wanted to oust the union (*Clinton Herald,* March 29, 1980). Union leaders were convinced that management had made the decertification literature available to these

Table 3.2. *CCPC bargaining demands, June 1979–April 1980*

Date	Demands
June 11, 1979	• Language changes concerning discipline, layoffs, and grievance procedures: (1) change steps in discipline procedure; (2) lay off by skill or training, not seniority; (3) grievances not resolved in fifteen days to be dropped
July 16	• COLA to be capped, modified, or eliminated • Economic package below the federal government 7 percent guidelines
July 25	• Presentation of company's final offer • July 16 economic package • Modified COLA • Arbitrator to determine who pays cost or pro-rated costs when there is no clearly defined loser
July 31	• Agree to additional $.20: (1) $.10 up front and $.05 each year across the board; (2) money cannot be taken during vacation or used for paid personal leaves or leaves of absence
August 7	• Final offer of July 31 withdrawn • Company right to discipline strikers; discipline can be grieved but not arbitrated • Replacement workers to retain positions after settlement; striking union members to be placed on preferential hiring list
September 6	• Mechanical force to be eliminated and the work contracted out: production jobs clustered—loss of two hundred union jobs • Elimination of language regulating layoff procedure; layoff by skill or training • Threatened plant closing
October 9	• Elimination of serverence pay and pensions for union members ineligible to return to work following strike
November 12	• All concessions requested to this point had to be met before any formal agreement could be reached
December 18	• No change
January 9, 1980	• All previous demands and (1) new agreement to cover three-year period from date of signing; (2) July 16 economic package; (3) language same as July 25 plus all subsequent modifications; (4) no retroactivity on negotiated items
January 24	• Company discontinues local negotiations
Early April 1990	• All previous demands and (1) no plan for recalling strikers; (2) economic package from August 7 offer but with cap on COLA: $.75 second year, $.60 third year; (3) dismissal of nineteen union members including local president; and (4) five-year contract

workers, had helped some of them contact outside counsel, and had coordinated the petition effort (Frielinger interview). Nevertheless, company officials expressed surprise at the petition drive and took no public position on it.

In June 1980, replacement workers and union members who had gone back to work voted 567 to 48 to decertify Local 6; some 414 votes cast by striking union members were challenged by the company, but the NLRB made no ruling on them because they would not have changed the outcome even if they were all no votes on decertification.[12]

Product Strategies and Labor Relations

Aggressive labor relations policies at the Clinton Corn Processing Company enabled the company to defeat a historically militant local union in a strike and eventually to eliminate it in a decertification election. They also enabled management to exercise greater control over production processes and labor costs and, indirectly, over product market revenues. This point is important to an understanding of the Clinton dispute: CCPC's containment and control of labor were critical to SBI's larger strategy of corporate restructuring and reorganization to overcome product market problems and improve financial performance.

SBI's reliance on Clinton's revenues from HFCS in the early 1970s had encouraged SBI to make the necessary capital investments to expand capacity. By 1975, however, when the new group of executive officers took over, conditions had changed in the natural sweetener market. Previous management decisions to increase short-term profits by selling licenses to produce HFCS to rival firms had increased industry supplies dramatically at the same time repeal of the Sugar Act had depressed the demand for and price of corn sweetener. For these reasons, the new SBI executives considered their Clinton subsidiary a low-performance, short-term cash cow. Clinton's status thus diminished significantly inside SBI under the 1978 zero-based planning strategy. Its earnings continued to further the parent company's redefined goals, however, because they were earmarked for reinvestment in new product ventures rather than for modernization or expansion of industrial sweetener production.

Thus, as SBI management saw it in 1979, the best available strategy was to gain complete control of the production process at its Clinton plant and maximize short-term earnings and minimize labor costs. The alternatives—closure, sale, or relocation—were either impossible or unattractive. Plant closure was inadvisable because SBI executives (and the industry) believed that HFCS markets would recover and become profitable again once the Sugar Act was reinstated. Closure in that event would have meant throwing away SBI's considerable sunk investment in Clinton. Selling the plant was impractical during a period of sluggish demand for HFCS, low prices, and industry overcapacity. Under these circumstances, few buyers would have been forthcoming, and certainly none would have made handsome offers. (Later, in 1982, SBI did try, unsuccessfully, to sell the Clinton plant.) Finally, relocation of SBI's HFCS operations was not economically feasible because of the plant's proximity to its principal raw material, corn, as well as the extensive capital costs that would have been involved in such a move.

For these reasons, SBI had to stay and fight the union if it was going to get control over the labor process, minimize labor costs, and maximize Clinton's operating flexibility. Labor costs, which had never been a problem when the operation was running smoothly, were now problematic. CCPC's objective in Clinton was to maximize short-term profits, but union standards and contract language were seen as obstacles to improved cost-revenue margins and overall management control. This was particularly true following the 1976 negotiations, in which Local 6 broke the industry wage pattern and improved union job security considerably.

In addition, contract administration costs had increased steadily during the 1970s as the union became more demanding, the company more resistant, and negotiations more intractable. The rising incidence of wildcat strikes and demands for more wages for time not worked, improved health and safety conditions, and greater employee training promised higher labor costs in the future. Probably more important, contract provisions prevented or discouraged management from subcontracting bargaining unit work and reorganizing production processes without union participation. The contract also provided generous financial compensation to union members who were adversely affected by work force reductions.

The confrontation that followed shows that labor relations can be part of a corporate strategy just as easily as they can be affected by a strategy. Thus, as Beat Hotz-Holt (1988:70) concludes, "Adjusting industrial relations and labor market structures becomes itself part of company strategy, although implementing change might need quite some time."

In this case, management apparently wanted to alter the union's status over time and in that way reduce or eliminate union and contractual constraints. The accumulation of grievance and arbitration cases beginning in 1975, management's punitive response to the wildcat strike, and its attempt to maintain production with supervisory personnel during the 1976 dispute signaled a change in policy, even if union members and officers did not perceive or appreciate the changed environment. In any event, by 1979, the shift in CCPC's labor strategy was clear to everyone as a result of the number and severity of its concession demands and the lengthy and (for the union) destructive impasse that resulted.

CCPC combined concession demands that would weaken the union on the shop floor and at the bargaining table with refusal to bargain over items that were acutely important to the union and the workers. As a result, rifts occurred among the members and the union was destabilized internally. CCPC then escalated its concession demands and hired replacement workers, a strategy that enabled it to exploit the region's high unemployment levels—10 percent at the time of the strike. The effect was to give CCPC a permanent and uncompromising advantage in the 1979 contract negotiations. As the company continued to gain leverage, its escalating concession demands transformed the dispute from a contest over the terms and conditions of employment to a war of attrition over union survival.

CCPC's readiness to set aside more money but its unwillingness to put it into fringe benefits rather than direct wage increases suggests an intent on its part to move toward an open-shop environment in which improved terms and conditions of employment reflect management goals and objectives and to discredit the union as an effective representative of rank-and-file interests. Nonunion workplaces typically pay wages that are comparable to those in union shops but have fringe benefits that are less costly, partly because they hire younger workers whose medical, pension, and other benefit costs are lower than those of higher-seniority workers. Thus, after the union was decertified and the company enjoyed unilateral control in these matters, CCPC granted wage increases (not paid-time benefits) to the replacement workers. The company also substituted job clusters for separate skill classifications and pay grades, subcontracted plant maintenance work, and introduced the team concept into the labor process.

CCPC's new corporate development strategy and its new labor policy reflected GE's influence on the new management team. Certainly its 1979 bargaining strategy is reminiscent of the aggressive labor tactics first introduced in the late 1940s by Lemuel Boulware to play GE unions off against one another. Managers were instructed to offer best and final offers directly to union members and then, with the union in a state of turmoil, to give union negotiators time limits within which to respond before the offer was rescinded and replaced by one even less desirable. In its original form Boulwareism was ruled an unfair labor practice, but, in a more sophisticated form and assisted by a sympathetic administrative law environment, the approach proved to be effective in the late 1970s.

The success of management tactics in labor relations depends a great deal on the perceptiveness and response of the union involved. The union in this instance was not perceptive and did not respond appropriately, no doubt partly because management's tactics were not yet common in American labor relations and therefore not easily recognized and fully understood. Thus, throughout the transitional period of the late 1970s, Local 6's focus remained where it had always been—on the immediate interests of its members. Beyond that, however, neither the officers nor the rank and file showed interest in or appreciation for CCPC's new operating strategy, its changing corporate structure and behavior, or its shifting position in the natural sweetener market. Moreover, they seemed to ignore cumulative evidence that CCPC was following a more aggressive, purposeful labor relations policy and dismissed it as nothing more than the conflict phase of the normal cycle of labor-management relations under collective bargaining, to which union members were accustomed.

This was a reasonable but costly interpretation.[13] Local 6 had been effective at the bargaining table and in the workplace throughout the 1960s and most of the 1970s. Despite the punitive firings in 1975, the 1977 settlement clearly favored the union and confirmed its bargaining power. Members therefore had reason to believe they could resist the company's unusual and unexpected demands in 1979. Tradition and misplaced confidence caused the union to underestimate the company's power and left it unprepared to handle the events that followed.

CCPC successfully baited union leaders and members both before and during negotiations. It manipulated union militance to its own advantage and systematically enhanced its own bargaining position. First, by working with the joint committee, management gained information from the questionnaire on standards and plant working conditions. Management thus knew the relative importance of various union bargaining demands and could construct an appropriate bargaining agenda. Second, by appealing directly to the membership during negotiations, the company elicited a premature signal from the union that it would strike, thereby giving CCPC time and opportunity to prepare to maintain production with replacement workers.

Third, although local union officials reportedly warned the membership that a strike probably would trigger a fierce company response (Krajnevich interview, 1981), union members refused to believe that the company's initial actions were but a prelude to the use of more aggressive tactics later.

It was as if union workers at CCPC did not take into account the obvious before leaving their jobs: that the company had legal grounds to replace them; that CCPC could demand union concessions that were institutionally and politically unacceptable to union officers and members, and then make acceptance of these demands the price of settling the dispute and going back to work; and that the legal process they had started eventually would give others (i.e., permanent replacements) the opportunity and authority to nullify the original workers' contract and decertify their union.

By the mid-1970s, SBI's diversification strategy was relatively commonplace in American industry, but its labor relations were not yet widespread. Thus, they were an early prototype of the sophisticated, aggressive bargaining practices that surfaced and flourished in the 1980s. Local 6 leaders and members were vulnerable to the new tactics because they did not recognize them or appreciate their significance.[14] A better understanding of the changing environment might have enabled the local to preserve some or most of its contractual labor standards and its legal status as bargaining agent. If so, the union might have been able to negotiate a termination agreement when Standard Brands decided to lease the Clinton plant to an industrial competitor in 1982 and in doing so might have protected bargaining unit members during the transition period.

Chapter 4
The Closing of Wisconsin Steel

David C. Ranney

We had this big meeting with the President and some of his associates. He says, "We are having this meeting to tell all you people who work for Wisconsin Steel not to worry about the mill shutting down. All this talk is just rumor. . . . This plant is going to be rolling right along. So don't have no fears about its shutting down." Two days later I call up to get my schedule. The guy tells me, "There is no more plant. We are shut down. . . . Your job is over. You lost everything."

—Former Wisconsin Steel worker, 1984

We're lean and mean. Today we have a future.

—Donald D. Lennox, chair,
Navistar Corporation, 1986

FOR SEVERAL MONTHS BEGINNING in late 1979, rumors spread among the workers in Wisconsin Steel in Chicago that the mill was about to close. By March 27, 1980, with morale low and talk of a shutdown persisting, the mill's management called an unprecedented meeting of the entire work force of thirty-five hundred to announce the end of a strike against International Harvester that had seriously affected the demand for Wisconsin Steel's products. The main reason for the meeting, however, seemed to be to assure the workers that the mill would not close. Frank Lumpkin, a black man who had worked for thirty years at the mill and who was a key leader of the movement to prevent its closing, recalls that meeting (interview, Jan. 12, 1990):

> I'll never forget it. The night of March 27 they come to us at a mass meeting at 1033 [the Republic Steel union hall] and have the management and the foremen all on the platform. They're saying, "We made it!" And they say the strike is settled. Everything is going to be perfect. And congratulations to the union and the workers because it was us pulling together that was able to make this thing a success. Everybody went home—union and management—happy. And the next day they put a lock on the gate.

Indeed, on March 28 when the second-shift workers arrived, the gates were locked and a small sign simply said "Closed." One first-shift maintenance worker who had been working overtime had to find a guard to let him out. He did not know about the mill's demise until he got outside.

The quick and brutal closing came after International Harvester, which had sold the mill in 1977 to a subsidiary of Envirodyne Industries, foreclosed on coal and iron mines that had been put up as collateral for the purchase. Chase Manhattan Bank, upon hearing of Harvester's action, immediately sent an armed security force to Chicago to close the mill in order to secure the assets behind a $35 million loan that it had made to Envirodyne. Suddenly, despite all the assurances to the contrary, thirty-five hundred women and men found themselves without jobs. Furthermore, Envirodyne filed for bankruptcy and the courts immediately froze the company's assets, including payroll funds and pensions. Paychecks already issued but not yet cashed bounced and the workers found themselves at the end of a very long line of creditors.

All plant closings are hard on the work force, but this one, because of its speed and because the pensions and payrolls were frozen, was particularly devastating. One former worker commented on the situation four years after the closing:

> I know fifteen guys who got divorced on account of this. I know quite a few guys who turned out to be drunks. I know four guys that committed suicide. The situation is bleak and getting bleaker.[1]

Another worker who lost everything described his feelings:

> When I go to bed I get the pressure. When I get up I got the pressure—the same thing. I don't know if it's really through or what. But I feel so little when other people work. I feel like they are saying you are nothing. You're a nobody. And that's the way I feel myself. So I just kept to myself.

The union at Wisconsin Steel was not able to mount an effective resistance to the closing or to fight for the rights of the workers afterward. The Progressive Steelworkers Union (PSW) was an "independent union" set up by International Harvester in 1937 as a way to avoid the militant organizing drive of the Congress of Industrial Organizations (CIO). PSW had historically never been a militant organization and had close ties with politicians in Chicago's 10th Ward, where the mill was located. In the 1970s, black and Latino workers attempted to make the union responsive to their needs and eventually succeeded in electing a coalition slate that resulted in Latino, white, and black officers. Nevertheless, in 1977, the president of the union signed a contract that seriously compromised the workers' pension and severance pay rights. When the plant closed so suddenly, the union essentially became defunct and the workers continued to be divided along racial lines.

An alternative organization, the Wisconsin Steelworkers Save Our Jobs Committee, was organized by Frank Lumpkin after the closing. The group took three busloads of workers to Washington, D.C., to secure pension rights guaranteed by the Pension Benefit Guarantee Corporation (PBGC). It also launched a campaign to reopen the mill and initiated a lawsuit against International Harvester to gain contractual benefits and punitive damages for what the group claimed had been a fraudulent sale of the mill to Envirodyne. The suit against International Harvester was not settled until 1988, however, and additional litigation in connection with the closing continues. In the meantime the mill was closed permanently. A $62 million blast furnace that was nearly completed but never fired up was dynamited and sold for scrap.

Although the closing of Wisconsin Steel appeared to be quite sudden, in reality the events leading up to it began in the mid-1950s. The workers at the mill were victims of a process of industrial restructuring that included a string of corporate decisions spanning more than three decades. The "lean and mean" Navistar Corporation (formerly International Harvester) was at the forefront of that process. In the course of restructuring, the number of workers employed by the once-giant corporation dropped from a high of one hundred thousand to about fifteen thousand. Thus, the closing of the mill was a piece of a much larger picture. In telling the Wisconsin Steel story, I will explore several questions: Why did Wisconsin Steel's management and parent corporations, International Harvester, Envirodyne, and EDC Holding Corporation, do what they did? Can their actions be explained as part of some "natural process" on the road to a "postindustrial society," or are there alternative explanations related to specific corporate management strategies? This case study points to the latter explanation. Harvester's strategy historically was to be the lead firm in a number of oligopolized product markets (markets with a limited number of competitors). Success depended on strict control of costs, an ability to use profitable operations in one area to feed other operations, and an expanding economy.[2]

Another question this case study explores concerns the ability of workers to resist a plant closing. Workers could see manifestations of corporate decisions that led to the closing long before the closing itself. Had there been an effective, militant, and unified labor organization, these early warning signs could have been the basis of actions that would have made the closing quite costly for International Harvester and Wisconsin Steel management and less costly for the workers. A weak company-oriented labor organization and a racially divided work force prevented a timely and militant resistance.

Three characteristics of the history of International Harvester and Wisconsin Steel are useful in understanding the corporate decisions that led to the closing of the mill. All are part of a corporate ideology that greatly influenced the nature of the restructuring process. The first was a tendency to attempt to limit competition and dominate the resulting struggle among a few competitors for the control of market shares. Harvester's management practice from its very founding could best be labeled an "oligopolistic mentality"; corporate priorities were focused more on expansion and marketing than on product quality or design. The second characteristic of Harvester's corporate ideology was its open hostility toward organized labor and a tendency to deal with labor militancy either with the velvet glove of paternalism or the iron fist of repression. The third characteristic was that racial relations were historically tied to the company's attitude toward organized labor. All three characteristics of Harvester's approach to corporate management contributed to the demise of Wisconsin Steel and the particularly cruel form that this closing took.

Historical Background

Before there was International Harvester, there was the McCormick Harvester Machine Company, founded in Chicago in 1847 by Cyrus McCormick. For its first fifty years, the company faced increasing competition from eighteen separate companies and a challenge from a growing organized labor movement that was demanding a shorter work day.

After McCormick died in 1884, his son took over the business and immediately attempted to achieve dominance on both labor and corporate fronts. On the labor front, he attempted to crush the National Union of Iron Molders, Local 233, which was the strongest force in his plant, thereby touching off the famous Haymarket riot of 1886 (Ozanne 1967:3–29). With respect to his competition, his efforts were directed toward creating a giant trust that would limit the number of competitors and enable the McCormick Company to dominate the reaper industry (*Crain's Chicago Business*, Nov. 8, 1982, 22).

Before the death of Cyrus McCormick, Sr., McCormick's policies toward labor favored paternalism. A coalition of Democratic party industrialists supported the policies of Chicago's mayor, Carter H. Harrison, which allowed labor considerable leeway in the conduct of strikes. Harrison's goal was to bring labor leaders into the party fold while at the same time avoiding mass strikes by confining militancy to ethnic neighborhoods (Schneirov, n.d.). Typically, police were assigned to factories in the neighborhoods where they lived, which caused them to side with the workers. While Cyrus McCormick was not a supporter of Harrison, he generally supported his paternalistic approach to dealing with labor strife.

The younger McCormick took a different approach. First, he attempted to cut wages. With the complicity of the Irish police assigned to the plant, however, the workers won the strike that resulted. Next, he attempted to automate the molding process to get rid of the troublesome molders. That effort failed, and the molders returned only to organize the entire plant for a strike. At this point, McCormick made a deal with Harrison. Political support was traded for a replacement of Police Commander O'Donnell with Inspector John Bonfield, who was known to be an uncompromising antilabor police officer with no ethnic ties to McCormick's largely Irish work force. When the strike broke out, violence erupted and two workers were shot to death. It was a protest over that action that led to the Haymarket events (Ozanne 1967:22–24).

On the corporate front, both McCormicks attempted to eliminate competition through buyouts. Several efforts made in the late 1880s failed. In 1902, however, McCormick was able to merge with his most formidable competitor, William Deering. Deering's company was second in size to McCormick's, but it included something extra—a steel mill and some coal and iron mines. These were important to withstand the price pressures imposed by the new steel trust, the U.S. Steel Corporation. McCormick now stood at the helm of the largest manufacturer of farm equipment in the world. Further, his was an integrated firm with its own steel-making facility and its own source of raw materials to make the steel. The new firm was called International Harvester.

Harvester consolidated its position by buying more and more firms and expanding into other product markets, including heavy trucks and construction equipment. Overseas operations were developed for all product markets. Soon, Harvester dwarfed its competitors. Only John Deere, which was itself buying up smaller firms, was competitive in farm equipment. Caterpillar began producing farm equipment just before World War I, and Ford was competitive in trucks, but Harvester made all three products and had established itself as a major U.S. corporation.

The aftermath of the Haymarket executions had a chilling effect on organized labor. McCormick moved to consolidate his gain on the labor front with a burst of paternalistic policies designed to promote labor peace. He instituted a special employee benefit association, an internal social security system before there was national Social Security. He also provided health and accident insurance and opened a credit union. Trade unions, however, were forcefully resisted.

In the 1920s, Harvester employees were forced to join company-dominated "industrial worker councils," which they termed "independent unions." These persisted until they were declared illegal under the Wagner Act in the 1930s. Harvester then turned its efforts to encouraging independent unions, mixing the velvet glove of paternalism with the harsher iron fist, but despite the efforts of Harvester's management, CIO industrial unionism had an impact on the company. Two unions emerged and vied for control: the United Auto Workers and the radical United Farm Equipment and Metal Workers of America (FE).

Racial policies during this period were heavily influenced by efforts to avoid unionization. Following World War I, labor shortages and the availability of black workers favored their integration into the work force. Harvester's labor relations department specifically discouraged their hiring, however, on the grounds that blacks had been active in efforts to organize American Federation of Labor unions.

In 1925, Harvester did a study of the impact of black workers on those firms where they were employed. The results showed blacks to be more productive and to have lower turnover rates than whites. Nevertheless, the company continued to discourage the hiring of blacks until the 1940s, although it left that decision to local plant superintendents. At Wisconsin Steel no black people were employed until 1943. Labor shortages were met by hiring Mexicans recruited by the mill from as far away as Kansas City (Ozanne 1967:184–85).

While Harvester's efforts to avoid the new industrial unions by organizing independent organizations generally failed, they seemed to work in a few notable instances. One of these was in the steel division. The Progressive Steelworkers Union was formed at Wisconsin Steel in 1937 at the time giant U.S. Steel recognized the United Steelworkers of America (USWA). A number of other steel companies, known as "little steel," attempted to crush the new union by force, resulting in the Republic Steel massacre on Memorial Day of 1937.

Harvester avoided such confrontations by engineering a succession from its outlawed industrial workers council to the new PSW. The deal offered by Harvester was to meet the settlement deals of other USWA locals without the expense or aggravation of militant strikes. Workers at Wisconsin Steel never (until the last few years of its existence) had to punch a clock; informal work scheduling permitted workers to change hours of work with one another; coal and electricity were supplied to neighborhood churches; and company-sponsored baseball teams and picnics were common. Furthermore, the pay and working conditions matched those of other area mills. Thus, during the major steel strikes of 1919, 1937, 1941, and 1959, Wisconsin Steel workers did not go out. Further, by keeping black workers out of the plant until forced to stop doing so in the early 1940s, Harvester was able to strengthen its paternalistic grip by promoting a "family" atmosphere.

Postwar Expansion: Prelude to Modern Restructuring

After World War II, Harvester again faced major competition on several fronts. Deere threatened hegemony in the farm equipment business and Caterpillar in construction equipment. Harvester countered with further expansion, made possible by the general economic expansion following the war. Consumer demand was high and interest rates low.

Despite the recession of 1954, conditions remained good until the late 1950s, when the economy was jolted with back-to-back recessions accompanied by higher rates of inflation and interest, all of which affected Harvester's main lines of business: farm equipment, construction equipment, and steel. Table 4.1 shows trends in the value added by the manufacture of these three products during the 1950s. Using constant dollars, value added can be used as a rough measure of demand. While farm equipment was hit hard by the recessions at the end of the 1950s, construction equipment and steel production were not.

Table 4.1. Value added by manufacture of farm equipment, construction equipment, and steel at International Harvester, 1951–60 (in billions of 1977 dollars)

Year	Farm equipment	Construction equipment	Steel
1951	$3.0	$2.1	$11.5
1952	3.0	2.4	9.7
1953	2.9	2.4	12.6
1954[a]	2.3	2.0	11.7
1955	2.8	2.7	15.7
1956	3.0	3.3	16.3
1957	2.9	3.1	16.0
1958[a]	2.3	4.3	14.4
1959	2.4	5.0	16.2
1960[a]	1.9	4.4	15.7

Source: U.S. Department of Commerce, *Annual Survey of Manufactures.*
[a]Recession years.

Motivated both by the positive economic conditions and by its general strategy to be the lead firm in a variety of markets, Harvester responded to the competition in the late 1940s from Deere and Caterpillar with an unprecedented expansion on all fronts. It organized construction equipment business as a separate division, and heavy capital investments were made. A new business was started to produce refrigerators, which it sold through its farm equipment dealerships. The company also expanded some farm equipment plants and built new ones. There was little investment in steel, however, since the Wisconsin Steel mill was able to handle the booming production demands. All together, International Harvester spent $184 million and added thirty thousand workers between 1947 and 1949 (*Crain's Chicago Business,* Nov. 8, 1982, 32).

During the 1950s, Harvester's efforts focused on sales. A tight network of dealerships was established between 1951 and 1959. Initially, three thousand new dealerships were started; three thousand more were added in 1955. During the recession years of the late 1950s the number was cut back to forty-five hundred, but despite the recession, the dealerships that remained were modernized.

Combating Labor Militancy

During this expansion there were other developments on the labor front that reaffirmed Harvester's historical approach to organized labor. Between 1945 and 1958, there were more than two thousand work stoppages at Harvester, and from 1954 to 1958, forty-eight thousand grievances reached the highest level (Ozanne 1967:209). To overcome this militancy, Harvester turned to a specialist. William Reilly had come up through the ranks at Wisconsin Steel. In fact, he had been president of PSW there.

Reilly took a hard line in the 1952 contract negotiations. His weapon was to exploit a rivalry between the United Auto Workers and the Farm Equipment Workers that went back to the 1940s. The UAW had engaged in extensive red baiting of FE union officials. Reilly played one union off against the other. The result was an agreement that left the UAW the sole representative of the workers and a contract designed to ensure labor peace. The union got minimal wage increases and an agreement to end involuntary overtime. To effect the deal, however, the UAW had to maintain former FE officials in their previous positions. This would come back to haunt Harvester and ironically play a role in the eventual closing of Wisconsin Steel.

Labor Policy and Race

Corporate racial policies during the postwar period were closely related to Harvester's fear of organized labor. As noted above, before World War II,

Harvester management resisted the hiring of blacks, probably because they were perceived to be more militant. Thus, by 1940, only 4.5 percent of Harvester's workers were black. In the following year, however, President Franklin Delano Roosevelt established the Fair Employment Practices Commission (FEPC) and issued an executive order prohibiting racial discrimination in firms that wished to do business with the federal government (Ozanne 1967:188). Harvester's initial response was to integrate its segregated plants by moving several black workers from its other factories. At Wisconsin Steel, the percentage of blacks went from 0 to 11.2 percent. Many of the black workers who started at Wisconsin Steel in 1942 were transferred from McCormick Reaper.

Eventually, Harvester moved to a policy of containment of blacks within the company and even hired a special human relations person, Sara Southall, who had been employed by the Chicago Urban League and had served on the FEPC. By 1959, the percentage of blacks at Harvester had risen to 14 percent and the company, including its locker and eating facilities, was declared to be fully integrated. Frank Lumpkin (interview) recalls this period:

> Republic Steel was strictly organized on the basis of black and white unity. But Wisconsin Steel just sat there with no blacks until the FEPC made them put some in. One guy tells me how there were no benches for people to sit on. This black guy was sitting down anyway and a white guy says, "You can't sit there." The black guy says, "Can't I? Just watch!" And they stood up to the fight and got the benches. Most guys understood the militancy of the black workers once they come into Wisconsin Steel. They changed the whole pattern of the way they treated everyone.

By the 1950s, Harvester's traditional attitude of paternalism toward workers at Wisconsin Steel had been upset by the new racial composition. The company's racial policies reinforced divisions within the plant insofar as blacks were confined to certain classifications and departments. In addition, Harvester refused to protect its black workers from mob violence being inflicted on blacks in the vicinity of the mill. The violence had erupted in 1954 when a black family attempted to move into the Trumbull Park Housing Project, a few blocks from Wisconsin Steel. For two years gangs of whites attacked any blacks who came near the neighborhood. According to Lumpkin (interview):

> The mill was pretty racist when I got there in 1950. I had come out of the merchant marine and was a steam engineer. I was hired at Wisconsin Steel as a chipper. At the time they had a lot of steam-driven machines. . . . I tried to get out of the chipping department and into the steam and power, which was all

> white. I had to get the superintendent's permission to transfer, but I couldn't get it and had to remain a chipper. . . . The racism came to a head when they had Trumbull Park. When the black guys come they'd stone the cars and break the glass. In the parking lot they'd attack black guys going out and coming in. For a long time this thing went on—two years! The [white] guys wouldn't buy this for the guys in the mill because they worked together. But they could go along [with the notion] that outsiders were coming in as troublemakers.

The racist job classifications and the fact that the white workers could accept that mobs were attacking black workers who wished to live in the neighborhood where the mill was located was a source of division among the workers that interfered with the establishment of the unity needed to fight against the closing and gain legitimate rights after the closing occurred. The company did nothing to prevent its workers from being attacked and actively perpetuated discriminatory job classifications. It seemed to be a policy of divide and rule.

Oversights and Reorganization

Harvester apparently overlooked some major demographic and economic trends crucial to the future of the corporation. One was the increasing rate of urbanization. In 1950, the percentage of U.S. residents living in rural areas was 55 percent. By 1960, it had declined to 42 percent. Further, there was a trend toward large-scale mass production in the farm industry that increased the need for farm machinery. The average farm acreage grew by 38 percent between 1950 and 1960. As a result, farmers found it more advantageous to plow, plant, and cultivate four or even six rows simultaneously rather than the standard two rows of a decade earlier.

Harvester failed to respond to these trends. It stayed with an outmoded distribution system based on small dealers in rural communities at the time the family farm was in decline. Furthermore, its lack of product development meant that while Deere was introducing large equipment to handle more rows of crops at a time, Harvester was still producing the smaller equipment designed for a different era.

During the recessions of 1958 and 1960 Harvester found itself in a difficult position. While it was ahead of its competitors in sales and profits, absolute profit had declined by $20 million during the decade, while Deere's and Caterpillar's had increased. Furthermore, Harvester's profit margins fell by more than 20 percent and its return on assets by more than 40 percent (*Crain's Chicago Business*, Nov. 8, 1982, 35). Harvester was also financially overextended, and it had outmoded products and some very old production facilities.

The initial response to these difficult conditions was to cut back. In 1955, Harvester sold its refrigerator business to Whirlpool. In 1958, it trimmed the number of sales outlets from six thousand to forty-five hundred, and in 1959 it closed five factories, including the original McCormick Reaper plant on Chicago's West Side. At the same time it tried to make up what it had lost to Deere and Caterpillar through further vertical integration. A new firm was purchased that made turbo engines, which Harvester hoped to develop for its trucks. Harvester also began to make larger farm equipment and to retool production lines for that purpose.

In the early 1950s, output at Wisconsin Steel continued to be geared to Harvester's expansionist policy. There was little capital investment, but the mill was generally considered to be an important contributor to overall performance. That began to change in the mid-1950s. The mill simply was not prepared to produce the steel products required for the larger farm equipment that Harvester was finally manufacturing.

By the 1960s, Harvester was purchasing much of its steel elsewhere, and only 35 percent of Wisconsin Steel's sales were to the parent company. Another 10 percent went to Harvester suppliers and the remainder to its competitors (*Crain's Chicago Business,* Nov. 8, 1982, 39). This was a turning point for the mill. To increase its capacity to serve the parent corporation (its original purpose), it had to retool the mill. To compete with other mills, it had to develop a market niche outside. Neither course was taken.

To workers in the mill, things looked fine. Even within the company, no one raised serious questions about current or future viability of Wisconsin Steel. But once Wisconsin Steel could neither satisfy Harvester's steel needs nor develop a product market niche outside Harvester's vertically integrated production process, the mill was in fact no longer a viable part of Harvester's corporate structure. The situation became more and more serious as Harvester's cash needs grew.

THE 1960s: THE DECLINE OF INTERNATIONAL HARVESTER

In the early 1960s, Harry Bercher became chairman of International Harvester. Bercher had once been general manager of Wisconsin Steel and considered the division to be special. Workers at the mill knew Bercher and considered his rise to the top to be fortunate for them.

Bercher was chairman between 1962 and 1971. These were relatively good times economically. Nonetheless, it was clear at Harvester that the company was losing ground to its competitors in two areas—Deere in farm equipment and Caterpillar in construction equipment.

Between 1961 and 1967, investment conditions were favorable. The rate of interest was relatively low (between 4.5 percent and 5.6 percent), and inflation ran between 1 percent and 3 percent. Furthermore, the demand for steel, farm equipment, construction equipment, and trucks was strong, as table 4.2 illustrates. The value of shipments for construction equipment expanded throughout the period. For farm equipment, steel, and motor vehicles (a separate breakdown for trucks is not available), shipments grew until the recession of 1968. The value of farm equipment shipments doubled during the period; construction equipment nearly tripled. These conditions gave Harvester an impetus to try to stop the decline in its fortunes relative to Deere and Caterpillar. The corporate gaze remained firmly fixed on market shares.

Bercher began his tenure with substantial investment in two areas. One was construction equipment. The other was steel, Bercher's major interest. His background at Harvester caused him to look for market shares in steel even though the mill had become a relatively minor part of the business. There was every indication that he intended to retool the mill so that it could both become competitive in the steel industry (which was expanding at the time) and serve Harvester's cost-control needs by supplying more steel to its other divisions. Bercher thus began a modernization program at the mill through the purchase of a modern basic oxygen furnace and a new technology—a continuous caster. In 1968, the mill upgraded its coke production facilities by purchasing forty-five modern coke ovens. The new furnace and caster cost a total of $29 million—nearly a third of Harvester's capital spending budget.

Table 4.2. Shipments of farm equipment, construction equipment, motor vehicles, and steel, 1961–69 (in billions of 1977 dollars)

Year	Farm equipment	Construction equipment	Motor vehicles	Steel
1961[a]	3.9	2.7	22.5	23.1
1962	5.0	4.8	30.3	24.3
1963	5.8	5.4	32.1	25.9
1964	6.3	6.3	32.8	28.3
1965	6.6	6.9	40.8	30.4
1966	8.1	7.0	32.9	29.7
1967	7.8	7.5	28.3	27.6
1968[a]	7.4	7.9	33.4	29.1
1969[a]	6.8	8.0	30.7	28.6

Source: U.S. Department of Commerce 1971.
[a]Recession Years

Bercher also put money into the construction equipment business and into farm equipment and other parts of the corporation. Harvester's competitors, by contrast, specialized in only one major product that demanded attention and resources. As a result, its competitors outspent Harvester in every area throughout the period.

By the end of Bercher's tenure, inflation and interest rates had doubled, a recession was in full swing, and Harvester was not any better off than before he took office. It was still spread thin and having cash-flow problems. Although Wisconsin Steel had begun to be modernized, the job was far from complete. Steelmakers came from far and wide to see the state-of-the-art coke operation, the new basic oxygen furnaces, and the caster. But behind this outward display much of the mill was old and unable to produce for the parent company or to compete fully with other integrated mills. Wisconsin Steel was of no use to Harvester. It was neither a major player in a growing product market nor a source of profits that could be put into other divisions. In fact, Wisconsin Steel was draining Harvester of badly needed cash.

Dumping of Wisconsin Steel, 1971–77

Harry Bercher retired in 1971 and was replaced by Brooks McCormick, a descendant of McCormick's founder. When he took over, the company was in trouble and the country was headed for one of its most serious economic downturns since the 1929 crash. His tenure was marked by major corporate reorganization, austerity that included streamlining and cost cutting, and an emphasis on business planning. Trying to dominate several oligopolized product markets was out of the question; the goal at this point had to be survival. Profits had reached a high point in 1966 and fallen each year since then. Between 1966 and 1970, profits declined by 42 percent (*Crain's Chicago Business*, Nov. 8, 1982, 41).

Conditions were far from ideal for saving the corporate giant. In 1974, there was a major recession that for the first time featured simultaneous high unemployment and double-digit inflation. The prime interest rate, which banks charge their best customers, reached 10.8 percent, also a historical high. And for the first time in U.S. history there was a negative balance of trade, representing the decline of U.S. world hegemony.

It was under these most unfavorable conditions that McCormick set out to save Harvester. No sooner had he taken office than the Wisconsin Steel Division was calling unfavorable attention to itself. In 1970, Congress passed the Clean Air Amendments. Whatever innovations were made in the mill during Bercher's tenure, pollution control was not among them. Wisconsin

Steel was cited with numerous violations and ordered to clean up or shut down. Pollution control for Harvester's steel operation did not fit with McCormick's streamlining plans. Neither did any other investment in Wisconsin Steel. The entire mill modernization effort initiated by Bercher was scrapped.

Although Harvester's annual reports in the early 1970s did not include profitability figures on the mill, Wisconsin Steel executives claimed that it was still a profitable operation (*Crain's Chicago Business,* Nov. 15, 1982, 21). Furthermore, demand for steel was relatively strong. Between 1971 and 1974, the value of steel shipments in constant dollars grew by 60 percent and employment by 5 percent. Government forecasters were predicting a 3 percent growth in shipments in 1971 and a 10 percent rate of growth in 1972 (U.S. Department of Commerce 1971). To International Harvester's management, however, Wisconsin Steel was now evaluated from the perspective of what it had been before the Bercher years. The mill had to be a viable part of an integrated production process or earn sufficient profits to feed the corporation's cash appetite. While the objective in previous years had been to help Harvester take the lead in its various product markets, in 1971 Wisconsin Steel and all the other divisions had to contribute positively to an effort to save the corporation from extinction.

In fact, Wisconsin Steel had become a liability. There was simply no way at this point that Harvester could continue Bercher's program and survive. The corporate cash-flow crisis was too great. Bercher's modernization plan had been a tactical error from the perspective of Harvester's needs as they had developed since the 1950s. The workers at the mill would have been better off if Bercher had sold the mill instead of modernizing it. But Bercher too was looking at the mill as a means to an end. From his steel-oriented perspective, he thought that the revival of the mill would enhance Harvester's position. He was wrong.

In 1973, McCormick hired a consultant to determine how much it would cost to get Wisconsin Steel to operate efficiently. The price tag including pollution control was put at $250 million. But that was not all. It was also determined that it would cost almost as much to close the mill as it would to make the needed capital investment and keep it open. The main expense of a shutdown was $62 million in unfunded pension liabilities. In addition, the union contract called for severance pay and pension supplements that amounted to $25 million. Since Harvester would have to write off nearly $200 million in assets, an out-and-out shutdown was unthinkable (*Crain's Chicago Business,* Nov. 15, 1982, 21; Bensman and Lynch 1987:45).

Although the timing was far from ideal, McCormick decided to sell. The decision was made secretly in 1973, but by the time McCormick got his people in motion to look for a buyer, the economy was in recession. Between 1974 and 1975, the value of steel shipments in constant dollars fell by 22 percent (U.S. Department of Commerce 1975). Furthermore, McCormick's entire business was under duress. Deere was outperforming Harvester in the farm equipment industry. Caterpillar was way out in front in the construction machinery business. Harvester's plants were aging; many of its products were not competitive. McCormick decided to focus on the one bright spot—the production of trucks—which accounted for half of all sales. Steel was not even in the picture.

Because the mill had become a liability, it was necessary to get rid of it. The question was how to sell an aging mill that needed heavy capital investment and had large unfunded pension liabilities at a time when even a good steel mill would be hard to sell. That was the problem McCormick gave James Doyle, one of his top executive officers.

Between 1973 and 1975, only Harvester and Wisconsin Steel insiders knew the effort to sell was under way. Finally, in 1975, it became general knowledge. At that point a buyer had been located, McLouth Steel Corporation of Detroit. An agreement was reached in September, but a month later, after a number of visits to the mill, McLouth pulled out. Charles McDonald, general manager of Wisconsin Steel, stated that McLouth officials had raised questions with him about why repairs were not being made: "I couldn't tell them that Harvester has shut us off, that we don't have a capital budget for any products" (*Crain's Chicago Business*, Nov. 15, 1982, 22). Perhaps the officials got the message anyway and that contributed to the collapse of the deal.

By this point, the workers in the plant had begun to worry. Bercher's start at modernization had come to a halt. There was no announcement, but it was obvious to anyone working in the plant. As one long-time production worker put it: "They didn't ever fix things properly. If there was a breakdown, they would just patch things up" (interview, anonymous worker, spring 1984).

Another worker added:

> They were getting set to shut the mill down to begin with. They had this in the planning stage for maybe six or seven years before the mill closed. I thought that Harvester was going to sell it, because the mill was actually rundown. In order for the mill to stay running, you had to put a lot of money into it. So my way of thinking is that they just probably wanted to get rid of it (interview, anonymous worker, spring 1984).

Lumpkin (interview) commented as well:

> There was a lot of pride in making high-quality steel until the company came in and really made us put stuff out. When I started, you didn't order steel on a weekly basis. It was monthly because that's how long it took. When Brooks [McCormick] came in you could order steel and he would supply it in a week. His plan was production on demand and not on a schedule where you could get the thing right. Around 1976 there was this whole relaxing of quality control. It was a matter of getting the stuff out. Rushing! Rushing!

These changes were even more apparent to the foremen. One supervisor during the McCormick years recalled that

> in the seventies you could see the change from quality to quantity. They'd call a supervisors meeting. They'd say we're going to talk about production. And they'd just say, "We want twenty-five ton a man and anyone who thinks he can't do it just leave your white hat on the rack." It wasn't a meeting where you'd discuss the possibilities of what you thought could be done or how you thought it could best be done. No such thing. What bothers you so much is you got the guys who condition the steel and they almost cried. "Look! This ain't right. Why do I have to let it go out this way?" (interview, anonymous worker, spring 1984).

As management pushed the mill to produce, James Doyle found the solution McCormick had been looking for. The scheme was nearly foolproof. In 1977, Doyle was having lunch with George Sealey, an old friend who was president of Envirodyne Industries. Envirodyne had been organized by an engineer named Ronald Linde whose strategy was to buy companies with promising technological processes and use his company's engineering prowess to develop and commercialize them. At the time Doyle met with Sealey, Envirodyne had purchased eighteen firms through stock swaps. Each had patents on unique technological processes, including the use of high-frequency sound waves as a clean energy source and pollution treatment technology. None had anything to do with steel.

Doyle did not realize it when he went to lunch with Sealey but his friend's company was looking for a major acquisition that would enable Envirodyne to jump into a larger scale of operations. Indeed, the firm's profits the previous year had been a meager $264,400 on revenues of $24.4 million (*Business Week,* Sept. 12, 1977, 96–97). Unexpectedly, Sealey asked Doyle if he knew of any major industrial facilities. Doyle had what Sealey was looking for, but how could a small company with no background in steel making afford to buy Wisconsin Steel? Rumor has it that Doyle and Sealey worked out the deal on the back of a paper napkin.

As that deal was being worked out, another offer came in. This one was from the workers at Wisconsin Steel, who now knew Harvester intended to sell their place of work. Harvester was asking $75 million for the mill, but a study commissioned by the Progressive Steelworkers suggested it was worth less than that. The union offered $55 million; the money would come from the federal government. Thirty-five million dollars alone was promised by the Department of Commerce under its minority business program. Harvester turned down the offer. Management had found a better plan that would absolve Harvester of the expense of either running or closing the mill.

Envirodyne would buy the mill, including the mines and ore freighters, for $65 million. The purchaser would be a limited-liability subsidiary of Envirodyne called EDC Holding Company. EDC would borrow $50 million of the purchase price from Harvester with 8.5 percent notes that did not require any payments for ten years. Collateral for the loan would be the mill's iron and coal mines. EDC would pay the remaining $15 million in cash. In fact, the cash did not come from Envirodyne but from a $35 million loan from Chase Manhattan Bank. The collateral for that loan was Wisconsin Steel's inventory, which was considerable because it always had a supply of coal, iron, and coke on hand. As part of the deal, EDC assumed all of Wisconsin Steel's liabilities, including the unfunded pension obligations.

This deal was clearly sweeter for Harvester than the one the workers had offered. And the decision to accept it was clearly not made on the basis of any consideration of who had the better chance of making the mill profitable. When the general manager of Wisconsin Steel expressed his reservations to Harvester officials, he was accused of "negative thinking" (Bensman and Lynch 1987:42). Another executive recalled the time shortly after the deal was put together when the chairman of Envirodyne, Ronald Linde, and his wife toured the mill:

> They seemed surprised that all 3,000 workers were not present. I said, when you work at a steel plant, you work 21 turns in primary operations, so you have four crews—three working in the day and one off. That's where a lot of people are. Home sleeping. And they asked, Does that mean you work Saturdays and Sundays? And I told them it never stops. They didn't know that, a fundamental of the business, and I thought, Uh-Oh, we're in big trouble (*Crain's Chicago Business*, Nov. 15, 1982, 22).

The deal was pushed through nonetheless. There were some potential glitches, but eventually they were all smoothed over. A major hurdle was preventing the Pension Benefit Guarantee Corporation, the federal agency in charge of protecting pension funds under the 1974 Employee Retirement Insurance Security Act, from challenging the sale. If Wisconsin Steel went under and EDC Holding Company could not pay, PBGC would be responsible for $50 million in pension funds. McCormick decided to overcome this obstacle by commissioning a study of the viability of the deal. Lehman Brothers was initially selected. Its answer was negative. Envirodyne had neither the funds nor the expertise to survive. A second consultant, Phillip Brothers, conducted another study and made a favorable recommendation. While its report enabled the sale to go through, it was later learned that Phillip Brothers had an interest in the deal. If the mill went bankrupt, Phillip agreed to buy its inventory from the creditors, which it could resell at a profit (Bensman and Lynch 1987:50).

PSW Responds

Both Harvester and Envirodyne still had to deal with the union. An existing contract with Harvester contained provisions for financial restitution in the event of a plant closing. And there was the matter of a new contract with Envirodyne's EDC Holding Company. Harvester's reason for selling the mill rather than simply closing it was at stake. The negotiations would have a major impact on the closing and its aftermath.

The Progressive Steelworkers had for a decade been a focal point of a movement among both black and Latino workers for better treatment at the mill. That movement had been sparked by both local conditions at Wisconsin Steel and a national struggle of mostly black steelworkers who had formed caucuses that operated outside the union structure but connected workers in different mills in loose informal networks. Black workers in Alabama, New York, and Maryland filed suit in the early 1970s claiming that departmental seniority in their steel mills was discriminatory. In 1973, an Alabama court ruled in favor of the workers there. The potential disruption to production, union procedures, and costly settlements caused the black workers to consolidate their suits and accept a consent decree and financial settlement.

At Wisconsin Steel, black and Latino workers got together and began looking to union leadership for a solution to the problem of discrimination. Into the breach stepped "Fast Eddie" Vrdolyak, the alderman of Chicago's 10th Ward. His constituency was made up predominantly of white workers of Serbian and Croatian descent and some Latinos. Vrdolyak was a politician who had freely exploited racial fears to get elected and had presented himself as a white populist. This time, however, a close associate, Tony Roque, became the president of PSW by promising black and Latino workers a better deal. Roque was elected in 1973, the same year as the favorable ruling on the suit in Alabama. Vrdolyak became the union lawyer, and PSW made regular contributions to his political campaign. Later he would attempt to unite white workers in an effort to defeat Harold Washington, a black leader, in a racially contentious contest for mayor of Chicago.

When the consent decree was extended, unions in mills where similar discrimination patterns existed could file for relief. PSW did not file. Lumpkin (interview) recalls Roque's position:

> The union said we had access to jobs throughout the plant and there was no restriction on where black workers could go. But when [the consent decree] happened there were no blacks in the electrical shop, no blacks in the carpenter shop. One guy who was a skilled bricklayer worked as a laborer, and when he applied to be a bricklayer they refused. Then they laid off laborers. If he had gotten the other job, he would have had enough seniority to stay on. He took it to court and lost. I told Roque, "Why didn't we get the consent decree?" He said it's because we don't discriminate.

Two years later, blacks at Wisconsin Steel formed an "Afro-American caucus" and put up a slate that included the Latino Tony Roque plus a white and a black. The black candidate was defeated by another Latino. Finally, in 1977, Roque was reelected president, a white worker was elected treasurer, and a black was elected secretary.

Whether these elections represented genuine union reform or were merely evidence that PSW was undertaking a new form of its historic role in stemming the tide of labor militancy is unclear. What is clear is that the union eventually smoothed out potential problems in the Envirodyne deal. Not only did Harvester have $65 million in unfunded pension liabilities, but it had contractual obligations for severance pay, accrued and extended vacation pay, supplementary unemployment benefits, and pension supplements for workers forced to retire before age sixty-two. These amounted to $24.5 million (Bensman and Lynch 1987:54). In a new union agreement, Roque waived rights to the $24.5 million and Harvester agreed only to guarantee the $65 million in pension liabilities, presumably already guaranteed by PBGC. In reality, Harvester's contractual liability amounted to only $5 million. Later Roque would claim he had been tricked.

EDC Holding Company Takes Charge

On July 31, 1977, the deal was consummated. Wisconsin Steel was owned by EDC Holding Company, a firm with no expertise or experience in the steel business, with virtually no assets other than the mill, and in hock to Harvester and Chase Manhattan Bank. In September, EDC negotiated a new contract with the union. Roque balked at proposed wage and benefit concessions, but he did give the new company a freer hand in determining production rates and job assignments, a concession that would boost worker productivity (Bensman and Lynch 1987:55).

The changes that the new contract brought about were more than evident on the shop floor. There was clearly a new style of management. Also the faster pace of work that had resulted in lower-quality steel over the previous few years was intensified under the new regime. To many workers these changes were the beginning of the shutdown. Here is how one worker saw it:

> We had good foremen but they were getting old and the company wanted to kick them out and they got all these kids from school. A lot of the old ones had thirty to thirty-seven years, but the company didn't want them. When they kicked those guys out that had the knowledge, they found out different. That's when they started to close (interview, anonymous worker, spring 1984).

Another worker made a similar observation:

> Envirodyne bought it and started firing all the foremen and started bringing in their own men who didn't know anything about making steel. And the plant slowly deteriorated and shut down (interview, anonymous worker, spring 1984).

The years of disinvestment at the hands of Harvester combined with work speedup and new supervision came together for workers as they perceived changes in the quality of the product they were producing. A man who had worked for thirty-nine years in the mill in a variety of jobs explains:

> For Harvester it was like a tax reduction because they never remodeled the mill. They just patched it together. The pipe mill was obsolete. We had customers for the bar mill, but the steel ain't too good a grade. For alloy, you have to cool off thirty-six hours—put it in boxes and let it cool slow so it won't lose grade, the temper. So now they come and take the steel out in twenty-two hours. Hey, that's fourteen hours that it should have stayed there! The superintendent said, "I want this done." And he didn't care how they did it. The superintendent didn't know quality (interview, anonymous worker, spring 1984).

In part, the changes perceived by the workers were the result of the new owner's lack of knowledge about steel making. In part, they represented an increasingly desperate effort to halt operating losses to give the company time to raise badly needed cash so that the mill could run efficiently. Just before the sale in 1977, workers attempting to repair faulty equipment had been injured in an explosion. Later, four men had been killed by gas fumes as they attempted to get an old blast furnace working. One coke battery had to be permanently closed to meet Environmental Protection Agency requirements. In 1979, a key blast furnace was seriously damaged when hot iron got through its wall of brick. The three-week shutdown of that furnace forced the cancelation of millions of dollars worth of orders (Bensman and Lynch 1987:60).

In September 1978, EDC Holding Company completed a business plan that called for a $74 million capital improvement program. EDC put together a complex financing package that depended on government-guaranteed loans. The key guarantor was to be the Economic Development Administration (EDA). Additional working capital was to come from a special Urban Development Act Grant from the Department of Housing and Urban Development (HUD). By law, 10 percent of the EDA-backed grant had to be guaranteed by the private sector. Phillip Brothers, which had initially done the study enabling Harvester to sell to Envirodyne, fulfilled this role. The loan was not approved, however, until November 1, 1979.

The reasons for the delay had to do with the EDA's concern about the viability of the loan package. A consultant to the EDA raised questions about EDC Holding Company's ability to proceed. HUD refused to extend the Urban Development Action Grant for working capital. Further, congressional rules prohibited any government assistance because EDC was in violation of the Clean Air Amendments and the civil rights acts as they applied to discrimination against women. Phillip Brothers pulled its 10 percent guarantee, and the EDA insisted that Harvester relinquish its hold on coal and ore mines to the EDA. Harvester refused but did agree to guarantee $30 million of the loan over a twenty-year period. The environmental compliance problem was solved politically through negotiations involving the local congressman, the EPA, and Envirodyne. The civil rights violations were resolved when Envirodyne hired the first women production workers at Wisconsin Steel.

As these problems were being resolved, production costs were skyrocketing. This caused EDC Holding Company to revise its loan application twelve times and to increase the amount sought to $90 million. That the loan application went through at all is remarkable. The EDA's consultant, Peter Bohn, continued to paint a gloomy picture of the mill's prospects. Intense political pressure, led by Congressman Morgan Murphy, a close associate of Alderman Vrdolyak, made the difference, so it was Murphy who announced at a press conference that the loan had been guaranteed. With him were an aide to President Jimmy Carter, Chicago mayor Jane Byrne, and Vrdolyak. (For discussion of these negotiations, see Bensman and Lynch 1987:56–70.)

During the two years that it took to secure the loans for the badly needed capital, the mill nearly became inoperable. This was, of course, obvious to the workers and line foremen. By summer 1978, two blast furnaces were down, which made it impossible to fill orders. The company bought raw steel from area mills in order not to lose customers, while the hole they were digging got even deeper. Frank Lumpkin (interview) recalled that workers borrowed parts from other sections of the mill, fabricated others out of whatever was available, and hosed the walls of the blast furnaces with cold water to keep them from burning. Another worker also recalled the situation:

> Everybody over there was always passing the buck. When orders came in and they were not met, all the top management and my foreman could think of was to make excuses and to make themselves look good. So customers got split orders here and split orders there. Quality suffered a lot. Lots were mixed up, and customers got the wrong specifications. They sent orders back, and that cost the company a lot of money. The mill was obsolete (interview, anonymous worker, spring 1984).

A third worker observed: "They spent money foolishly, and it came to nothing. They tried to blame it on the employees—that we were lazy and didn't know the job" (interview, anonymous worker, spring 1984).

Once the loan came through, some of the needed investments were made. Construction of a new blast furnace was begun, and a continuous caster was put into operation. But events at International Harvester led to the final blow to Wisconsin Steel.

Closing of Wisconsin Steel

In 1977, the year Wisconsin Steel was sold, Brooks McCormick handpicked his successor, Archie McCardell. During McCormick's tenure, sales had been close to those of Caterpillar and better than Deere's. Profits were still far below Wisconsin Steel's competitors, but they had improved, from less than $50 million in 1971 to more than $200 million by 1977, mainly through cost cutting.

McCardell's policies were similar to McCormick's. He immediately launched an aggressive campaign of cost cutting matched by increased capital spending and improved research and development. Between 1977 and 1979, capital spending increased by 70 percent, from $168 million to $285 million. Research and development spending in 1979 totaled more than $240 million, a 33 percent increase.

Although demand for trucks and farm and construction equipment was reasonably strong from 1977 to 1980, economic conditions generally were not propitious for McCardell's program. By 1977 the country had not fully recovered from the 1974–75 recession. Yet inflation and the rate of interest were climbing into the double digits and unemployment remained high. In

1979, inflation was at 11.3 percent and rising, and the prime rate of interest was nearly 13 percent.

McCardell's number-one priority was cost cutting. And a major part of that cutting involved labor. According to *Crain's Chicago Business* (Nov. 15, 1982, 35):

> McCardell saw Harvester's contract with the UAW as a perfect target for his cost-cutting campaign. In fact, he identified the contract—a product of compromises that had ended the labor turmoil of the 1950s—as the culprit most responsible for the competitive gap between Harvester and rivals Deere and Caterpillar.

From the beginning of his tenure as chairman, McCardell made several forays on the labor front that were successful from his point of view. He took serious disciplinary action against wildcat strikers in Illinois and broke a five-week strike in Louisville. He also began preparing for a strike over new contract negotiations nationally. Months before the negotiations, McCardell hinted at a strike, and six months before the strike began, Harvester started an unprecedented inventory buildup. From April to November 1979, the Harvester subsidiary that financed equipment sales to domestic dealers experienced a 30 percent increase in wholesale receivables, compared with 5 percent the year before (*Crain's Chicago Business,* Nov. 15, 1982, 31, 34).

Barbara Marsh and Sally Saville, in an analysis of the strike, claim (*Crain's Chicago Business,* Nov. 15, 1982, 34) that Harvester and McCardell underestimated the resolve of the UAW workers and leadership and thereby discounted the role of the old Farm Equipment Workers Union radicals, who still controlled many locals in 1979. In any event, Harvester negotiators made a series of demands they said they would not relinquish. These focused on diminishing worker control over the pace and place of work, including increasing the number of weekly shifts, requiring some overtime, and increasing management's right to limit transfers within the plant. When these demands were laid on the table, the chief union negotiator said he knew there was going to be a strike.

Inside the company, several long-term executives also were alarmed over the hard line being taken. Some went to Brooks McCormick and asked him to intervene on the grounds that a strike would be the ruination of the company. McCormick refused, and the strike lasted six months. The union essentially won, and Harvester ended up in deep operating trouble.

To Wisconsin Steel the strike was the final blow because the mill still depended on Harvester for 40 percent of its orders. The strike began at the same time that money for the modernization program became available. Even though McCardell had been planning for a strike for six months, he failed to inform the management of EDC Holding Company about it. He must have known, given the condition of the mill, that a strike would probably mean the end of Wisconsin Steel. Indeed, in the end it was Harvester that administered the coup de grace by foreclosing on the iron and coal mines.

PSW's response was to have black, Latino, and white workers meet separately with "their own" union representatives to listen to speeches by Mayor Byrne, Alderman Vrdolyak, and other politicians eager to decry the closing. Lumpkin (interview) recalls that day:

> They called me for a meeting and I said that Save Our Jobs would be there. Then I get a call from the union secretary saying that this one was only going to be for blacks. He said that he was representing the blacks, the union president was representing the Mexicans, the vice president the whites. I said, "What do you mean! You're going to have a meeting by nationality group?" He says, "Yes, that's the way it goes." I said that Save Our Jobs is black, Latino, and white. And we all want to come. He says, "Well, I want to tell you whether you want to come or not, there ain't going to be no whites in there and there ain't going to be no Mexicans. So that is your problem." So we went to the meeting and began hollering, "Why not all the nationalities?" It was a big fight. We had some Mexican guys that went there and they wouldn't let them in. . . . For a long time they kept it going like that but it eventually died.

Wisconsin Steelworkers Save Our Jobs launched a campaign during the strike to reopen the mill and to secure workers' benefits lost through the sale of the mill and in union-management negotiations. By then it was too late for the campaign to reopen the mill to be successful, but the group's rearguard action to secure benefits continues. In February 1981, Save Our Jobs filed a lawsuit against Harvester to gain more than $40 million in lost benefits and was recognized by the courts as the workers' sole representative in the class-action suit. In February 1988, the group settled for nearly $15 million but nevertheless continued to picket Harvester to protest the handling of ongoing grievances from the effects of the shutdown. By 1992, another lawsuit against EDC/Envirodyne was in the courts.

Conclusion

This case study follows two main lines of inquiry. One is the reasons the mill closed. The other is the nature of the resistance to the closing. The first responds to two conventional explanations of plant closings—that they tend to be part of a national economic restructuring in the move toward a postindustrial society and that they are the result of mismanagement. My conclusion is that neither explanation is appropriate in the case of Wisconsin Steel.

It is true that the closing of Wisconsin Steel came on the eve of a major downturn in the steel industry that eventually devastated mills throughout the Calumet region. The closing of Wisconsin Steel had nothing to do, however, with the market for its products nationally. The mill's function from the beginning was connected to Harvester's strategy of dominating a number of oligopolized product markets. Achieving this objective required very strict cost controls to maintain a flexible and adequate cash flow. If the corporation began to slip in one product market, it needed to take funds from other operations to prop up the slumping one. Vertical integration (in this case making its own steel and truck engines) was part of that cost-control strategy. Wisconsin Steel's original goal was to avoid the price uncertainties that came about with the organization and market power of U.S. Steel.

Several developments contributed to Wisconsin Steel's loss of viability within Harvester's corporate framework. One was a change in the scale of Harvester's products. Larger sheets were needed than the mill was tooled to produce. Thus, the parent corporation began to buy much of its steel from other firms. At this point, Wisconsin Steel either had to be retooled to serve Harvester or modernized to compete well in other market niches and thereby become a source of badly needed cash for other operations. Neither was done in a timely fashion. By the time Harry Bercher began to modernize the mill, other forces had doomed his effort.

Harvester's strategy of focusing more on market shares than on product and process innovations in a number of different markets eventually caused Harvester to falter in all operations at once. Not only did Harvester lack an innovative outlook in each of its several operations, but it also became financially overextended. Cash-flow problems in firms employing this strategy are most severe during periods of economic decline. Serious recessions, first in 1969–70, just before Bercher's retirement, and again in 1974–75, put Harvester in a desperate situation in which further modernization of the steel mill was out of the question. The mill was no longer viable as a part of Harvester's corporate structure. Harvester's labor and racial policies were manifestations of the cost-control needs dictated by its overall corporate strategy. The closing is thus better explained in terms of corporate strategy to minimize the cost of reorganization, rather than by pointing to an individual, in this instance Harvester's president, Archie McCardell. Rather,

McCardell's actions were consistent with the strong sense of corporate self-justification that dominated nearly all of Harvester's regimes.

At the same time, labor and racial policies played a major role in shaping the character of the only labor organization at that time that could have upset Harvester's plans for divesting and then closing the mill. PSW was organized by Harvester as an antidote to militant industrial unionism in the 1930s. The union traditionally went along with company policies and practices, including those that discriminated against some of its members. In the course of the shutdown of Wisconsin Steel, PSW was clearly ineffective. But that raises the question of whether any labor organization could have been effective under the circumstances. Can labor resistance stop plant closings or ameliorate their most damaging effects?

One determinant of the effectiveness of any resistance to a plant closing is how much time workers have to organize and develop a resistance strategy. Plant-closing legislation since Wisconsin Steel offers some relief. But a few months' notice does not compare to the time it took Harvester to plan and carry out the shutdown. Nevertheless, this study shows that early warning signs were abundant long before the mill actually closed. Plant closings are generally preceded by periods of deterioration. In this case, the mid-1950s—when Wisconsin Steel needed to be retooled so that it could either serve Harvester better or compete with other mills—was a turning point. Harvester's decision to do neither was a very early warning of trouble. The next clear warning did not come until 1971 when Brooks McCormick stopped Harry Bercher's modernization program. By 1975, workers saw clear evidence of deterioration in product quality, supervision, and plant maintenance. These changes accelerated after EDC took over in 1977. Finally, the sale of the mill to a firm with no assets or steel-making experience was another warning that a closing was likely. Despite all these signs, PSW failed to organize against the shutdown.

A strong and militant labor organization could have mounted an effective resistance that could have pressured Harvester to sell Wisconsin Steel earlier and might have saved the mill. At the very least, organized resistance might have prevented the worst aspects of the closing—its suddenness and the loss of benefits. Because the reason Harvester dumped the mill and closed it had to do with the expense of the pensions, supplemental unemployment, and severance pay and the need to write off the mill's assets, timely resistance could have made it very difficult for Harvester to avoid these costs. Resistance could have forced Harvester to take a different approach.

PSW was historically and structurally weak. It had never initiated a labor action, and it had avoided strikes even when all the other workers in the industry were out. That was how and why PSW was set up by Harvester in the first place. Racial division, supported by the job classification privileges of white workers, were evident in the mill from the time blacks came in until the presidential order outlawing workplace segregation in 1941. The racism at the mill was brought into painful focus during the Trumbull Park attacks in the 1950s. In the late 1960s, when black and Latino workers formed caucuses to push for an end to discrimination and better working conditions, Wisconsin Steel workers tried to effect change in their plant. Since the 1940s, black workers had been a relatively militant force in the mill. Their approach in the 1970s was to try to reform the union by electing new leadership. First a Latino, Tony Roque, was elected. But that did little to ease the problems. Later a black worker was made an official. But this by itself did not turn the union into an effective and militant organization. Not only did the union fail to heed the early warnings and develop a resistance strategy but it actually aided Harvester's efforts by making contractual concessions.

Finally, Harvester successfully exploited racial divisions as a way to contain worker militancy. PSW complied by instructing its members to meet only within a racially segregated union structure. Thus, even though considerable evidence and advance warnings were available to workers before the sudden closing, the historical character of the union and racial divisions within the mill prohibited PSW from responding in an effective and timely way to the destruction of workers' livelihoods at Wisconsin Steel.

Chapter 5
Relocation of a Torrington Plant

Keith Knauss and Michael Matuszak

IN OCTOBER 1983, the local South Bend, Indiana, newspaper reported that the Torrington Company, a subsidiary of Ingersoll-Rand (I-R), was closing its South Bend bearings-manufacturing plant. The article noted that "the end of the line for the 55-year-old facility had not been unexpected" (*South Bend Tribune,* Oct. 13, 1983) because it had been operating at a fraction of capacity for some time. On the surface, this shutdown appeared to be yet another example of industrial decline in the rustbelt, caused by shrinking markets, aging plants and equipment, obsolete technology, obstinate unions, and high labor costs.

Closer examination reveals another story. In fact, just fifteen months earlier the same newspaper had reported on a speech by Torrington's president to the South Bend workers in which he had promised that, in view of recent gains in productivity, there were no plans to close the plant (*South Bend Tribune,* July 21, 1982). Either something had happened to production costs that prohibited continued operations or company officials had deliberately misled the workers and the community into believing that the plant would stay open when the company intended to close it all along. A careful review of the events surrounding the shutdown supports the latter interpretation.

This case study describes and analyzes I-R's relocation of its Torrington bearings operation in South Bend. It argues (1) that during the postwar era Torrington had only reluctantly accepted unionization of production workers and an adversarial bargaining relationship; (2) that by the early 1980s Torrington/I-R's operating diversity and capital mobility gave it the option to undermine and eventually terminate the bargaining relationship; (3) that managers in I-R's corporate headquarters chose to exercise this option and closed South Bend as part of a nationwide relocation of bearings production to obtain a more favorable business climate in the South, to avoid labor contracts and negotiated labor standards, and to employ an unorganized work force; (4) that Torrington/I-R persistently misled employees, union officials, and the public regarding its day-to-day operations and long-term plans; and (5) that Torrington/I-R executed the South Bend closing in a way that confused and divided both the workers and the city and prevented either from responding effectively.

Thomas A. Kochan, Harry C. Katz, and Robert B. McKersie (1986) describe the process by which multiplant employers rid their operations of unions and collective bargaining over time. This case explains how they use diversified corporate structure, established bargaining relationships, and heightened community concern over industrial dislocation and job loss to do so at minimum cost and inconvenience to themselves. It demonstrates that the postwar collective bargaining system cannot survive intact the structural, environmental, and behavioral changes occurring in corporations, communities, and governments and why traditional union structures and procedures are inadequate to ensure industrial democracy in the workplace. In view of the determination and methods with which Torrington/I-R achieved nonunion production, it also suggests that there will be no industrial democracy in America's restructured industries in the absence of revitalized unions and collective bargaining.

Torrington's Reluctant Acceptance of a Union

South Bend already was a factory town in 1928 when Bantam Ball Bearing decided to relocate its entire industrial bearings operation there from Connecticut. Craft unions had been active in South Bend for some time, but manufacturing employers had little difficulty practicing paternalist, open-shop labor relations. Indeed, the Chamber of Commerce promoted South Bend as being free of labor trouble because it was "peopled largely by home-owning folks." Citing the city's close proximity to midwestern customers, favorable labor conditions, and good distribution facilities, Bantam took advantage of the chamber's offer of free land and guaranteed loans for new equipment (Craypo 1984: 61–62; *South Bend News-Times*, Feb. 14, 1928).

Bantam grew steadily, even through the 1930s depression, in part because of its state-of-the-art production processes and wide range of industrial bearings products. By 1935, Bantam announced plans to increase its manufacturing facilities by more than half. Later that year, it disclosed plans to merge with the Torrington Company, a much larger firm with diversified operations in this country and abroad (*South Bend News-Times,* Feb. 16, 1929, May 30, 1935, Sept. 23, 1935).

In 1936, along with industrial workers across the United States, Torrington's work force in South Bend, which was experienced, skilled, and reliable, demanded union recognition. For a time the company was able to resist recognition using the standard antiunion practices of that time: red-baiting the union and firing union leaders, engineering a successful back-to-work movement when the union struck for recognition, dividing the workers by establishing a company union, and threatening to relocate production if protests continued. Nevertheless, by 1938, Torrington had recognized and was bargaining with United Auto Workers (UAW) Local 590.[1]

Plant labor relations were not entirely peaceful despite labor's wartime no-strike pledge. R. B. Nichols, a company official, blamed a 1944 job action by the local on a few agitators who were discrediting "our loyal employees" and causing the vast majority of workers "who were willing and anxious to work to be sent home." As the war drew to a close in 1945, South Bend Torrington workers struck the plant for more than a month over the discharge of two union members. The following year the local struck for sixteen weeks over unsettled grievances and what it perceived to be company attempts to curb union participation on the shop floor. When the strike was over the union claimed victory and management called for harmony (*South Bend Tribune,* March 12, 1944, July 20, 1945, Jan. 16, 1947; Gard interview). Thus, management reluctantly accepted the union and collective bargaining, not because it sought to co-opt labor or because it preferred that approach to industrial conflict but because the parties had comparable bargaining power. During this period of reluctant tolerance both sides became more professional in negotiating and administering labor contracts.

Nichols soon became president of the South Bend heavy bearings division for Torrington, while Don Gard served as president of Local 590. Gard later observed that Nichols "put up a good front" but actually resented organized labor and on at least one occasion had threatened to "break the union." Gard and other union officers got along well enough with the industrial relations staff and, as a result, the parties negotiated regular two-year contracts without incident throughout the 1950s (Gard interview).

The local occasionally demonstrated its muscle, and this aggravated company officials. In one instance, it called out the entire production work force to discuss union matters, forcing an embarrassed management to cancel a plant tour for local teachers. Nichols was incensed. He accused the union of using the tactic as a means of harassment and of reaching "a moronic low by provoking such a disgraceful procedure." More important, he noted that Torrington was in the midst of a capital expansion locally but now he was "almost sorry that we decided to expand in South Bend" (*South Bend Tribune*, April 17, 1953).

The union had called out the members in response to management's refusal to accept a union wage demand. Local earnings already averaged $.50 an hour more than the rest of the industry. The following year Torrington therefore proposed to reevaluate all incentive piece rates, an initiative the union rejected out of hand on the grounds that the company intended to reduce rates by 25 percent and restrict worker seniority and job rights. Management retreated but continued to raise the issue at every opportunity and, as it did during the 1936 organizing drive, threatened to relocate jobs or even close the plant if it did not get relief on incentive earnings and union work rules (letter, Lyle E. Hughes, industrial relations manager, to UAW Local 590 bargaining committee, April 27, 1954; Gard interview).

A former plant-level manager, who agreed to be interviewed on the condition of anonymity, told us that such threats were rhetorical insofar as the South Bend plant was consistently profitable during this time and company officials knew that Don Gard could be relied on to prevent more serious, open conflict. Moreover, Torrington had no alternative plants to produce industrial bearings and the technology that would enable it to replace experienced, skilled workers with low-wage labor was not yet available.

STRATEGY IN THE 1960s

Before 1960, Torrington's domestic plants were concentrated in the unionized Northeast and Midwest. After that, it built new plants and bought existing ones in southern open-shop states. It also acquired companies operating nonunion plants in states with union security. This strategy was intended, in part at least, to discipline union bargaining units. Torrington demonstrated the new strategy in 1961 when it built an expensive, state-of-the-art (nonunion) plant in Clinton, South Carolina, but made only minimal expansions in its aging (union) flagship bearings plant in Connecticut. It followed this approach, according to the company president, because the environment in South Carolina would "better enable the Torrington Company to meet competition."

There was a clear message for the union in this decision, he added:

> Anything in a community or state that increases the cost of doing business has an immediate adverse effect on a firm's competitive position and its ability to maintain or expand production and jobs.

> Tax inequities, restrictive labor practices, inadequate transportation facilities—all these things can, and do, affect the cost and attractiveness of doing business in a particular location. Such cost factors, among others, constitute the economic "climate" of a community. The difference between a favorable and unfavorable business climate often means the difference between . . . expansion or contraction and sometimes between remaining in a community or being forced to move (*Torrington Register,* May 31, 1961).

Citing Connecticut's high unemployment insurance benefits compared with those in South Carolina, he said that future Torrington decisions would be influenced by "competitive labor costs, realistic governmental regulations, prudence in tax structures [and] cooperative attitudes in the community and among its leaders." Noting the unlikelihood of a labor strike occurring at the South Carolina plant, he concluded that "capital tends to move where the possibility of a reasonable profit return is greatest" (*Torrington Register,* May 31, 1961).

The company's southern strategy soon influenced union bargaining in South Bend. Torrington made a major plant expansion there after contract settlements were reached without a strike in 1961 and 1963 and the company reported record profits in 1962. And, although there were three strikes during the 1960s—ranging in length from one week to a month—each was settled without picket-line incidents or company attempts to continue production. Nevertheless, Torrington continued shifting the balance of power against its unions by building and acquiring southern plants, including a heavy bearings facility in Union, South Carolina (*South Bend Tribune,* Sept. 16, 1965).

Becoming Part of Ingersoll-Rand

I-R, a huge U.S.-based machine manufacturer, acquired Torrington in 1968 as part of an ambitious diversification strategy intended to give I-R capacity in several new and related product lines. In the process, however, it was restructuring itself as a nonunion firm by adding facilities in mainly southern states (*Wall Street Journal,* June 13,1985, 1). In 1960, all of its U.S. production workers were covered by union contracts. A decade later, the ratio had fallen to 80 percent, by 1980 to 60 percent, and by 1990 to 25 percent. I-R's policy thus was similar to that identified frequently by Kochan, Katz, and McKersie (1986) in their survey of changing industrial relations in America during these years.

I-R's strategy was confirmed publicly as early as 1981 when its vice president for human resources told a college audience it was business's responsibility to "stop unions from forcing us to do things." I-R, he boasted, was expanding in open-shop states, implementing a new approach to traditional labor-management relationships, and fighting union organizing drives: "Where we don't have unions, we tell workers we want to remain union-free" (*Chicago Sunday Sun-Times*, May 10, 1981, 62). Unions interpreted this approach differently, however. To the International Association of Machinists (IAM), I-R had become a "textbook study of a union-busting operation" that "ha[d] blatantly declared class warfare on its workers" and was now "ideally suited to lead corporate America's charge toward a 'union-free environment' " (*Machinist*, Aug. 1982, 16).

Subsequent events in South Bend therefore should be interpreted in the context of I-R's corporate labor policy, an overall strategy we refer to as the Ingersoll-Rand Plan, the basic goals of which are to build or buy domestic plants in open-shop states and acquire companies whose operations are partly or wholly nonunion; to relocate existing production from union to nonunion plants; and to use labor and community relations techniques to bypass existing local unions and union officers, to encourage union decertification attempts, and actively to oppose new unionization efforts.

Given that both I-R and Torrington had policies aimed at minimizing union representation, the acquisition was a good fit. Its impact was not felt immediately in South Bend, however. For example, management of the local plant was still not able to get rid of incentive rates. A year after the acquisition, piece rates in South Bend averaged $.50 an hour more than for the industry nationally, although South Bend workers paid on day rates averaged $.30 an hour less than the rest of the industry. The overall difference between incentive and day rates in South Bend averaged $.81 an hour in 1969 and by 1971 had widened to $1.25, causing resentment among day workers and obvious political problems within the union.

After the 1972 contract was settled without a strike, wages at South Bend Torrington were still higher than wages in the bearings industry in general. This was due to the proliferation of low-wage, nonunion bearings plants in the Southeast, which were pulling down average wages in the industry. The largest and highest-paying bearings plants employed more than a thousand workers and patterned their wage settlements after the UAW's Big Three contracts. The middle tier, including South Bend Torrington, employed between five hundred and a thousand workers. Most were unionized, but their wage and benefit patterns were somewhat different from those in the auto industry. The lowest paying were the runaway "greenfield" shops in the South, most of which were owned by northern-based manufacturers.[2] The rapid growth of the low-wage tier reflected changing industry attitudes toward unions and collective bargaining—from postwar acceptance, albeit reluctant perhaps, to increasingly aggressive opposition.

The shift in industry attitudes toward unions and collective bargaining is reflected in three recommendations an executive from Federal Mogul, one of the largest domestic producers of bearings, made to other industry representatives at a conference in the early 1970s: "One, we must make government understand our industry; two, anti-trust action is needed where we must break up a monopoly—and that monopoly is organized labor; and three, let's reward those who can earn it" (*Industrial Distribution*, June 1972, 44–45).

Beginning of the End

Torrington may have decided eventually to close the South Bend plant after a relatively violent strike (compared with those after the 1930s) occurred there in 1975. Seven years later, an internal I-R evaluation of its bearings division concluded that the 1975 walkout, and a shorter one in 1978, had caused "irreparable damage to South Bend" and adversely affected the entire division "because the South Bend plant has not been contributing its share of profits and . . . has hurt our image with customers with severely sub-standard levels of on-time performance" (Confidential Task Force Report, March 1982, Heavy Bearings Division, 1).

The 1975 strike violence occurred when Torrington attempted to continue production with office and management personnel and tried to get freight trucks back and forth through picket lines. In the melee that followed, individuals on both sides were injured and police arrested several strikers.

As the strike wore on, the company sent letters to the homes of strikers in which the amount of wages being lost was calculated and they were urged to convince their officers to end the stoppage. Shortly afterward about 10 percent of the bargaining unit members signed a "back-to-work" petition.

After eleven weeks of being on strike, members approved a settlement that the company said was its final offer. It was almost identical to the offer that had been on the table when the strike began. The union accepted this offer, in part, because the company was able to continue production and divide the workers, much as it had during the unsuccessful organizing strike in 1936. Torrington's tactic in 1936 was to establish a company union, whereas in 1975 it maintained production in its nonunion plants in the South. Management clearly had reverted to earlier antiunion norms and tactics in labor relations.

As he prepared for what would be his final round of contract negotiations in 1978, Don Gard was therefore convinced that the balance of power had changed sufficiently that the union should strike only as a last resort.

Members nevertheless chose to strike over company efforts to reevaluate incentive standards, to substitute binding arbitration for the union's right to strike over grievances, and to narrow the wage gap between incentive and day-rate workers, which now averaged $2.63 an hour. After six weeks on strike, the union accepted an offer to raise wages significantly in return for a tightened grievance procedure, notification requirements before the local could strike over unsettled grievances, and an agreement "to negotiate a revision of the existing incentive system" as early as possible.

Although the proposal did not receive approval from the Internal Revenue Service and therefore could not be implemented, the parties also had agreed to a bonus for retiring workers to be paid for out of Supplemental Unemployment Benefits (SUB) funds. During the 1960s they had negotiated two SUB funds to be financed through company payments of $.05 an hour: one of the funds was to supplement benefits during short-term layoffs; the other would accumulate when the first fund became fully funded and would be distributed among the members in the event of a plant closing. The decision to use fund number two for retirement bonuses reflected the belief of the officers and members of Local 590 that the chances of Torrington South Bend closing were remote.[3]

New Management, New Bargaining Committee, New Problems

By the late 1970s, top managers no longer came up through the ranks of Torrington's northern plants and no longer accepted unions and collective bargaining as the norm. Norman Cook was the new assistant general manager of Torrington's Heavy Bearings Division, and Bernard Randall was industrial relations director. In a confidential internal company report, Cook was credited with having turned around the company's heavy bearings plant in Union, South Carolina—called the Tyger River plant—and with successfully resisting a union organizing drive there (Paterson and Company [Los Angeles] Productivity Improvement Study, Torrington Company, South Bend, Oct. 29, 1981, 41; hereafter cited as the Paterson Study; also see 207 NLRB 257). Thus, when negotiations in South Bend stalled over a new incentive system, Cook and Randall began communicating directly with members about productivity issues through plant billboards, newsletters, and group discussions on paid time (*Torrington Topics,* Sept./Oct. 1979, 1).

On the union side, Gard retired because of illness and a slate of largely inexperienced bargaining committee members was elected, an expression of membership dissatisfaction and division within the local. Finally, however, both the old and the new committees met with management on the incentive issue until an agreement was reached and approved by the membership. It included protections to ensure equitable standards for union members but also met company demands for controls on average incentive payments. Management forecast a bright future for the plant, including additional work assignments from the bearings division, now that the long-awaited reevaluation plan was in place.

A few weeks later, however, company officials told a meeting of supervisors and workers that Torrington South Bend would soon lose its small bearings production line. At the time they said the loss to the plant would be offset by new heavy bearings work, but that work never materialized. Instead, this became the first in a series of phasedowns that eventually ended in the plant's closing.

One effect of the loss was to reduce productivity in South Bend regardless of worker effort. Increasingly, the plant became a job-shop operation as large, standardized production orders were removed and only short-run two- and three-piece orders remained. This work required machine operators to devote much of their time to setup rather than direct production. The adverse effect on productivity of these irregular, small product runs, when productivity is measured as the change over time in product output divided by hours of labor, was magnified when management began estimating output in "pounds per man hour" rather than sales dollars generated. In addition, according to in-plant sources, many new employees were put on jobs for which they had little training or experience; the number of plant janitors was increased from about twenty to more than fifty; and management suddenly suspended piece-rate payment in departments and work areas being converted to the recently negotiated incentive system.

The last labor contract at Torrington South Bend was negotiated peacefully in 1981. In large part, this was because company negotiators painted a bleak picture of the future of the Heavy Bearings Division in the absence of tighter incentive standards and work rules. Concerned about continued frictions among incentive, day-rate, and skilled trades workers and that morale had been lowered in the bargaining unit following the earlier two strikes, union negotiators began a program to better inform members about the issues and trends at stake in the negotiations and to involve them more in the decision-making process.

When the membership overwhelmingly authorized the committee to strike if necessary to preserve key contract language and standards, officers of the local consolidated the union's demands rather than let the company separate them and try to divide the membership by strategically granting some demands and rejecting others. Included in the package was extensive protection against a possible plant closing. Company negotiators rejected the language, saying they had no intention of closing the plant but would do so before accepting such restrictions. The union succeeded in getting very favorable economic terms but no additional protections against a future shutdown, although Torrington said, in a separate memorandum of agreement, that it would inform the union in advance of a closing and bargain over its effects on the bargaining unit.

Another development during this time reflected the increased tension between labor and management. Over the local's objections, the company implemented a quality circle (QC) employee-involvement program. Management claimed, prematurely and erroneously, that the union favored the program, which encouraged union officers to reject the plan and prohibit officials of the local from participating, although they did not object to individual rank-and-file involvement. The company nevertheless went ahead with compulsory departmental meetings aimed at improving production efficiency. Union officers did not interfere at the outset because they did not want to give the company an issue in the 1981 contract negotiations or an opposition slate inside the local a platform in upcoming local elections. Later, however, Local 590 officials formally refused to cooperate in the QC program after the company linked it to the reevaluation of incentive standards. Torrington also alienated rank-and-file support by simultaneously eliminating its traditional (and popular) practice of giving financial bonuses to employees who made cost-saving suggestions. The QC program nevertheless remained in place because, according to the company, too much money had been invested for it to be abandoned.[4]

When management finally got its program to reevaluate the incentive standards under way, the workers were inclined to resist the changes insofar as the old standards had evolved over years of shop-floor negotiations. Union officials persuaded them to cooperate, however, on the grounds that the new standards would be fair and acceptable to both sides. This became doubtful when experienced machinists complained that the company engineers assigned to set the new standards were insisting on machine speeds that were so fast that there was a risk that equipment would be damaged, the product ruined, and workers injured. Thus, the reevaluation, like the QC program, proved to be unsuccessful in the form insisted on by management. Afterward, former workers said they were convinced the company was not really interested in setting new production rates but merely wanted accurate documentation of production methods and capabilities in order to do the work elsewhere.

Planning for the Shutdown

As 1981 contract negotiations drew to a close, I-R made Thomas Bennett the new president of Torrington. A career I-R manager, Bennett came out of corporate planning and development. Not surprisingly, therefore, one of his first acts was to arrange for a feasibility study of the Heavy Bearings Division. The results were contained in a confidential report (the Paterson study) prepared by a West Coast management consulting firm, which evaluated productivity at the South Bend plant against that of Torrington's South Carolina bearings plant. The report concluded that South Bend's performance problems were "behavioral and cultural" and observed that the absence of these problems was precisely the reason the South Carolina plant could reach its performance potential. Managers at the South Bend plant agreed that its problems could "only be marginally improved" even though "South Bend's production equipment [was] in general effective although somewhat older" than that in South Carolina.

The study went on to note that the revised incentive system probably would not improve performance at South Bend because "peer pressure in this union shop tends to move productivity towards the lowest common denominator." There were, it claimed, "serious cultural barriers to productivity [that were] union and regional related," and even though community leaders were trying to improve the situation, "cultural change is a very long, slow process." As a result, South Bend management had to cope with a "depressed" regional culture in which "workers are mainly interested in job security, preservation of the status quo, in a highly unionized environment." The South Carolina plant, in contrast, "is nonunion, has a positive employee work culture, and is in a region noted for its work ethic." Things were so bad, it said, that "decertifying the union at the South Bend Plant would not change the regional culture." The cost differential between the two plants was "prohibitive," and "the reward is not worth the risk, nor the opportunity worth tying up good men to achieve," it concluded. Bennett responded to the consultants' report by commissioning Norman Cook to head a management "task force" that would make recommendations to Bennett. Coincidentally, Jim Banks, a former colleague of Bennett's from outside the Heavy Bearings Division, was appointed plant manager at South Bend.[5]

Although the Paterson study had not yet surfaced, at the plant, rumors about the task force study soon circulated. And, quite by accident, the bargaining unit became aware of some of the findings. A shop worker and active union member came upon a trash bag of shredded documents. A piece of shredding he picked up contained a reference to the union, so he began to take bits of papers home. With intense concentration, he pasted together significant parts of what are now known to be portions of drafts of the I-R task force report on the South Bend plant. A part of the reconstructed shredding stated: "A change in plant managers was made on January 1, 1982. The new manager, Jim Banks, has been directed to mount a bold program which will improve profits as he prepares the plant for final closing."

We have no evidence that this report was seen by union officers or members before the announcement of the closing; however, the reconstructed material contained key findings and recommendations comparable to those contained in the final report of March 1982.[6] Among them were the following:

- The South Bend plant has been a cash generator but has not received a proper level of reinvestment.
- The area culture and the influence of the UAW have been working against the plant; the work ethic drove the company into a noncompetitive posture.
- The plant has been the victim of a badly deteriorating incentive pay system installed in 1946 and out of control by 1975.
- The plant's productivity, which was never outstanding, started a slide in 1975 that has continued; the catalyst for the slide was the 1975 strike.
- Labor relations have been improving since the union elected a new team in July 1980; relations are at their best level because of good feelings between the new plant manager and the union committee.
- Fringe benefits are a factor in South Bend's problems since it has a senior work force; the plant's unfunded pension liability is about $5.6 million, which makes it an important consideration.
- The current plan would retrench factory employment to 275 to 300 and reduce output for the year to $40 million by shifting production to other plants by the end of 1982.
- The company should not seek cost concessions from the union in 1982 since the prevailing mood of the United Auto Workers is to consider temporary takebacks only with company guarantees for job security.
- The South Bend plant should vigorously pursue a cost-improvement program through all of 1982 while at the same time preparing to

close in late 1983 but defer until late 1982 a final decision on the future of the plant.

There is evidence that Torrington's management had plans for the South Bend plant even before the October 1981 Paterson study was released. In a confidential memo to I-R written one week before release of the Paterson study, Torrington outlined its strategic plan for 1981–85. Torrington indicated the following:

- It planned to use cash to increase capacity, but not at South Bend.
- It would most likely recommend constructing another new plant and some rationalization of the South Bend plant.
- It intended to improve significantly its relationship with its unionized employees by building more trust and mutual respect.
- It expected to encounter high startup costs in putting the new Shiloh (Rutherfordton, North Carolina) plant on line but that its major operating problems were the high costs and poor productivity of South Bend.
- With a capital-intensive business, improved productivity could be gained by building new facilities in the Southeast, thereby capitalizing on the more favorable work rules.
- Among other factors, the potential for success depended on an analysis of the probability of improving productivity at the South Bend plant and of benefiting from worldwide rationalization opportunities, as well as the achievement of low-cost producer status for standard items through the development of Shiloh and similar facilities.
- Opportunities to be pursued included reducing the costs associated with standard products through such process and productivity changes as cell manufacturing, CAM, and rationalization.
- The risks involved included the company's commitment to making capital investments since the business was capital intensive, an inability to maintain stability and the strong work ethic in its southern plants, and the uncertainty of improving productivity at South Bend.

No evidence suggests that the contents of the memo were shared with any union officer or member. Many of these issues were similar, however, to those outlined in the reconstructed task force report that was circulating in the plant and causing concern and confusion among both the rank and file and the officers of the local. In particular, the local bargaining committee faced difficult decisions about strategy and tactics for responding effectively to the company's threats.

Dialogue Committee

On February 2, 1982, Torrington announced the closing of South Bend's brass cages foundry. The union was told it was cheaper to contract out the brass cages because of the depression in the foundry business. A similar foundry Torrington had built in 1980 adjacent to its Tyger River plant in South Carolina continued to operate, however. The company also said it might reopen the South Bend foundry when the general economy picked up.

The knowledge gained from reconstruction of the shredded documents, the ongoing layoffs, and the closing of the foundry led local union leaders to urge members to work harder and increase production. In mid-February, members of the bargaining committee also agreed to a request by Banks for weekly meetings of a "dialogue committee," consisting of them and five management representatives. The purpose was "to assure continued full operation of the South Bend plant" (minutes, dialogue committee meeting, Feb. 17, 1982). Initially, union leaders were enthusiastic about the meetings. They particularly appreciated management's willingness to share information on the plant's performance, including monthly productivity and profitability reports.

Further, Banks instructed company time-study representatives and supervisors to resume negotiating piece rates with the operators. The union had always insisted that negotiating with the operators was more realistic and acceptable than the reevaluation program. As the union predicted, a dramatic increase in the performance of the South Bend plant followed the change.

Although Banks later stated that he had not seen the official task force report until the summer of 1983 and had seen only the reconstructed shred version that was circulating in the plant, at an April 23, 1982, grievance meeting he told the bargaining committee that all plans to close the plant were "out" because of its recent solid performance (deposition, James H. Banks, Oct. 9, 1986, Torrington, Conn., in Civil Action no. S85-00483, *Winard Anderson et al.* v. *The Torrington Company,* 23, 24). Although this reassured some committee members, others were convinced that the task force material was accurate. Rumors of the closing persisted.

Perhaps because of their long experience with idle company threats, some former union officers accused the bargaining committee of yielding unnecessarily to scare tactics. They maintained that the plant would never be closed because its skilled work force could not be duplicated elsewhere. These internal union conflicts were reflected on the shop floor. Officers and members who suggested that the plant might close, or that the union should respond to this threat, were not favorably received or encouraged. Many of the workers believed company statements that the information in the task force report was "old news." They were reinforced in this view by an April 27, 1982, letter to the bargaining unit from Banks and Jerry Amm, president of Local 590, that urged workers to "lay aside the old antagonisms and destroy the barriers between Labor and Management because rebuilding job security is a joint venture that can only succeed in an atmosphere of mutual trust."

Plans, Productivity, and Promises

Shortly thereafter, the prospects for mutual trust worsened. Within a week the *South Bend Tribune* (May 4, 1982) reported that the company denied that "business lines are being shifted to other Torrington plants." Responding to this misrepresentation, the union announced that "contrary to the company's denials, [Torrington] is moving up to a third of the plant's product lines from South Bend to facilities in North Carolina and South Carolina."

The company newsletter attempted to dispel the rumors that the plant was closing (*Torrington Topics,* June 1982, 1). Norman Cook, now the general manager of the Heavy Bearings Division, denied the company planned to close the plant, and Banks indicated that the company had no plans to seek concessions from the union and praised the union bargaining committee for its "contributions to turning South Bend around." The newsletter also included an extensive account, with photographs, of a cookout provided by the company "in appreciation of the excellent performance of the South Bend Plant personnel over the past 5 months." Spirits at the Increase in Productivity Celebration were dampened, however, by a *Tribune* article (June 9) in which the president of Torrington, Thomas Bennett, claimed he had "tons of data . . . showing that the [South Bend] plant is getting worse all the time" and that it was plagued by "high wages and benefits, yet comparatively low productivity."

The next day division management attacked the article: Bernard Randall, director of industrial relations, told the *Tribune,* "It is beyond my belief that someone would shut down a profitable business." Bennett later tried to minimize the effect of his statement in a letter to the *Tribune* that the paper did not print but that was circulated in the plant. He said the newspaper's report "that productivity was . . . 'going downhill' [had failed] to recognize my statements of the improvements since January 1."

The company nevertheless requested that the union reopen the contract to renegotiate the average earned rate provisions. At the same time, however, management said things that reinforced the union's opposition to reopening the contract. Banks, for example, briefed the union on a presentation he planned to make to higher corporate officials in an effort to get more work for South Bend. He indicated that plant productivity (pounds per man hour) was on the rise, that annual gross profit was running at 30 percent, and that direct labor costs in South Bend were only 10.8 percent of each $1.00 cost of sales. On the basis of these figures, bargaining committee members concluded it was neither rational nor necessary to make concessions.

On July 20, Bennett visited the plant and spoke to the assembled workers at the loading dock. The following day the *South Bend Tribune* reported on the speech under the heading "Torrington Promise: Plant to Stay Open." The paper quoted Bennett as saying that "as of today, there is no intent to close," but, since he could not predict the future, "whether or not we ever find the need to leave South Bend is a question to be decided in the future." In a copy of his speech given to the union, Bennett claimed that the task force had been assembled before the turnaround of the South Bend plant:

> Last December management had given up, they were willing to throw in the sponge, they were close to closing this plant. Today I find no one who really wants to close this plant. The important thing to me is that this didn't happen because we had some outside consultant come in and tell us how to do it, or because we made massive capital investments in new machinery, it happened because both sides changed their attitude towards each other and began a process of trusting one another.

Citing the many improvements since December, the speech assured workers "that you people have earned the right to keep this plant open, and we are going to keep it open," and "that before any decision to close this plant will be taken in the future, you will be given a fair opportunity to work with us in developing remedial programs directed at saving jobs in South Bend." Bennett summarized six reasons "for not wanting to close this plant": (1) improved operating performance; (2) vastly improved labor-management relations; (3) the unique bearings made in South Bend; (4) the workers' skills and expertise, which were at least as good if not better than those of workers at any other bearings manufacturer; (5) the eventual end of the recession, which would lead to a need for greater plant capacity; and (6) the $60 to

$70 million it would cost to duplicate the operation and additional costs to duplicate the skills of workers at South Bend.

Bennett's speech concluded with an invitation for "all of you . . . to make a personal effort to contribute in your own way. Do something meaningful to help us succeed with this program. In the last analysis, I won't decide this plant's future, you will."

Later that day he and other Heavy Bearings Division and plant managers met with members of the Local 590 bargaining committee, but Bennett did not provide them with a copy of the task force report. Even if the union had officially demanded the information, in connection, for example, with the company's request to renegotiate the average earned rate, it appears unlikely that the report's contents would have been clear and convincing to a majority of the union members or officials in light of the company's comments, commitments, picnics, and promises from May through July.

Regardless, the company's promises seem hollow at best when compared with the contents of another document that management did not share with the union. A full two months before the loading dock speech, Bennett had reported to I-R's top three officers on the results of the Paterson study and the internal task force report comparing plant performance levels in South Carolina, South Bend, and Darlington, England. In response to these findings, Bennett wrote, the task force would "study the various alternatives available to us in addressing the problem of extraordinarily high costs and accompanying low productivity at the South Bend location. . . . It had [now] become quite evident . . . that the longer view [made] it virtually inevitable that operations at the South Bend plant should be discontinued." Therefore, he concluded, "We believe the attached [task force] report makes a compelling case for the closing of South Bend. . . . We are recommending and seeking your approval to close the South Bend plant" (letter, Bennett to the executive vice president, president, and chairman of Ingersoll-Rand, May 20, 1982).

Introduction of Cell Manufacturing

In late 1982, management proposed the introduction of a cell-manufacturing process. Simply described, the idea was to group machines into cells in which several, previously separate machining operations would be performed. According to the company's proposal, some nineteen job classifications would be reduced to three or four. To make the idea attractive to the union, Torrington offered a list of possible cell names (including EXCEL 590) from which the bargaining committee could choose. The company also was willing to conduct a plantwide contest to name the cells.

Although the committee accepted the concept of grouping machines into cells, it objected to combining job classifications. Since there were numerous laid-off union members whose classifications would be eliminated, the committee insisted that existing classifications, seniority provisions, and established practices be followed in assigning workers to the cells. Plant manager Banks charged that to adopt cell manufacturing within the confines of the labor agreement would defeat the whole concept.

The bargaining committee then offered to accept cell manufacturing in return for a guarantee that the machines in, and the products from, the cells would not later be transferred to Torrington's southern plants. The company adamantly rejected the proposal and later moved the machinery targeted for the cells to the shipping dock, while announcing that the work and jobs would be leaving the South Bend plant because of union obstinance. Some workers condemned the leaders of the union and went to management officials with the advice that they ignore the union and post the jobs for bid. Using a broad management rights clause to proceed without union agreement, Torrington posted the cell jobs and workers swamped the personnel office to apply. Job bidders saw this as a way to avoid layoff; they disregarded union solidarity in favor of what they believed to be individual job security.

Last Union Election

Management continued to tie ongoing layoffs to the recession and predicted that employment would be back up to about five hundred employees, but 1983 brought no improvements. In April, the president of Local 590, Jerry Amm, wrote to all working members urging them to "take all remaining vacation time . . . during this vacation year [since] this would require the Company to recall our laid off members . . . to meet . . . production needs." He reminded workers "of the things the Company has done [such as] offering overtime instead of calling back workers and the six week [Christmas] shutdown to avoid paying holiday pay." He pleaded for working members to "think of your fellow members who are on the street" who would benefit from being "able to receive paychecks and insurance benefits, items not readily available in our community today." In contrast to Amm's plea for solidarity among workers, the spring 1983 issue of the *Precisionist* (12–13), Torrington's company magazine, carried a scathing antiunion article that blamed labor organizations for the decline of the United Kingdom as an industrial power, the decay of American railroads, and the inability of the

American steel and auto industries to compete on a worldwide scale. It condemned labor strife, labor monopolies, and the "social sanctity of labor negotiations by threat, strike and interfamily war." It also predicted that in those U.S. companies that survived, labor unions would become primarily company unions.

A union election campaign letter put out by incumbents on the local bargaining committee illustrates the continuing conflicts in both the shop and the union:

> In 1981 we negotiated our contract. We feel we brought our membership a good settlement. We made some improvements in areas such as vacation pay and night shift premium that had not been changed for twenty (20) years. We also made improvements in most areas of the contract with no one group receiving the major share of improvements. This was most important to us, that we all benefit as equally as possible. The contract was also accomplished without a strike.
>
> Look at our plant compared to others in the area. Most have had major layoffs and many have given concessions. Our own plant faced a poor profit picture when we took office. In 1981 our plant only made .2% profit but with changes in union-management relations and changes within management itself, the plant is running at a respectable 25–30% profit. Because we did not resist all changes our members have not had to concede anything.
>
> We promise to do what is best for all of our membership. Our only goal for negotiations in 1984 is the same goal we had in 1981 and that is to negotiate the best agreement we can. Job security for all of our members is the number one issue. And if the company is after take-aways as they have hinted at then they better be prepared to secure all of our jobs in writing for we have no intention of giving up anything merely to increase the company's profit margin.
>
> Think of the past administrations this local has had and the past contracts. We have members who refused to go to union meetings because they were ridiculed and laughed at for speaking what was on their minds. We have also had strikes based on an officer's promise of what he would get from the company and rather than admit defeat at contract expiration he would do it after a strike. We are proud to have taken this union out of these outdated methods and do not believe that our members wish to return to them.
>
> These are the reasons we ask for your support in the upcoming election. We hope that your vote on May 11th and 18th (if needed) will show what kind of administration and future you want for our union.
>
> **Special Note**
>
> For our opponents and others who like to spread unfounded rumors—*NONE* of the expense for this letter or its mailing came out of union funds.

Because membership on the bargaining committee gave relatively junior employees superseniority in the event of layoffs, and would have allowed them to bump more senior workers, many members openly voiced their intent to vote for the more senior candidates running against the incumbents.

It is not surprising therefore that in the May 1983 election all these incumbents were defeated.

END OF THE LINE

Once again, information not known to the workers and the union might have affected the election and other events that followed. President Bennett later said that his May 20, 1982, letter to senior I-R management recommending that the South Bend plant be closed had resulted in a decision "to try to keep it going" and that he had not received I-R's approval to proceed with the closing until May 12, 1983. Moreover, he said that he had not told this to the South Bend workers at the time because corporate headquarters requested that the information be kept confidential until after the announcement of I-R's second-quarter earnings (Bennett deposition, 70–73, 116, 121–23). On August 9, 1983, Torrington announced that it was relocating the headquarters of the Heavy Bearings Division from South Bend to Torrington, Connecticut, but it waited until October 13 to notify the union and the community that the manufacturing operation would also be relocated (*South Bend Tribune*, Aug. 6, 1983, Oct. 13, 1983).

To help supervisors explain the shutdown to workers, Torrington management gave the supervisors a fact sheet. The following excerpts are from that document:

> Q. *Why is the South Bend plant closing?*
> A. The Company simply has too much unused capacity in the Heavy Bearings Division and our business projections through the next several years indicate that will continue to be the case. We've tried to hang on as long as we could but we can't keep three plants operating indefinitely when we don't have enough volume to really keep two going.
>
> Q. *Why hasn't the company asked the union for concessions?*
> A. The reasons for the plant closure aren't related to labor costs. They're related to our having too much capacity. The Union can't control that condition.
>
> Q. *Isn't it true that the real reason South Bend is closing is due to the fact that this is a union plant and labor costs are higher than in the South?*
> A. No. The union and employees have tried to cooperate with management over the last several years and, though labor costs are higher at this plant than in the South, that wasn't the basis for this decision. The reason is that even if labor costs were the same as in the South, the age of the plant and its equipment and the other contributors to cost such as layout, facility maintenance and so on would still dictate that the decision would go against South Bend given the basic problem of overcapacity.
>
> Q. *Is the company willing to negotiate the decision to close South Bend?*
> A. Neither the Union nor the Company can affect the factors causing this

closure. If they could, there would be something to negotiate; but they can't and so there's no basis for negotiations over the decision. However, the Company is willing to negotiate with the Union over the effects of the plant's closing and invites the Union's Bargaining Committee to meet with Company representatives as soon as it's reasonably convenient for them to do so.

Q. If the company and union are still bargaining over the effects of the plant closing on April 30, 1984, and haven't reached agreement, will the company stop bargaining at that point?

A. The Company will continue to bargain until an agreement is reached or until an impasse is reached.

Q. Is there anything that we as employees can do to change the company's decision to close the plant?

A. Unfortunately no.

Responses to the Announcement

Although about seven hundred shop workers and five hundred salaried personnel had been employed at South Bend at the end of 1980, on October 15, 1983, the *South Bend Tribune* noted in an editorial that "the shock of the pullout [was] cushioned both by anticipation that it would happen and by the gradual decrease in the number of persons employed at the local operation. This community has weathered industrial closings before. The story has become familiar in recent years. Torrington is rather typical." It also predicted a "bright future" for the community because "times have changed and South Bend is changing with them. . . . South Bend has a lot going for it. . . . We have a Project Future organization constantly seeking out prospective industries and businesses, and we are not devastated by unemployment." The editorial went on to commend "members of Torrington Local 590, United Auto Workers [because they] cooperated with the company in trying to make it feasible to retain production here, a fact that should reinforce our labor image—workers who care about their products and employers and who will cooperate."

Torrington workers expressed a different reaction to the announcement of the closing. Sixty-year-old Ben Kaznia complained about the decision to close after workers had "gone out of our way to improve productivity." Fifty-seven-year-old Bill Fabyan pointed out the irony of the company decision to consolidate production at its southern plants when "the South Bend plant was the mother company that made the profits to finance the Sunbelt plants." Questioned "about the dilemma of competing with lower-paid, non-union workers in the same company," sixty-two-year-old Jim Foulk responded, "This plant has turned out good work and we feel like we're worth it" (*South Bend Tribune,* Oct. 14, 1983). A former plant manufacturing services director also criticized the company's decision to shut down: "From a business standpoint, I thought Torrington was missing the boat leaving this area. . . . It was still profitable. . . . It was still making money up to the day they pulled out" (*Indianapolis News,* Jan. 21, 1985).

At the first monthly union meeting after the announcement of the closing, John Dandino, president of Local 590, said that members of the bargaining committee were as shocked and surprised as the rank and file. Discussion centered on questions about the distribution of severance pay from SUB fund number two. There was little mention of strategy or tactics to combat the closing. By late October, however, Dandino and Vice President Arnold Friebe were consulting with higher levels of the UAW, as well as with resource people within the community. We were among those contacted. Keith Knauss was asked to provide information and ideas based on several years of plant-closing research. Michael Matuszak, a political rival of Dandino's who had been defeated in the May election of bargaining committee members and had been laid off by Torrington, was asked to become involved.

Matuszak proceeded to call on leaders in the labor community, to draw up an economic impact statement on the closing, and to outline a strategy based on the widely reported actions being taken at the Morse Cutting Tool plant in New Bedford, Massachusetts. In November, he met with UAW Local 590 officials and South Bend's mayor and city attorney to discuss these ideas. After that meeting, Matuszak was no longer asked for his advice.

It appears that neither union nor city officials believed a successful Morse Tool–type campaign could be mounted to stop the closing. Instead, their efforts to keep the plant in South Bend open revolved around a presentation to Torrington/I-R on the benefits of South Bend's new urban enterprise zone (UEZ). It was hoped that the UEZ's tax incentives, along with union concessions, would entice the company to reconsider its decision. Nevertheless, the local newspaper reported that at a mid-December meeting Torrington officials called the decision to close "irreversible" but promised to cooperate with city efforts to find new owners to operate the plant. A city economic development planner prepared a business plan to attract such investors, but no action was taken to implement the plan. Six years after the closing, Torrington "agreed to donate the building" to the UEZ for use as an "industrial incubator" (*South Bend Tribune,* Dec. 15, 1983, Feb. 4, 1990).

Matuszak's initial groundwork led to the formation of the Save Our Jobs Campaign, a group of concerned South Bend–area citizens and displaced workers. In late November, it held a well-publicized gathering at a union hall that was attended by about seventy union officers and activists, clergy, and laid-off workers. Workers were challenged "to fight for their jobs—even if the fight sometimes resembles shadowboxing a faceless opponent—[through a] community-wide effort to keep manufacturing businesses in the area." A public rally was planned, and the vice president of Local 590, Arnold Friebe, promised that "together we can get something done" (*South Bend Tribune,* Nov. 29, 1983).

According to the newspaper account, the rally attracted "more than 200 workers and supporters [who] weathered a numbing, 15-degree cold Saturday afternoon to express frustrations with plant closings, concessions, absentee management, and Reaganomics" (*South Bend Tribune,* Dec. 18, 1983). Relatively few Torrington workers attended, however, and Friebe was the only major Local 590 officer present. Besides the frigid weather, other factors affected the turnout of Local 590 members. Torrington had scheduled overtime work for that day, and some union officers discouraged workers from participating. Further, after initially agreeing to help fund the rally, Local 590 withdrew its pledge. At a membership meeting a few days before, the local president said that the international UAW had directed him not to contribute to Save Our Jobs. Other union and community officials openly expressed concerns that such demonstrations would anger the company and ruin chances for a good closing agreement.

Although Save Our Jobs continued to publicize plant-closing problems, its activities dissipated as the Torrington closing neared. Another community organization, the Citizens Action Coalition, drew attention to the company when it "charged Torrington [was] leaving behind groundwater and soil pollution." The "county environmental officer [said] the Torrington Company will be held responsible for any hazardous materials found at the site [but that] you can't just jump on industry . . . until you've got some specifics," (*South Bend Tribune,* April 5, 1984, April 25, 1984). Six years would pass before the specifics of these "environmental concerns about the property" once again received public attention. In 1991, the estimated cleanup cost was $2.5 million (*South Bend Tribune,* Feb. 4, 1990, June 13, 1991).

Both Local 590 and the international UAW took various actions in response to the closing. Eventually, these included pursuing grievances, demanding extensive information for the closing negotiations, filing charges with various government agencies, securing an outplacement and retraining program funded by Job Training Partnership Act money from the governor of Indiana, and initiating lawsuits. Unfortunately, none of these actions resulted in a reversal of the decision to close. The 1981 contract expired and the plant officially closed on April 30, 1984. Although the parties met at least a dozen times after the closing announcement, the union rejected the company's final offer of July 17, 1984.

Results

Workers whose jobs were destroyed in the shutdown suffered consequences similar to those reported in other plant-closing studies. An article in the local press summed up these experiences: "Because of seniority at the unionized plant, many of those last workers were veterans [of] other South Bend factories that closed in the 1950's and 1960's. [These] older workers face depression, [a] drop in a long-accustomed standard of living, [and] discrimination in the job market. Other Torrington workers didn't survive the initial depression" (*South Bend Tribune,* May 6, 1984).

A lawsuit filed in November 1984 revealed the extent of union and workplace conflict during the plant's final years. After exhausting the internal appeals measures, fifty-one "former employees . . . with 10 years or more experience" sued the joint company-union board of administrators of the SUB fund number two over claims to "separation pay benefits." They understood that the plan was meant to pay severance to employees with ten or more years of seniority who were either working or laid off and still eligible for recall when the closing was announced. But the board of administrators had ruled that the only employees to receive a payout were those with ten or more years who were working on the day of the closing announcement. The suit was not settled until March 1988 with the distribution of $1.4 million to 127 plaintiffs and to 119 employees previously found to be eligible (*South Bend Tribune,* Nov. 13, 1984, March 21, 1988).

Although union complaints to government agencies were vigorously pursued, such as those filed with the Occupational Safety and Health Administration by union vice president Friebe, most were eventually dismissed. By May 1991, the only remaining major litigation financed by the UAW had been settled. Originally filed on August 22, 1985, this suit charged Torrington with age discrimination and pension retaliation in the South Bend closing. The settlement would distribute about "$1.1 million to 336 participants in the class action lawsuit" and provide a health insurance option to some of them. "At least 33 former Torrington workers . . . filed objections to the proposed settlement" (*South Bend Tribune,* Dec. 31, 1989). Many of the provisions of the final settlement were similar to those found in Torrington's July 17, 1984, final offer.

Since the shutdown, former UAW Local 590 members or their survivors have attended meetings about the litigation efforts. A longtime member described one such gathering two years after the closing: "We had like three hundred people there. I'd worked for many years with most of them. I looked around and everyone seemed to have aged ten years. Their faces were like bare walls, and their eyes were staring straight ahead. It's as if they still didn't believe what had happened" (interview, Bill Fabyan, by Keith Knauss, South Bend, Feb. 10, 1987).

Six years after the closing, the financial and emotional impact persisted. At the January 1990 federal court hearing on the proposed age discrimination settlement, forty-seven-year-old Lawrence Noens told the judge a typical story. After the closing, "he was unable to find work for a long time, and when he did, the pay was much lower. [This] financial crisis led to a divorce. 'I lost my family. It's all gone.' "

Bill Fabyan said that Torrington "abandoned faithful workers who had given their lives to the company." Referring to Noens, Fabyan, and other ex-Torrington workers who spoke, the judge said, "The courtroom today rang with an eloquence not usually heard" (*South Bend Tribune,* Jan. 27, 1990). Unfortunately, that eloquence did not result in the reopening of the plant; nor did the judge's approval of the settlement provide the justice these ex-workers so fervently sought.

Lessons from the South Bend Torrington Closing

We believe that this case study can be used to help unions and workers develop better foresight. We hope these suggestions will be used as they evolve strategies to deal with such grand designs as the Ingersoll-Rand Plan.

1. The events in South Bend illustrate the shortcomings of relying on an employer's public statements in making union and community decisions. By the time an employer publicly announces a closing or phasedown, it is often too late to develop an effective response. Workers, their organizations, and their communities must improve their methods for monitoring employers and exposing inappropriate behavior. Unions cannot afford to give concessions; nor can communities afford to grant incentives automatically without enforcing standards for corporate accountability.

2. Both the Paterson study and management's task force report claimed there were productivity problems at the South Bend plant. Based on this conclusion, both recommended that the plant be closed. As we have shown, many of these "problems" resulted from management decisions on basic investment and production matters. Although the union made vigorous efforts to enhance and protect workers' wages, hours, and working condi-

tions, it never mounted a serious challenge to mismanagement. During the postwar era many major manufacturing employers reluctantly accepted the existence of unions and collective bargaining. In that period, labor law, corporate structure, and union goals all interacted to create "management rights." Today, workers and their unions should resist further ceding such rights to management.

3. At least one reason that the full potential of Save Our Jobs was not realized is that the union did not maintain an official role in it. Though union members may have honestly believed that making waves would negatively affect closing negotiations, such logic was questionable. Torrington/I-R's grand design had already eliminated the need for the labor of its South Bend work force, so that the union's traditional source of bargaining power was gone. Other sources of strength were essential; Save Our Jobs could have provided such strength. The union most directly affected has to play a central role in any community coalition efforts.

4. Although Local 590 participated in meetings with unions from other plants in the bearings industry, it had little contact with unions at other I-R facilities. Thus, there was an unrealized potential for coordinated action, especially after I-R's antilabor offensive became evident. Organized labor at all levels—local unions, national and international unions, labor federations, and international trade secretariats—must restructure their policies, practices, and procedures to account for global corporations and capital mobility. They must increase their communication, consultation, and cooperation across national boundaries, as well as by industry and employer. These actions must include enhanced opportunities for local labor leaders to interact with their peers throughout the world.

5. Fundamental to balancing the bargaining power of workers and their employers is the need to organize the relevant work force. The 1936 union effort at Torrington South Bend was defeated by an array of employer tactics common to that time, but because of their courage and determination, the workers eventually established a union that lasted for forty-six years. Today the strategies and tactics of the Ingersoll-Rand Plan pose significant obstacles to unionization, but there is still no substitute for revitalized organizing activities.

6. Employee-involvement programs, such as quality circles, and technological changes, such as cell manufacturing, are not neutral elements in the workplace. Such innovations have a dramatic impact on the sociotechnical system and the collective bargaining relationship. They must therefore be extensively researched, cautiously developed, and carefully negotiated so that

they result in an improved quality of work life and enhanced employment security.

7. The union's litigation efforts illustrate some of the weaknesses in current labor policy, legal procedures, and remedies. These include the variability in labor law interpretation and enforcement, the lengthy delays in reaching resolutions, and the significant financial burdens. U.S. labor legislation reflects assumptions and values from an era in which the bargaining power of employers and unions were seen as relatively equal. The Ingersoll-Rand Plan makes that judgment obsolete. U.S. unions must look to the labor relations systems of other advanced nations for a model that could be promoted in the public arena while also increasing the use of creative concerted activities in the workplace and communities.

8. As representative democracies dependent on voluntary participation, unions experience all the tensions inherent in democratic decision making. These normal conflicts were magnified by Torrington/I-R's antiunion corporate culture in the plant's last years. Although it is no panacea, a structured continuing education and leadership development process must be integrated into the fabric of daily union and workplace life. Given the large number of informal and formal labor education opportunities available today, this should be the first lesson to be learned and the easiest to complete.

Chapter 6
Cui Bono?

David Fasenfest

THE 1970S AND 1980S were rocky times for the U.S. economy as the United States experienced fiscal crises in its states and fiscal crises in its cities (O'Connor 1973; Alcaly and Mermelstein 1977). Its economic base was eroded as the heavy industries that drove U.S. prosperity in the 1950s and 1960s began to collapse under the weight of inadequate capital reinvestment and foreign competition (Bluestone and Harrison 1982). The once-booming industrial cities of the Northeast and Midwest became humbled as people and businesses moved to warmer climates and the former became known as the rustbelt (Sawers and Tabb 1984). To slow or reverse this decline, cities and states now compete with one another in new forms of regional economic warfare (Markusen 1987; Howland 1988) by offering bigger and better incentives to keep existing businesses and attract new investments both from other parts of the country and more recently from Japan and Europe.

A plant closing usually means the loss to a community of high-wage industrial employment. Local income and property tax revenues are reduced at a time when the demand for social services is increasing. Indirectly, the closing reduces sales tax revenues and jobs in supporting industries and firms (a reverse multiplier). Communities have had to face this new urban reality and devise responses to industrial restructuring and economic downturns (Peterson 1985; Logan and Molotch 1987).[1] A crisis of confidence emerged in the ability of local, regional, and national governments to respond

This chapter could not have been written without the research assistance of J. B. Hoover, who collected material used in the chapter and commented on drafts of the manuscript. The editors of this book provided especially useful suggestions for improving this article. Any problems or oversights are strictly the result of my own stubbornness.

effectively. New growth strategies were adopted and coalitions formed as communities turned to economic movers and shakers for guidance (Swanstrom 1985; Cummings 1988).

In the 1980s, a view of disinvestment and deindustrialization began to take shape. Communities experiencing the decline of heavy manufacturing blamed too much government regulation, high corporate and property tax rates, overpriced union labor, and unfair competition from Asia and Europe. Incentives were needed to lower the cost of doing business in urban areas in order to retain existing plants and promote new investment.

Creation of a better business climate was the goal of most communities faced with plant closings. Economic enterprise zones, tax abatements, tax-increment financing, and industrial development bonds became weapons in the economic development arsenal of city managers and economic development officials of cities large and small. Job creation became the benchmark with which to measure both economic policy success and community decline. Failure to keep jobs from leaving a community could mean political ruin for incumbent administrations, and promoting job growth was part of every campaign promise.[2] When small business startups were identified as the major source of new jobs, everyone favored a new era of entrepreneurial activity in their communities.[3]

The 1980s began with the election of a president who was committed to getting government out of the way of business, who promoted the virtue of supply-side economics and (more quietly) the trickle-down effect, and who was unafraid to show workers without jobs the help-wanted columns. If we ensured that business could get on with the business of making money, the reasoning went, then employment would increase and eventually everyone's income would rise.[4] This philosophy led to a decade-long process of increased reliance on the private sector to lead the economic recovery while the public sector was rationalized and streamlined. Jobs, any jobs, at almost any cost to the public, guided the business climate approach to solving the problems of industrial decline and sluggish growth.

Absent a clear national policy to reverse industrial decline, public officials pursuing this strategy began offering generous incentive packages to businesses in the hope of keeping existing plants and attracting new ones. The most publicized, although far from the only example, was the bidding war for the General Motors (GM) Saturn plant. Ever-larger packages of free or low-cost sites, low- or no-cost financing, worker training grants and subsidies, tax abatements, and public financing for site improvements were offered to GM to locate in a given state. This circus culminated in the appearance of several state governors on Phil Donahue's TV show to promote the virtues and assets of their respective states in an effort to sway corporate decision makers.[5]

Such a business interests–first environment creates problems for the public sector. Firms doing business in a community that has just offered a large economic inducement to another producer might understandably ask for a similar package from the community or threaten to leave. Was it not reasonable then for the Chrysler Corporation, for example, to demand a large subsidy from Wisconsin after that state offered GM one to get the Saturn plant?[6] And what is to keep a firm doing business in a suburban area from moving into the central city (or the reverse) simply because the other community is offering attractive incentives to businesses willing to relocate? Such competition does nothing to improve overall employment but can cost both communities financially. How can communities differentiate which corporations will go out of business or have to relocate without subsidies and which will view subsidies as a free good and a source of profits? Even the business press identifies some incentive programs as "corporate food stamps" (*Barron's,* Aug. 17, 1981, 7; Aug. 16, 1982, 9) and applies all the pejorative implications usually reserved for individual recipients of government aid.

This chapter focuses on three cases in which public monies were used to promote jobs, on the demands and promises the firms made to get the subsidies, and, most important, on what happened afterward. It examines in detail arrangements between the city of Detroit and General Motors to develop an industrial site in an area commonly known as Poletown, discusses the industrial revenue bond the city of Chicago provided the toy maker Playskool to retain jobs there, and reviews the efforts of state and local authorities in Duluth, Minnesota, to recover jobs and monies lost when Diamond Tool relocated operations after receiving financial incentives to stay. It concludes by analyzing the cases discussed.

Poletown: Do You Get What You Pay For?

In early 1980, the General Motors Corporation approached the city of Detroit about finding a site for a 3-million-square-foot plant to replace aging Cadillac and Fisher body plants. At stake was a proposed "6150 jobs which would have otherwise been lost to the Detroit area . . . [and] a potential $15,000,000 in new property tax revenues" (Detroit, City of, 1980: 11–14). In addition, Detroit faced the prospect that the loss of both old and new GM facilities would accelerate an ongoing process of deterioration of its manufacturing infrastructure (Hill 1978, 1981). The direct support services created around automobile manufacturing (e.g., automotive design, machine tool manufacture and metal-bending operations, trucking and rail services) were a vital part of the revenue base of Detroit. Consequently, the loss of these GM plants meant more than just the loss of six thousand jobs. It could well signal an end to the hope that Detroit would ever recover as a manufacturing employment center.

In response to the challenge posed by GM's announced plant closing, the Detroit Community Economic Development Department (CEDD) began to search for a site that would satisfy General Motors' needs and therefore ensure construction of the new plant in Detroit. This process raised the question of what price the people of Detroit would pay for the plant. Given time constraints imposed by General Motors (General Motors 1981), the city selected a site in and around the neighborhood commonly called Poletown (because of its predominant ethnic composition) and proposed using its powers of eminent domain (the right of government to take private property for public use) to acquire more than 460 acres for the new facility. The city of Detroit proposed to move 3,438 residents in 1,362 households, 143 institutions or businesses (including 16 churches, a hospital, and 2 schools), and to demolish 1,176 buildings (*Detroit News,* Oct. 16, 1980, A1; Detroit Community Economic Development Department 1981a).

This approach reflected conventional thinking about how to respond to a threatened plant closing. Specifically, the response was to find ways to lower the cost of doing business in Detroit to ensure General Motors' continued presence. At issue in such a calculus is the overall cost to the city, who pays those costs, whether the benefits outweigh the costs, and whether the benefits compensate those who pay the costs (Fasenfest 1986).

Once plans to close the Fisher and Cadillac plants were announced, and GM's desire to replace them with a new facility was made known, three issues were brought before the Detroit City Council: (1) where to situate the proposed plant; (2) how to finance the project; and (3) what special tax abatements, if any, to offer GM. The first issue required approving the proposed site for the plant and ruling that the project was vital to the city of Detroit, thereby enabling the city council to use available legislation (Michigan Public Act 87) to approve the rapid acquisition of private land by the CEDD. The second issue concerned the use of urban development action grants (UDAGs) and grants from the Economic Development Administration (EDA) for site-preparation costs. These monies, already granted and earmarked for specific communities and other purposes, would be redirected for the proposed project (Detroit Community Economic Development Department 1981b). In addition, future UDAGs and EDA grants would be mortgaged as loan repayment guarantees. The third issue involved granting a tax abatement to GM for new plant construction. Under Michigan law, a municipality can grant abatements to encourage construction of new manufacturing facilities.

The overriding concerns for Detroit can be summarized as follows: What were the best interests of the people of Detroit, which actions were in those interests, and how were the actions to be implemented? Each neighborhood within the city was concerned with the effect of the project's direct and indirect costs: What funds would now be unavailable for community development if the city diverted monies to the project? What would be the effect on the community chosen as the site of the project?

Similarly, each community had to weigh the costs against potential benefits: Would there be more jobs for the city as a whole? Would these jobs specifically help members of the community? Would overall taxes be lower because the plant would be in the city? Would the project stop the economic erosion of the city?

Clearly, not all communities and neighborhoods had to be concerned about more than the broadest questions affecting the city as a whole. But the decision to finance and build the plant was made with little input from any of the city's communities. Rather, the decision was the product of pressure brought to bear by GM and a willing administration seeking to provide GM with a good climate for its investment.

The city council was excluded from the process that resulted in the initial decision to close the two operating plants and replace them with a newer, more productive one. GM stated clearly that current rules and tax laws made it economically unreasonable to renovate and maintain the existing plants (*Detroit News,* June 28, 1980, A1). The city was limited to a variety of options, all in the interests of GM as a corporate entity. The council's actions therefore focused on preparing and turning over a suitable site for the new plant. It never raised the questions of when and under what conditions GM would build the plant and what type of plant it would be.

GM had unilaterally planned to replace its older facilities and maintained that it was interested in, and even committed to, remaining in the Detroit area. GM would wait until only October 1, 1980, however, before it would review the progress the city had made in its search for a site and make a decision. In this way, the company defined the parameters and timetable of the problem and the options available to the city—no site meant no plant and no jobs.

Decisions affecting the city as a whole thus came to be controlled solely by the logic of GM's internal accounting practices. As a result, within two months the city had committed large sums of money earmarked for other community projects and had applied for additional funds in the form of grants and loans from various agencies (with the council's reluctant approval)—all because the city had to make suitable progress by the beginning of October.

On October 7, GM reportedly added tax-abatement guarantees to its demands. Four days later, the city's CEDD and GM signed an agreement calling for the terms and price under which GM would buy the site. Any sale was contingent, however, on the city having clear title to the property, razing all buildings, completing necessary site improvements, and granting GM a twelve-year 50 percent tax abatement. Notably absent was any commitment by GM to build a plant and put people to work. The council realized the degree to which it was being forced into a position in which it no longer made policy decisions and instead was treated like a rubber stamp (*Detroit News,* Oct. 11, 1980, A1).

By the end of October, the council had diverted $60.5 million in current HUD grants for the project and had committed $51.5 million in future UDAG monies to repay additional loans. The latter commitment was made in spite of CEDD staff recommendations that it estimate the effects of the new plant on communities losing grant monies and that it link tax abatement to guaranteed levels of employment—at least six thousand jobs to be created and maintained for the life of the abatement. Meanwhile, GM predicted that future automation could trim the new plant's work force significantly (*Detroit News,* Oct. 21, 1980, B4), and Mayor Coleman Young conceded to the council that a new plant would not necessarily create new permanent jobs, claims of "thousands of jobs" were not accurate, and an original payback estimate of fifteen years presented to the council did not take the tax abatement into consideration (*Detroit News,* Oct. 22, 1980, A1). Nevertheless, the council approved the site and the associated financing (see table 6.1) on the grounds that there was a clear and immediate need to act.

Finally, the council had to consider whether to grant GM a tax abatement for its proposed plant. In the interest of the city's financial crisis, GM had agreed to accept only a 50 percent reduction of taxes for twelve years (*Detroit News,* March 16, 1981, A1)[7] rather than ask for either a 100 percent abatement or for a 50 percent abatement over a longer time period.

To gain approval, pressure was brought on a reluctant council. First, the company pointed out that many other communities would welcome a GM plant, so that if the tax abatement were denied GM would have to reconsider.

Table 6.1. Financial summary for the Poletown Redevelopment Project (in millions of dollars)

Costs	
Land acquisition	62.0
Occupant relocation	25.0
Demolition	35.0
Road preparation	23.5
Rail preparation	12.0
Other site preparation	38.7
Professional service fees	3.5
Total	199.7
Funding sources	
HUD section 108 loan	100.0
HUD UDAG	30.0
EDA grant	30.0
EPA grant	6.9
State road funds	38.7
State rail funds	17.8
State land bank loan	1.5
Urban Mass Transit Administration	1.4
Community Development Block Grant	2.0
Other grants	66.1
Proceeds from land sale to GM	6.8
Total	301.2
Funds set aside for loan payment guarantees	(101.5)
Total financing available for project	199.7

Source: Community Economic Development Corporation, "Central Industrial Park Project Plan," Sept. 30, 1980, 11.

Second, Emmett Moten of the CEDD argued that GM was technically entitled to the abatement according to the earlier land-transfer agreement, in which an abatement was a precondition to the transfer. Third, Mayor Young asserted that the absence of any written commitment to build was not a problem, noting that GM was "doing the city a favor" by building the plant in Detroit in the first place (*Detroit News,* April 16, 1980, B1).

Not surprisingly, the council granted the abatement. The only constraint placed on GM was that it create no fewer than three thousand jobs within four years. Just before the finalization of the property transfer, the city announced that the project area had been designated a "tax-increment financing" district in which all tax revenues generated by the project would be removed from the general fund and earmarked to repay the more than $200 million spent on the project. Consequently, there would be no direct revenue to the city of Detroit as a result of the project for fifteen to twenty years (*Detroit News,* April 30, 1981, B1).

If there was no opposition from the city council to GM's plans, the residents of Poletown were not so agreeable. Organized as the Poletown Neighborhood Council (PNC), residents challenged the need for GM to acquire such a large site. The PNC solicited architects' support and proposed alterations in GM's site plan that would have reduced the size of the site and thereby saved most of the homes, businesses, and buildings slated for the wrecking ball. GM rejected the modifications, however, which called for a multistory parking garage and reduced green space around the plant, and the Poletown project moved forward.[8]

The mayor's office refused to force GM to accept the modifications for fear it would jeopardize the project. The PNC thus found itself cut off from institutions that had represented residents' interests. As Jeanie Wylie (1989) notes in her account of the Poletown story, the UAW told the PNC that the union could do nothing on the community's behalf and the archdiocese of Detroit rejected pleas for help from the predominantly Catholic community. In fact, the archdiocese tried to silence the parish priest who helped organize the community and then sold the parish's churches to the city over the community's opposition. Powerless, members of the community had to watch as GM's plans were realized and their community destroyed.[9]

On May 1, 1981, the site was sold to GM. Within weeks of the property transfer, the company announced that the changing economic climate required a review of all its capital expenditure plans (*Detroit News,* May 17, 1981, H1), although research and investments in plant robotics and automation would continue. In response to criticism that the city had proceeded without GM's binding commitment to build a plant, Mayor Young stated that "if we waited for all the silly guarantees, nothing would get built" (*Detroit News,* May 31, 1981, B8). In spite of Mayor Young's assurances, the local press reported on November 3 that GM planned to delay completion of its plant for at least another year and hoped to get the plant on line for 1985 car production provided the economic climate for the industry improved.

Eventually, a plant was built, and GM began operations for its luxury Cadillac, Riviera, and Toronado lines with the 1986 model year. But the number of jobs created did not live up to the fantasy. Whereas Chrysler had employed as many as thirty thousand workers in and around its original Dodge Main plant on the Poletown site, the new GM plant, which is a state-of-the-art forerunner of its Saturn plant in Tennessee, employs fewer than five thousand at peak production with two shifts in operation. This is mainly because it uses 2,000 programmable devices, including 330 robots. The plant is so highly automated that entire sections of the assembly process require no human assistance. Just-in-time delivery of parts eliminated the warehousing jobs and weakened the need for traditional industrial links with closely situated firms. Research in robotics and the decision to delay the opening of the plant enabled GM to cut its labor force, lower production costs, and perhaps increase profits per car. GM also paid low taxes and had a plant built in part through contributions from the public coffers.

The entire process was constrained by two deadlines imposed by GM: October 1, 1980, to review site-selection progress, and May 1, 1981, to take possession of the site. There was no need for such urgency. In an atmosphere in which building a better business environment is the goal, and during a period of ready subsidies in which there is little examination of whether a firm needs them or simply demands them, corporations will naturally demand subsidies. The community is left to wonder whether the benefits will materialize and outweigh the costs.

Industrial Development Bonds: Financing Whose Future?

Corporations also received subsidies during the 1980s from local and state governments in the form of low-interest, tax-exempt loans designed to help firms make capital outlays for plants and equipment. Most recently known as industrial revenue bonds (IRBs), these loans used tax exemptions as an indirect way to subsidize corporate borrowing. A company usually made commitments to the community to maintain or increase the work force at its plants if the community would authorize an IRB to finance all or part of the capital-improvement project. Originally designed to attract businesses to depressed areas, IRBs were widely used to offset limitations or restrictions on access to capital imposed by commercial banks. Communities justified their increasing use on the grounds that they provided capital to increase local investment, boost job creation, and in general invigorate or ensure the financial status of expanding enterprises.

The IRB program has come under much criticism over the years as an inefficient capital subsidy tool[10] and for its poor record in generating employment (Pascarella and Raymond 1982; Marlin 1986; Pascarella 1986). Industrial revenue bonds have been widely used yet poorly understood. Until recently, community development officials used them at the behest of corporations in their communities or of corporations looking to enter a community without undertaking critical reviews of the corporations' experiences elsewhere. Publicized cases such as the suit by the city of Yonkers against Otis Elevator for misuse and abuse of its IRB did little to stem their use.

By the early 1980s, the business press was roundly criticizing IRBs for three main reasons: they raised the cost of other forms of government financing by creating competition in the general bond market; (2) they subsidized one firm at the expense of others; and (3) they represented an increasing share of tax-exempt financing (Harrison and Kanter 1981; Moore and Squires 1988). In fact, concern about the contribution of IRBs to rising debts finally prompted Congress to curtail the IRB program. Oddly, while business decried the unfair advantage some firms seemed to get from IRBs, local and state governments showed little concern that a major proportion of IRBs went to finance the expansion of retail chains such as McDonald's and K-Mart. These businesses did little to create jobs, and those they did create were usually low paying and part time.

To provide a better understanding of how IRBs are used and abused, and to demonstrate what some communities are trying to do to set limits, this section examines the IRBs given to Playskool, Inc., in Chicago and to the Diamond Tool and Horseshoe Company in Duluth, Minnesota. In both cases the companies identified capital investments and improvements that, if financed through IRBs, would have permitted them to retain local jobs. The economic costs of self-financing were prohibitive, and they would have had to consider closing plants or other actions involving job losses. These cases were unusual in that the corporate excesses that followed were too great to ignore and the companies were taken to court and forced to return their loans or fulfill their obligations under the loan agreements.

PLAYSKOOL

In September 1984, Playskool, Inc., a subsidiary of the Milton Bradley Company, in turn owned by Hasbro Industries, announced it would close its Chicago plant and lay off more than seven hundred workers before the end of the year. On its own this would have been nothing more than additional bad news to a city in which 110,000 jobs had disappeared between 1979 and 1984 (*Barron's*, Aug. 16, 1982, 9). In this case, however, the response was a public outcry that mobilized the community around a national boycott of Hasbro toys during the Christmas season, condemnation by Chicago's business community, and eventually a suit filed by the city of Chicago to stop the closing. What made this closing so different in the eyes of Chicago's neighborhoods, businesses, and government was that Milton Bradley had been awarded a $1 million IRB in 1980 to purchase equipment on the promise that it would create four hundred new jobs at its Chicago plant.[11]

Instead, employment during the period between the awarding of the IRB and the shutdown announcement had fallen from about twelve hundred to seven hundred employees (Giloth and Rosenblum 1987). The cost to the city of the closing and layoffs, as outlined in Alderman Miguel Santiago's resolution before the Chicago City Council, was $17 million per year in personal income, $7 million in bank deposits, 450 additional jobs in supporting businesses, the closure of seven retail establishments, and $10 million in lost retail sales. The reneged promise meant that Chicago lost 25 percent of the total job-creation and job-retention claims made for the entire 1980 IRB program. In addition, Alderman Santiago identified more than $200,000 in interest benefits that had accrued to Milton Bradley by 1984 as a result of the IRB's tax-exempt status (Chicago Department of Economic Development, Playskool Briefing memo, n.d.).[12]

Community opposition grew quickly. Within a week of the announcement of the closing, the West Side Jobs Network (WJN), a coalition of community and labor organizations, organized to bring pressure on the city and Playskool to keep the plant open. Public meetings informed the community about the events, and the pre-Christmas season added to the toy manufacturer's discomfort at being portrayed as heartless for laying off workers just before the holidays. Finally, Chicago Mayor Harold Washington drew sizable political support for taking a stand on the need for community development and greater equity. His campaign promises to maintain an open government and to build the city's job base translated into pressure that community groups could apply to get the city to act in innovative ways.

In December 1984, the city of Chicago filed suit against all parties (Playskool and its layers of ownership) to force Playskool to keep the plant open and honor the terms of the IRB agreement. To wit, the city wanted the company to operate the plant until February 1, 2000 (the IRB was a twenty-year instrument). It was the first suit of its kind by any government agency to recover its IRB or force a company to honor its loan obligations.

At the end of January 1985, Playskool made an out-of-court settlement with the city, which, in addition to returning the IRB, required that the company keep the plant open another year and maintain one hundred jobs at the plant; make its "best effort" to find another user for the facility; and establish relocation and training programs and funds for the displaced workers. The results were less than hoped for, and the out-of-court settlement precluded a legal precedent in the case. Some corporate obligations were implicitly acknowledged, and the community managed to postpone and blunt the blow.

The burden of the plant closing by Playskool fell on the workers and the surrounding community. Of the seven hundred workers who lost their jobs, 80 percent were black and Hispanic and 65 percent lived within five miles of the plant. It was located in a declining area (an industrial corridor being dismantled by commercial and residential development), and its loss further undermined the integrity of the last major manufacturing district in Chicago. Currently the site is subdivided and has an array of tenants. Although some jobs have been reclaimed, most do not pay the same wages workers received from Playskool (Giloth and Mier 1986).

Hasbro Industries offered several public rationales for closing the plant, including the need for corporate consolidation, the plant's inefficiency and poor condition, and the need for cheaper labor and fewer work rules. It generated profits and sales for the company (*Chicago Enterprise*, Nov. 1989, 10–11), but not enough.[13] A business climate approach accepts that an enterprise will seek the location and environment delivering the best return, independent of external costs imposed on the abandoned location.

Serious questions are raised about Milton Bradley's behavior in Chicago when one considers that the company also secured a $1 million IRB from the Massachusetts Industrial Finance Authority to renovate a plant to which the Chicago production was transferred.[14] Milton Bradley's original intention may not have been to close the Chicago plant, but the Massachusetts IRB paved the way for such a decision. Furthermore, a machine purchased for the Playskool plant in Chicago used labor-saving technology and therefore was transferred to the Massachusetts plant (Chicago Department of Economic Development, Playskool briefing memo, n.d.). The out-of-court settlement left unanswered questions of ultimate responsibility and underlying corporate intent vis-à-vis Chicago. But if Playskool's behavior remains cloudy in motive and intent, the Diamond Tool and Horseshoe Company acted in a manner that provides a clearer understanding of corporate opportunities to abuse access to public monies.

DIAMOND TOOL

A family-owned manufacturer of pliers and other hardware in Duluth, Minnesota, the Diamond Tool and Horseshoe Company was auctioned in 1981 after the founder's death. The winning bid of $20 million came from a Connecticut company, the Triangle Corporation. Triangle could not raise the necessary financing, however, so the city of Duluth agreed to issue a $10 million IRB to finance the purchase and an additional $750,000 Community Development Block Grant (CDBG) to finance planned equipment renovations and improvements (Giloth and Rosenblum 1987:23).[15] At the time of the purchase, Diamond Tool employed 757 workers and, as part of the UDAG grant, pledged an additional 145 jobs from the proposed improvements (*Duluth News Tribune*, June 28, 1988).

By 1987, however, the plant's labor force had fallen to 379 workers and management had asked the remaining workers for a $6 per hour cut in wages and benefits (Midwest Center for Labor Research 1987). At that point Diamond Tool's union, the Directly Affiliated Local Union (DALU) 18650, contacted the Minnesota Working Group on Economic Dislocation, an anti–plant-closing coalition, for assistance. Through the Working Group, DALU 18650 contracted with the Midwest Center for Labor Research (MCLR) in Chicago to research Triangle's actions. Using the rationale that GM used to delay construction of the Poletown plant, management insisted poor business conditions and a shrinking economy were forcing Triangle to consolidate its operations.

The MCLR report, however, uncovered a clear pattern of program abuse by the Triangle Corporation. Of the fourteen firms it had acquired before Diamond Tool, twelve had been sold or closed and one had been relocated. One also had been purchased with an IRB, only to be closed later, leaving the balance of the IRB unpaid (*New York Times*, June 24, 1988, B1). The report also showed that Triangle had used Job Training Partnership Act funds to train workers at its Orangeburg, South Carolina, plant for jobs that were then relocated from Diamond Tool in Duluth. In a controversial inquiry, the Department of Labor failed to find any abuse of JTPA funding provisions (Midwest Center for Labor Research 1987:4). Nevertheless, the Triangle Corporation acted as if local and national government subsidies were legitimate sources of funds to lower the cost of corporate acquisition and the dismantling of profitable product lines.

Most of the job loss in Duluth, according to the MCLR, was the result of the transfer of various production units to the Orangeburg plant (see table 6.2 for a chronology), not market downturns and low profits. More important, the MCLR suggested that the interstate transfer of equipment purchased with state funds violated Minnesota laws governing the financing of industrial development (*Employment and Training Reporter*, Feb. 24, 1988, 4). Triangle's actions, according to the MCLR's estimate, cost the community $228,998 in lost sales and income taxes and the state $867,048 in increased unemployment insurance benefit payments. Against this, and aside from the profits made from the products moved to South Carolina, Triangle received more than $2.25 million in savings on financing costs from the IRB and the UDAG.

Table 6.2. Chronology of job loss at the Duluth Diamond Tool plant, 1984–87

1984	Triangle Corporation begins to dismantle Duluth plier production department by moving solid-joint pliers. Duluth loses approximately forty jobs, including links to other departments, by the end of 1985.
January 1985	Diamond Tool's sales department is transferred from Duluth and consolidated into the Orangeburg sales staff. A number of key Diamond sales jobs, including vice president for sales, are lost as a result. Duluth loses approximately fifteen jobs.
March 1985	Sixty workers are laid off. At the same time, work in Orangeburg picks up as employees switch from partial to full workweeks and in some cases to overtime work.
October 1985	Sixty-five Duluth workers are laid off, in part because of a market downturn and overproduction. Workers are also laid off in Orangeburg.
November 1985	Twenty-five Duluth workers are laid off. None of the Duluth workers laid off in 1985 have been called back. The bargaining unit declines from 523 to 350 during 1985.
December 1985	A total of 360 workers are laid off to avoid paying them for the Christmas holiday; three hundred are recalled January 7 and the remainder two weeks later.
Fall 1986	The miniature plier line is transferred to Orangeburg; two broaching machines and two large Pacific presses are removed.
March 1987	Triangle announces the transfer of packing, warehousing, and shipping activities (approximately twenty-five jobs) and of machining and finishing of slip joint and groove joint pliers and finishing of adjustable wrenches (approximately seventy-five additional jobs) by end of 1987. Citing higher Duluth labor costs, company also blames "old and inefficient Duluth facility, and the high cost of doing business in Minnesota."
Spring 1987	Triangle moves two truckloads of plant equipment from Duluth to Orangeburg, including four Acme grinders, two broaches, four upright belt grinders, four snip grinders, a skin-packing machine, miscellaneous cutters, jibs, and fixtures for the broaches, two punch presses, the aviation tin snip assembly line, and two serrating machines.
Summer 1987	Two LaPointe broaches (larger, more expensive, newer models), two more punch presses, and one counter-sinking machine are packed for shipment to the Orangeburg plant.

Source: Midwest Center for Labor Research, "Partial Shutdown of Diamond Tool and Horseshoe Company: Analysis, Outlook and Options for Public Intervention," 8. Report prepared for Local 18650, Directly Affiliated Union, June 1987.

Armed with this report, the DALU pressured the Duluth City Council to act. The result was a suit against Triangle to force it to comply with the terms of the IRB and UDAG agreements and to restore the plant to its earlier level of activity or return the IRB financing. The original court ruling was in favor of the city's claim and ordered Triangle to return the equipment from Orangeburg. On appeal, the courts overturned the order requiring the return of the equipment but upheld the principle of forced compliance with IRB and UDAG promises by preventing any further erosion of the plant's operating capabilities. Although this outcome was less than ideal for those adversely affected, it did establish the right of a community to force a company to follow through on economic performance and job promises when the public sector finances its operations.

LESSONS FROM PLAYSKOOL AND DIAMOND TOOL

Chicago's experience with Playskool indicates the strength of the community's claim that a company should be held accountable for its actions when they have a negative impact on the community. Duluth's experience takes this one step further. First, it demonstrates that such a claim is legally enforceable because the IRB represents a promise to act on the part of the company in return for subsidized financing. This point is critical because so many communities still have outstanding IRB instruments issued for up to twenty years. Now communities have a precedent for enforcing the terms of those IRBs or recovering their investments.

Second, and perhaps more important, the Duluth experience clearly raises the specter that many companies look at IRBs, and at government subsidies generally, as easy money with which to finance plant closings and improve profit margins. Other suits were filed to force compliance and other examples emerged of proposed IRB financing in which it appeared that deals were constructed solely for the purpose of raiding public coffers (*New York Times*, June 24, 1988, B1). As the MCLR report shows, however, only diligence on the part of workers and early warning systems prevent abuses, whether intended or not.

The Playskool and Diamond Tool examples further demonstrate the importance of active community involvement. The political will of community leaders to take legal action against firms abusing incentive programs comes both from activism within and participation by the community and from a reform-oriented administration that has been forced to consider alternatives to the business climate approach to development.

The experience of East Chicago, Indiana, in the closing of a Combustion

Engineering (CE) plant is a case in point. In 1985, Combustion Engineering applied for and received an IRB based on its promise to purchase equipment that would save eighteen jobs. Within a year, however, the firm announced that it was closing the plant entirely. When workers and their union local informed the Calumet Project for Industrial Jobs (a local job-retention and anti–plant-closing community organization) that no such equipment had been installed, the parties called a press conference to alert the community. CE offered to return the IRB, but activists urged the mayor and city council to take CE to court for breach of contract. (Chapters 7 and 10 in this volume focus on the Calumet Project.)

Even though CE had not used its IRB to purchase the machinery it said would make the plant competitive, the city declined to go to court (*Barron's*, July 16, 1984, 14–22). The city attorney recommended against it on the grounds that he could not prove fraudulent intent. CE claims it lost money while holding the IRB in escrow; the Calumet Project and the union claim CE had the money in an interest-bearing account and earned up to $200,000 on the difference between the earnings and the low-interest loan (*Hammond Times*, July 15, 1986; *American Metal Markets/Metalworking News*, July 1986). Over strong opposition from the Calumet Project and the union, and contrary to another legal opinion urging the city to take action[16] (*Gary Post Tribune*, July 24, 1986), CE was allowed to return the IRB, to ignore workers' proposals of ways to keep the plant profitable, and eventually to close the plant.

In this case, despite some community presence and an activist local organization, East Chicago's political leaders lacked the will to pursue Combustion Engineering via the courts. Their refusal stemmed from their approach to local economic development, which emphasized improving the business climate for future investors. A lawsuit against CE would have jeopardized that policy, regardless of the legal merits of the city's claims. Unwillingness by the local government to oppose creation of a business climate at any cost meant the loss of jobs to the community and permitted a company to benefit improperly from its access to public-sector loans.

Conclusion

IRB financing was abolished in 1988, but there are still an arsenal of subsidies and loans to underwrite almost any corporate venture that promises to provide jobs, especially manufacturing jobs, to states and communities.[17] Sometimes the promise is to bring new jobs, and sometimes a negative threat is made to relocate old jobs. Both approaches are so effective that tax abatements and financing for construction continue to provide millions of dollars to firms that are able and willing to exploit the "incentives race" among governments. The Playskool experience notwithstanding, Chicago and the state of Illinois, for example, paid dearly to keep Sears headquartered in the city and built a reservation center for United Airlines at O'Hare Airport. These gambles may or may not return benefits greater than the costs, but that will be determined by the actions and strategies of firms independent of community efforts. GM's decision to locate its Saturn plant in Tennessee, where it got no major subsidies from the state, rather than in any of the surrounding states that were offering generous incentive packages, indicates that decisions key to overall corporate strategies are made for reasons beyond the size of incentive packages. Thus, GM may have built the plant in Poletown without the subsidies it received. Only the management of GM knows. And even after getting the subsidies and building the plant, it hurt the community in ways Poletown neither expected nor wanted.

Why are cities and states often disappointed in the results of financial incentive programs based on business climate strategies? The cases discussed in this chapter suggest why. First, as the Poletown case shows, in the competition for jobs, the public sector has to reveal its intentions and needs and commit its resources to the intended project without receiving corresponding information and commitments from the firm. In a very real sense, corporate strategies and options remain confidential while the public sector openly deliberates and acts on demands for huge expenditures that may or may not improve the lives of its citizens. As a practical matter, local and state governments know only as much as the firm wants them to know, have no way of requiring any meaningful public "debate" over the issue, and, in view of competitive offers from other communities, cannot force the firm to make enforceable commitments it does not want to make.

Second, the Diamond Tool case demonstrates how a company can use public subsidies to acquire other firms and transfer profitable product lines to low-wage locations. The incentive package Duluth assumed or was told would be the decisive factor in the company's operating decisions turned out to be just one of numerous calculations determining the final outcome. Knowledge, mobility, and resources (including public incentives) give companies the freedom to choose options; without knowledge and mobility, communities have only the resources with which they compete against other communities and gamble with hidden corporate agendas. The firm typically does not consider the interest or even the goodwill of a particular community in its decision making. Capital spending choices reflect overall business strategies unconnected to previous or historical corporate-community relationships, dependencies, and commitments. Mutual interest cannot be assumed in these matters, and the community that makes such an assumption is mistaken.

Third, the Playskool case shows that for communities to obtain favorable terms in their relations with firms, they must have a strong and militant local organization and a progressive and responsive local administration that is not vulnerable to public and legal pressure by the firm. In this instance, years of plant closings and broken promises had shaped community opinion and forced grass-roots activism against such practices. The political philosophy and constituency of Harold Washington's administration were consistent with efforts by the government to make Playskool accountable for its behavior. Further, the company's blatant abuse of public financing in its production relocations and the language it had agreed to in the subsidy exposed it to legal action. The result was that this outcome was the exception rather than the norm in these matters.

A conclusion to be drawn from these and other cases involving public-sector subsidies in return for promised job retention and creation is that policies designed to manipulate market-based decisions and outcomes by altering production costs in specified, desirable ways are in fact deeply susceptible to the law of unintended effects: they benefit the party that has more information, mobility, and resources—that is, the one with greater market discretion. The effect is that the firm's operating performance is improved without anything significant necessarily returning to the community (*Chicago Enterprise*, Nov. 1989, 10–11).

What does all this mean for community policy? To begin with, communities should reconsider the business climate strategy. By creating an environment that caters to corporate interests and needs in order to attract or keep jobs, a community is only inviting another Triangle Corporation or GM plant expansion project. Corporations are encouraged to demand subsidies simply because they are available. Communities need to find ways to encourage job retention and creation while providing safeguards whenever public monies are involved. They should take a more proactive stance to maintain current jobs and to ensure that job-creation programs are used properly. When firms seek public-sector financing, land acquisition, job training, or other subsidies, they should be required to provide information about long-term corporate plans and to document economic need.

Additional policies are needed after the firm qualifies for public assistance. First, specified quid pro quo arrangements are essential to identify the benefits from the firm to the community as a result of the subsidies. Once accepted, these benefits should then become standards against which the firm's subsequent performance and actions can be judged.

Second, communities need appropriate monitoring programs to determine progress toward the established goals. Early warning programs—like those promoted by the West Side Jobs Network in Chicago and the Calumet Project for Industrial Jobs in northwestern Indiana—help identify potential plant closings soon enough to encourage efforts to reverse decisions. Such monitoring alerts the community to potential problems and can be used to involve the firm in solving problems that threaten mutual objectives.

Third, and finally, communities must insist on adequate sanctions against firms to ensure that they repay loans and, in the event they fail to meet job and tax goals, compensate the community for lost opportunities. Such sanctions would guard against firms accepting public funds unless they intend to meet their promises to the community. Public monies can and should be used to improve the economic welfare of entire communities, not only corporate balance sheets (see Fasenfest 1988). Until there is more community involvement in deciding who gets subsidies, a shift away from a jobs-at-any-price business climate, and a greater political will for strict enforcement of subsidy agreements, we are liable to continue to see firms fattening at the public trough.

Chapter 7
SHUTDOWN OF A STEEL FOUNDRY

Bruce Nissen

FACED WITH A DECLINING product market, many companies choose to "milk" an existing facility for its remaining profits while choosing not to reinvest or develop alternative product lines to keep the plant viable. Ultimately, the plant is closed, and the company claims that market conditions made the shutdown inevitable.

This chapter details and analyzes one such case in northwest Indiana. The case involves an unusually rich and detailed set of occurrences that demonstrate the many ways a corporation can accomplish its ultimate goal. Because an alerted local union and community chose to contest the shutdown, the company was forced to employ a wide variety of methods to achieve its purpose.

Specifically, this case study illustrates (1) how a corporation used secrecy and misrepresentation in its dealings with the press to achieve predetermined goals; (2) how a corporation used a last-minute sale to avoid ultimate responsibility for a shutdown; (3) how a corporation manipulated politicians to obtain defense orders solely for the purpose of milking further profits before the shutdown; (4) the extremely limited effectiveness in a situation like this of public officials and economic development officials who follow a business climate approach to economic development; and (5) the role and possible power of labor-community coalitions in fighting plant shutdowns and job loss.

In the first section, I provide historical and economic background on the closure of the Blaw-Knox foundry in northwest Indiana. I then describe the two-year campaign to save the facility. Finally, I analyze the forces at work and summarize the possible sources of power for unions and communities in plant-closing situations of this type.

Background

The Blaw-Knox steel foundry in East Chicago, Indiana, began as the Hubbard Steel foundry in 1911. Located near the giant U.S. Steel mill in Gary, it produced castings for the local steel industry. Shortly before World War II, it was purchased by the Continental Roll and Steel Foundry Company; during the war it produced military tank hulls and turrets to supplement civilian production. After the war it was purchased by the Pittsburgh-based Blaw-Knox Corporation. Blaw-Knox then shifted production back to making steel mills and mill equipment.[1] The postwar years were good ones worldwide for steel mill construction, and the Blaw-Knox foundry was well positioned to do a substantial part of the work. In some years it constructed three to five complete mills.

In 1968, the Cleveland-based conglomerate White Consolidated Industries (WCI) acquired Blaw-Knox's parent company. White Consolidated was aggressively acquiring subsidiaries at the time, especially in the home appliance industry but also in a wide-ranging array of products in the industrial equipment, machinery, metal products, and home and office fields.

The acquisition prompted fears that the local plant might be sold or have its operations reduced. But in 1969 both national and local Blaw-Knox officials assured the local press that such fears were groundless. President R. J. Sherlock stated, "We have in the past spent more on the East Chicago plant than on others. We'll continue. This is our policy." Plant manager Frank J. Satek assured the community that the fourteen hundred employees were secure: "We are the only mill-builder in the Midwest. So as the steel industry grows, so do we" (*Hammond Times*, Nov. 9, 1969). Officials also claimed to be investigating new product lines for the plant but declined to specify any in particular. In subsequent years, none materialized.

Throughout the 1960s and 1970s, White Consolidated grew rapidly by absorbing other firms. Its specialty, in addition to buying healthy companies, was acquiring facilities experiencing financial difficulties and rapidly turning them around to profitability through drastic cost cutting and personnel changes. In 1967, the year before it acquired Blaw-Knox, WCI had net sales of $172.7 million, which grew to more than $1 billion by 1974 and more than $2 billion by 1979. During the same period net income grew from $11.25 million, to $38.5 million, and to $62.9 million, the last excluding an extraordinary item (White Consolidated Annual Report 1967, 1974, 1979). Much of this growth was attained through the aggressive acquisition of competitors, particularly in the Home Products Division.

Most of WCI's growth was in the Home Products Division, although this was not the line generating the most operating income. From 1974 through 1983, this division grew from 54 percent of total sales to 77 percent; during the same period its share of operating income grew from 48 percent to 97 percent. (Figures for the years 1974–83 are given in table 7.1.)

Table 7.1 shows that in the early period the Home Products Division consistently generated less income per dollar of sales than did the other two divisions: 59 percent of sales but only 44 percent of earnings. Income per sales in the General Industrial Equipment Division was above average, while the Machinery and Metal Castings Division (to which Blaw-Knox belonged) was about average until 1981–83, when it dropped precipitously.

Of the three divisions, Home Products was the one favored for expansion. The company's business plan, although it emphasized "balance" between consumer and industrial products, was firmly and strategically wedded to the home appliance industry. WCI's overall capital expenditures and acquisitions demonstrate the same pattern: from 1976 to 1983, the book value of all assets in the Home Products Division increased by 49 percent versus a 25 percent increase in the Machinery and Metal Castings Division and a 34 percent increase in the General Industrial Equipment Division.

Thus, the parent company was expanding most rapidly in the home products field and was expanding least rapidly in Blaw-Knox's division, machinery and metal castings. In addition, Blaw-Knox's main commercial customer, the steel industry, was ordering very little in the way of new mills or equipment. As early as 1977, WCI noted in its annual report (2), "The order level of equipment we manufacture for use by both the steel producing industry and the textile industry has remained depressed. Sales and income from these two areas have been below satisfactory levels although operations in these areas remain profitable." In fact, the division remained profitable through 1981.

In 1980, WCI aggressively began to divest itself of businesses. Within three years it would shed more businesses than it had in its entire prior

Table 7.1. White Consolidated's operating performance, 1974–83

Division	Sales		Earnings	
	1974–78	1979–83	1974–78	1979–83
		(percent of total)		
Home Products	59	69	44	66
Machinery and Metal Castings	26	19	27	6
General Industrial Equipment	15	12	29	29

Source: Computed from WCI annual reports 1974–83.

history, and this trend accelerated in the mid-1980s. Virtually all of these sales were in the two divisions other than Home Products. In 1982, WCI engaged the management consulting firm of McKinsey and Company to do a comprehensive analysis of the company so that it could formulate or redefine its long-term objectives and strategic plans. A goal was to streamline operations, which produced more candidates for divestiture (Annual Report 1983:3, 7).

The 1983 WCI annual report (4, 6, 8, 10) revealed three new strategic objectives. The first goal was an overall 20 percent return on stockholders' equity, that is, $.20 of profit on every $1.00 invested in the company. The second goal was to obtain a net profit of at least $.05 on each $1.00 of sales, that is, a "net margin" of at least 5 percent. The third goal was to produce a minimum of $1.60 in sales for each $1.00 in book value of assets, which is an "asset turnover ratio" of 1.6:1. Businesses that failed to meet these three "hurdles" would be candidates for divestiture, consolidation, or closure.

The data used to calculate return-on-equity figures for particular subsidiaries or divisions are not publicly available. It is possible, however, to estimate the performance of WCI's three major divisions regarding the second two goals. Figures for "net income" are not available on a division basis, but "operating income" figures are. The ratio of *operating* income/sales is higher than the *net* income/sales ratio, but it nevertheless indicates the relative standing of the three divisions on the latter ratio (assuming that the deductions reducing operating income to net income are proportionally allocated to the divisions). Percentages for 1974–83 are given in table 7.2.

From the table, it is apparent that as a whole the companies in the General Industrial Equipment Division clearly met WCI's second hurdle of 5 percent net income on sales. Home Products was marginal but was generally meeting this goal (in 1983, even if *all* general corporate expenses, interest expense, and an "unusual item" had been charged to this *one division,* it would have met the goal of 5 percent net income on sales). Machinery and Metal Castings, the Blaw-Knox division, had definitely met this goal before 1981

Table 7.2. White Consolidated's income/sales ratios by division, 1974–83

Division	Time period	
	1974–78	1979–83
Home Products	7.6	6.2
Machinery and Metal Castings	11.0	1.6
General Industrial Equipment	19.2	16.2

Source: Computed from WCI annual reports, relevant years.

but had rapidly deteriorated in 1982 and 1983. In both years it lost money on an accelerating basis, both proportionally and absolutely.

From the first two goals WCI set for itself (20 percent return on equity and 5 percent net margin on sales), it would appear that, as of 1984, the most likely candidates for divestiture or shutdown would have been in the Machinery and Metal Castings Division. Performance in meeting the third goal ($1.60 sales for every $1.00 in assets) pointed in the same direction. Performance on this measure is given in table 7.3.

Table 7.3 demonstrates that the Home Products and General Industrial Equipment divisions were each meeting goal 3 but that the Machinery and Metal Castings Division was not and never had. Again, this division was deteriorating after 1981.

At the time of its acquisition by WCI, the East Chicago Blaw-Knox foundry was producing primarily steel mills and rolls. According to company officials, this was the "main thrust" of production at the time. Plant manager Satek estimated that orders for military tanks accounted for only 15 percent of production at the foundry (*Hammond Times*, Nov. 9, 1969).

In the 1970s, the foundry shifted heavily toward production of the M-60 tank for the U.S. Army and U.S. military allies abroad. The buildup of orders began with the increase of hostilities in the Middle East in 1974; by the mid- to late 1970s, the plant was producing four to five tanks a day, operating three shifts, and employing approximately twenty-five hundred workers.

Meanwhile, construction of steel mills had leveled off and then declined. Foreign competition for mill construction also became a production consideration for the first time. The plant constructed its last steel mill in 1983. Occasionally commercial work for the foundry's extraordinarily large castings and machining work for construction and mining equipment or power generators was obtained, but all of this work plus regrinding of rolls for steel mills was estimated to represent less than 20 percent of Blaw-Knox's business by the early 1980s (Little 1985:II-2).

Table 7.3. White Consolidated's sales, 1976–83

Division	Average dollar sales per $1.00 of assets	
	1976–79	1980–83
Home Products	1.68	2.06
Machinery and Metal Castings	1.44	1.25
General Industrial Equipment	1.77	1.64

Source: Computed from WCI annual reports, relevant years.

Thus, by the early 1980s, the product mix was the reverse of what it had been in 1969: production of the M-60 had jumped from 15 percent to 85 to 95 percent of the total product. Steel mill construction had plummeted from being the "main thrust" of production to being virtually phased out.

In 1980, the U.S. government decided to replace the M-60 tank with the M-1. By the end of fiscal year 1981, the U.S. Army ceased all orders for the M-60. From then on, all M-60 tank orders were from foreign regimes allied with the United States, such as Israel, Egypt, and Taiwan. But these orders decreased gradually as other countries followed the United States's lead and abandoned the M-60 as outmoded. From 4 tank hulls a day in the mid-1970s, production at Blaw-Knox dropped to 1.5 per day by 1984. Blaw-Knox was not able to switch over to production of the newer M-1 because it was welded and fabricated and did not require the huge plate castings needed for the M-60.

As the foundry stopped producing most commercial castings and orders for tanks slowly fell, employment in the mill also declined. In 1978, there were 2,278 employees; by 1983, the figure had dropped to 1,137. Table 7.4 gives employment figures for the 1978–85 period.

Campaign to Save the Foundry

In 1984, a worker advocacy organization was started in East Chicago. Known as the Calumet Project for Industrial Jobs, it was a joint creation of the Chicago-based Midwest Center for Labor Research and an East Chicago community organization known as the United Citizens Organization (UCO). The Calumet Project's stated goal is to preserve well-paying industrial jobs in the northwest Indiana Calumet region. Toward that goal, it helps workers and unions identify the "warning signs" that a facility may be in danger of

Table 7.4. Employment at Blaw-Knox's East Chicago foundry, 1978–85

	Total employment	Hourly	Salaried
1978	2,278	1,997	281
1979	1,540	1,348	192
1980	1,668	1,479	189
1981	1,462	1,266	196
1982	1,353	1,172	181
1983	1,137	966	171
1984	992	830	162
April 1985	812	684	128

Source: Little 1985.

closing, builds labor-community alliances to fight plant closings, and pushes for greater worker and community involvement in economic development efforts.

In May 1984, Calumet Project researcher Tom DuBois saw an article in *American Metal Markets* that reported that financial analysts were speculating that White Consolidated intended to sell Blaw-Knox. The speculation stemmed from announcements made at the May annual meeting by Roy Holdt, the chairman and chief executive officer of WCI. At the meeting Holdt stated that White would move "as quickly as is possible" out of some of its steel mill machinery and steel-processing businesses (*American Metal Markets/Metalworking News,* May 7, 1984, 5). At the same meeting, Ward Smith, WCI's president and chief administrative officer, confirmed that the steel-related businesses were prime candidates for divestiture despite their past history of profitability (White Consolidated First Quarter Report 1984). Analysts considered the Blaw-Knox Foundry and Mill Machinery Company (with four plants including the East Chicago foundry) and the Aetna-Standard Engineering Company (one plant), which produced finishing equipment for the steel industry, to be the most likely candidates for sale.

In late September 1984, following a series of meetings and consultations with members of the Calumet Project, Clarence "Buck" Martin, president of Local 1026 of the United Steelworkers, sent a memo to eleven individuals regarding imminent layoffs and a possible shutdown of the facility. These individuals were the top district and national officers of the United Steelworkers, the congresswoman from the region, the governor, the mayor of East Chicago and his director of business development, an aide to the state's two senators, three key local and regional economic development officials, and a local minister who was chairing an East Chicago task force on economic development.

The memo noted that there was speculation that WCI would sell Blaw-Knox and pointed out that company officials refused to confirm or deny the rumor. It also stated that tank orders were due to run out sometime in the coming months and that no replacement orders were forthcoming. The conclusion was harsh:

> This seems to be an obvious case of disinvestment and "milking" of what has been a profitable operation, or at least one with a high cash flow. White Consolidated says in its annual report that parts of the conglomerate which have not shown large profits have been useful to the parent because "positive cash flows were usually produced through increased financial control. These profits and cash flows have been available to invest in our business and to support our development activities."

Martin also noted that the machine shop, the second largest in the Midwest, was due to shut down completely by the end of the month (more than 150 workers had been already laid off). A shutdown of the roll shop also was imminent; employment had declined from sixty to thirteen, and the union believed (correctly, it turned out) that equipment in the roll shop would be shipped out shortly after the shutdown.

On the basis of the above, Martin called for a meeting to consider how to respond, further investigation of company plans, the possible use of tools such as a court injunction or a feasibility study to save jobs, an investigation to determine the viability of employee ownership, an investigation of alternative product possibilities, and the utilization of the experience and expertise of others involved in "conversion" efforts.

The memo, an unusual action for a local union officer, prompted an immediate response. On October 12, local economic development officials promised to help, while White Consolidated denied any intent to sell the plant: "An official of White Consolidated Industries Inc., which owns the foundry, said he knows of no plans to sell the Northwest Indiana plant. 'As far as I know, tank production will continue through 1985,' said Charles Conlin, White's vice president of industrial relations" (*Gary Post-Tribune*, Oct. 12, 1984).

Less than two weeks later, on October 24, WCI announced that it was selling all of its foundry, steel machinery, and printing equipment businesses, including the East Chicago foundry (*Wall Street Journal*, Oct. 25, 1984, 20).[2] Ronald G. Fountain, White's treasurer and vice president, stated that he hoped the foundry would be sold to someone who wished to keep it running because "it's worth more that way." He refused to say, however, that the company would hold out for a buyer committed to keeping the facility open. Buck Martin responded to the sale plans negatively: " 'I can only feel the company came in when it was profitable, worked it until it no longer served a purpose for them and now they're going to sell it. . . . It isn't right to milk a company and then leave the membership high and dry' " (*Gary Post-Tribune*, Oct. 25, 1984). These sentiments reflected the feelings of many foundry workers; the ensuing campaign was based on this bedrock of worker sentiment.

On October 31, Jack Parton, the director of United Steelworkers District 31, called a meeting that was attended by the mayor of East Chicago and his two top economic development aides, state and regional economic development persons, and aides to state political figures, in addition to union and community representatives. White Consolidated was invited to send a representative but did not do so.

During the meeting a permanent Blaw-Knox Steering Committee was formed to save the plant. The first goal of the committee was to raise the money to finance a feasibility study to determine what could be done to preserve employment and keep the facility running. This could only be done, all agreed, by retooling for commercial market production as tank orders were phased out.

In November and December 1984, numerous activities occurred: the local congresswoman requested Defense Department aid in attempting a conversion to nonmilitary production; representatives of the Defense Department came to East Chicago for a meeting; funds for a feasibility study were sought; plans were made to secure an Economic Development Administration grant and/or an Urban Development Action Grant; the potential for employee ownership was explored; the mayor of East Chicago wrote the state commerce department requesting $60,000 for the feasibility study; the steering committee took a guided tour of the plant; and requests for proposals to do the feasibility study were sent out (*Gary Post-Tribune,* Dec. 3, 1984).

The Indiana Department of Commerce agreed to fund one-third of the cost of the study, up to $20,000. The Steelworkers local pledged $2,000; the international Steelworkers $5,000; the United Citizens Organization (the Calumet Project's "parent" community organization) $2,000; the city of East Chicago $10,000; and the East Chicago Economic Development Commission $4,000. On December 31, Congressman-elect Peter Visclosky wrote to WCI requesting that it also provide funding. In the end it was reported that WCI did contribute, but the sum was kept confidential (*Gary Post-Tribune,* Feb. 12, 1985). The "confidential" sum can be determined, however, simply by adding the other contributions to the study's final $50,000 price tag and subtracting the result from $50,000. Since the other contributions totaled approximately $40,000, White Consolidated must have contributed $10,000.

All of this activity at the steering committee level was occurring against a backdrop of union and community activism. On December 13, the union local, the Calumet Project, and the United Citizens Organization hosted a union-community meeting at a local community hall. Approximately two hundred workers and community residents attended, most of them Blaw-Knox workers. Representatives of the state's two Republican senators, an aide to the outgoing Democratic representative, Katie Hall, and the incoming Democratic representative, Peter Visclosky, all attended and addressed the meeting. Audience interest was high, and so was hostility toward the company. One union member launched into a tirade against the plant's industrial relations manager, who was present, accusing him and White Consolidated of lack of good faith in its dealings with the work force.

On December 27, the director of United Steelworkers District 31 called a meeting in his office at which members of the Blaw-Knox Steering Committee were requested to report on what they were doing. By this point, the union's and community's monitoring of and involvement in the effort to save the plant were great.

All the proposals to conduct the feasibility study were received by January 15; on the 16th, the Blaw-Knox Steering Committee met to begin evaluating them. Shortly thereafter, the district director of the United Steelworkers once again called a meeting so that the steering committee could update the union's district office and the press.

In late January, the finalists were interviewed, and in early February, a firm was selected. On February 11, the Blaw-Knox Steering Committee named Arthur D. Little, a Massachusetts consulting firm with extensive foundry experience, to do the feasibility study. The study was to be completed by the summer, but Arthur D. Little was required to give preliminary progress reports to the steering committee (*Gary Post-Tribune,* Feb. 12, 1985).

In March, members of the Calumet Project met with the leadership of Steelworkers Local 1026 to plan a strategy for an ongoing public campaign. The aims were to involve the membership of the local, to publicize the issues widely, to pressure politicians and economic development officials to continue to keep the *jobs* issue foremost, and to force WCI to reveal full information and to cooperate in transferring the facility to an owner committed to keeping it open. The Calumet Project and the union local made plans to hold a public meeting in conjunction with the United Citizens Organization, to speak on popular local radio talk shows, and to communicate with and involve laid-off workers.

These plans were only partially carried out, however. The president of the local was reluctant to involve lower-level leaders actively in ongoing work. He felt that he personally could handle any tasks the local needed to do. Consequently, much of the communication with the membership that was necessary for active involvement was never undertaken. For the most part, the local union never initiated anything after Martin wrote the memo that started the whole process.

To compound matters, union elections were conducted in mid-April. For personal reasons, Martin chose not to run for reelection as president and retired shortly thereafter. Tom Patterson, a thirty-year employee, ran unopposed for president and was elected along with a team that included many new officers. The leadership turnover made consistent union planning even harder.

After assuming office, Patterson took an even less activist role than had Martin. His main role was to express optimism to the press and to wait for the Blaw-Knox Steering Committee to take appropriate action.

Despite these problems, March through May were busy months for the local and for the Blaw-Knox Steering Committee. At a March 19 committee meeting, representatives of Arthur D. Little gave a preliminary report of their study. At the same meeting, Jon J. O'Connor, the plant's manager, reported that an order for 140 more tanks was likely—ensuring the plant would remain open through 1985.

The district director of the Steelworkers called a meeting of the steering committee and other interested parties for April 1. As was usual for a meeting at which attendance was broader than the official membership of the committee, this one was far from tame. Blaw-Knox workers in attendance lambasted White Consolidated, charging it with milking millions from local plants and refusing to take responsibility for the workers and the community. Strong pressure was brought to bear on the economic development officials on the steering committee to keep an unrelenting focus on job preservation as the number-one goal.

On May 1, the Blaw-Knox Steering Committee met and received a midterm report from Arthur D. Little. Two days later, the union local and the United Citizens Organization cosponsored a community forum at which the Little representatives again spoke. Approximately one hundred workers and community residents attended this meeting. Based on preliminary information, Little's spokesperson, John Reed, indicated that orders for military armor would indeed "dry up" shortly and that there was a very limited market for the extraordinarily large castings the Blaw-Knox facility had the unique capacity to produce. Thus, the only hope for future long-term production was for Blaw-Knox to develop a market for smaller commercial castings.

Workers at the May 3 community forum criticized Little for not consulting them. Local 1026 member Vern Felton noted that the union had partially funded Little's study but that the workers had not been contacted, making for a "one-sided approach." Workers also wanted Little to criticize White Consolidated for past disinvestment and "milking" policies. Lynn Strong, treasurer of Local 1026, said, "We're where we are today because White Consolidated did not want to reinvest." Reed refused to review WCI's past investment decisions. "We're looking at the plant as it is now," he stated. "We're looking for a viable option that an investor from the outside can say, 'Yes, that makes sense.' We're looking at it from the point of view of an investor" (*Gary Post-Tribune,* May 4, 1985). The workers in attendance were less committed to an exclusively investor-driven private-market approach; to them, long-term stability and job creation were the primary goals.

The Blaw-Knox Steering Committee did not meet again until July 12, when Little presented a draft version of its final report. In the meantime the Calumet Project worked with the local to prepare for the worst. If the Little study said that the facility was not viable under any circumstances, the Calumet Project wanted to be ready to initiate a broad-based community campaign against White Consolidated. The purpose would be to develop a broad public consciousness of corporate misbehavior on WCI's part and to force the company into providing generous assistance for retraining, severance pay, pensions, and the like.

Specifically, the Calumet Project claimed White Consolidated had

- dangerously narrowed the product line at the East Chicago facility, making it vulnerable to fluctuating trends in military production;
- disinvested in the facility over the years by putting in only money procured from the Defense Department;
- made enormous profits off the plant, only to invest the cash elsewhere (i.e., treating it as a "cash cow");
- not made large enough payments to the Blaw-Knox pension plans, leaving them underfunded; and
- failed to pay its property taxes to the city for the past few years, hurting local services, including the school system.

Available information supports most of these charges. WCI certainly had narrowed the product lines at the foundry until military production became its only source of survival. Although this may have been a good business decision for the company as a whole, it jeopardized the facility and local jobs.

Disinvestment is slightly harder to prove, but the charge appears to stand. Figures show that WCI expanded its Home Products Division at the expense of the other two divisions. This growth was more the result of acquisitions, however, than of uneven capital investment patterns in existing divisions. Table 7.5 shows the *net* investment (capital expenditures minus depreciation and amortization expenses) for the three divisions from 1977 through 1983.

Table 7.5 does not show an obvious pattern of milking one division to pay

Table 7.5. White Consolidated's net investment by division,[a] 1977–83

Division	Time period 1977–79 (millions of dollars)	1980–83
Home Products	35.0	53.4
Machinery and Metal Castings	25.2	55.0
General Industrial Equipment	11.2	13.1

Source: Computed from WCI annual reports, selected years.
[a]Capital expenditures minus depreciation and amortization expenditures.

for capital expenditures in another. Certainly Blaw-Knox's Machinery and Metal Castings Division as a whole was not being milked to pay for investments elsewhere. It was getting proportionally *more* than other divisions, especially in the later years. Only in 1983 did net capital investment in the Machinery and Metal Castings Division turn negative. In that year WCI disinvested in the division in the amount of $276,000.

Closer inspection, however, reveals that much of the investment in the Machinery and Metal Castings Division during this period was going into WCI's machine tool line, including new flexible manufacturing systems and automated numerical-control equipment, not its foundries. WCI did put approximately $30 million into its Blaw-Knox roll shop operations, but this investment all went to the Wheeling, West Virginia, facility, not to the one in East Chicago.

There was a clear case for disinvestment at the plant level. WCI had invested very little in the local plant, and of the little it had put in, most was from the Department of Defense. Virtually all of the equipment in the machine shop was 1950s and 1960s vintage—way out of date for modern competitive purposes. All the former workers I interviewed stated that WCI invested very little in the plant. A former manager told me that basically nothing had been put into the plant at company expense for years; finally, near the end, WCI agreed to invest a couple of million dollars, but that was nothing relative to the needs at that point.[3] This money may have been spent on innovative "vacuum-process" (V-process) equipment ($1.2 million) and a modernized electric furnace. According to workers, the Little report, and ex-managers, no one learned to use the new V-process equipment properly, so that even this expenditure was largely a waste.

In any case, company investment in the foundry was minimal for well over a decade. Nonetheless, the plant had been immensely profitable by any standard. Local union official Lynn Strong claimed that the Defense Department contracts were set at a cost-plus basis that guaranteed a minimum 15 percent profit on sales. A former management official confirmed that anytime the foundry ran into a problem it simply renegotiated more money from the Defense Department, which never failed to increase the payment.

In fact, Strong's estimate of a 15 percent profit on sales is almost certainly too conservative. Precise figures on the profitability of a particular plant are confidential, but considerable information has been obtained in this case, enabling us to estimate profitability. Plant manager Jon J. O'Connor provided the Blaw-Knox Steering Committee with year-by-year estimates of tank production at the foundry. These figures are given in table 7.6.

The figures for tank orders and dollar amounts in press accounts from 1981 through 1985 indicate that Blaw-Knox was being paid approximately $95,000 to $157,000 per tank. These figures are too low, however, either because the initial contracts were later renegotiated upward or because they reflect partial orders for only hulls or only turrets. When WCI put the company up for sale in late 1984, a prospectus was issued by its investment banker, Lehman Brothers. This prospectus gives financial data (table 7.7) for the East Chicago foundry.[4]

The figures show that the facility produced a 22 percent gross profit on sales in 1984. (They also show that the 360 tank orders resulted in revenues of $65.4 million, or $181,667 per tank, well above the figures quoted in press releases.) Conservatively estimating that the profit rate was the same in 1980–83 as in 1984, although it was probably higher, WCI reaped a gross profit of $82.53 million from this facility during 1980–84.

Clearly, this was a highly profitable plant. It easily exceeded WCI's three hurdles: with total assets in 1984 of $34.4 million and profits of more than $15 million, the facility was greatly exceeding the required twenty percent

Table 7.6. Annual tank production at the Blaw-Knox East Chicago foundry, 1980–85

Year	Tanks Produced
1980	500
1981	400
1982	360
1983	360[a]
1984	360
1985	265

Source: Estimates of plant manager Jon J. O'Connor.
[a]Annual report of General Dynamics, the firm subcontracting casting work to Blaw-Knox, indicates 367 tanks for this year, confirming the accuracy of O'Connor's estimates.

Table 7.7. Actual and projected financial data for the Blaw-Knox East Chicago foundry, 1980–86

Year	1980	1981	1982	1983	1984[a]	1985[b]	1986
	(millions of dollars)						
New sales	76.0	80.9	74.1	71.7	71.8	60.3	19.9
Net sales from tank armor					65.4	49.9	0
Gross profit					15.9	15.8	4.0
Profit/sales (percent)					22.0	26.0	20

Source: Lehman Brothers prospectus.
[a]Projections based on incomplete figures as of Aug. 31, 1984.
[b]Estimates for 1985 and 1986 based on projected future tank orders and refurbishing the number-2 commercial castings foundry.

net return on equity. Net profit on sales was three to four times the required 5 percent. And with a book value of $14.128 million, sales of $71.8 million meant $5.08 in sales per $1.00 book value, more than 3.5 times the required $1.60/$1.00 ratio.

Steel foundries in the United States reinvested 4.7 percent of sales into plant and equipment from 1980 to 1982. Had WCI done the same for the 1980–85 period, it would have made capital expenditures of $17.6 million. Charges of disinvestment and treatment of the facility as a "cash cow" therefore seem justified.

The Calumet Project was correct in its claim that WCI had not fully funded its pension obligations. The prospectus noted that White Consolidated had unfunded pension liabilities of $58.3 million, which it would retain in the event of a sale. As we shall see, pension obligations also became an issue in the sale of the plant.

Finally, Blaw-Knox was delinquent in its local property tax payments, as alleged. Property tax records in mid-1985 indicated that the company was delinquent in paying $107,516.53 in 1983 taxes payable 1984 and behind by $115,813.93 for 1984 taxes payable 1985, for a total of $223,330.46.

The particulars of the Calumet Project's indictment of White Consolidated were basically correct. It is not clear, however, whether a public relations campaign against the company would have been favorably received. Local politicians were firmly wedded to a business climate approach to economic development. They emphasized their desire to maintain a cooperative and positive environment for businesses; certainly they wished to avoid any confrontation with corporate interests.

Local economic development officials had a similar orientation. They very probably would have dissociated themselves from a "negative" campaign against WCI.

The United Steelworkers was a more likely ally, but its main goal was a strictly pragmatic one: saving jobs and preserving union pattern wage rates. As with most of the American labor movement, the union was not accustomed to wide-ranging "social movement" approaches to achieving these goals. Unless a campaign had a very high likelihood of achieving fairly immediate results, the union leadership was not likely to devote much energy to methods that it considered unorthodox. A highly motivated leader of the union local who was determined to stand up to the company and who had a strong view of corporate accountability to the workers and the community could have changed this attitude, but neither Martin nor Patterson was such a leader.

Only certain active members of the union local (none of them on the crucial Blaw-Knox Steering Committee) and allied community forces, organized through the United Citizens Organization, were activist enough in their orientation to be willing to initiate and develop such a campaign. As it turned out, the campaign was never undertaken; events intervened.

On July 12, 1985, Arthur D. Little presented a draft version of its final report to the Blaw-Knox Steering Committee. Exactly one week later, the Steelworkers' district director, Jack Parton, called an open meeting of the steering committee and the press to make the findings public. At these meetings and in its 130-page report, Arthur D. Little presented a mixed prognosis for the future of the facility. It recommended that the foundry operations shift from the Department of Defense market to the commercial castings market. If this did not occur, the plant would close as the orders for tank armor disappeared.[5]

It also recommended that the small foundry be consolidated with the large foundry. The large foundry was not viable standing alone because the commercial market for its large castings was depressed. At the same time, this foundry was the only one in the United States able to produce castings of more than half a million pounds. Although the market for these extraordinarily large castings was small and sporadic, the plant's capabilities in this area would be an asset in a refurbished small foundry.

According to Little, the key was for Blaw-Knox to operate as a modernized small-castings foundry (less than one hundred pounds to approximately five thousand pounds). This would provide the stable market needed to keep the operation viable. Little estimated that it would not be too difficult to capture 3 to 5 percent of the U.S. market in this size range, representing approximately fifteen thousand to twenty thousand tons per year. Supplemented by five thousand tons per year in large-castings work (8 to 15 percent of the

U.S. market), Little said the foundry should be quite viable. The small foundry would have to be highly automated and state of the art. Employment would drop drastically in the consolidated foundry to 100 to 200, compared with the 812 employed at the time of the study.

The cost would also be considerable: $3 to $5 million to upgrade the small foundry; $7 to $11 million total (including consolidation costs and minor upgrading of the large foundry).[6] Because of the depressed state of the small-castings market and the low returns to producers, Little estimated that $3 to $5 million of the $7 to $11 million total would have to come from public sources. With that degree of public funding, Little said there was a moderately good chance of finding a buyer. To keep costs moderate, the report recommended a 20 percent wage cut from the current $10.90 per hour average. Little also recommended that, to facilitate the change in ownership, WCI dispose of the facility at a "nominal" price of essentially the liquidation value and assume pension obligations rather than carry them over to the new owner.

The study confirmed charges of disinvestment in the portions of the plant not devoted to tank production. The machine shop equipment was of 1940s to 1960s vintage. Not one major piece of equipment in it had been bought since 1968, the year WCI bought the company. What was left of the roll shop was close to useless; all of the best equipment had recently been moved to the Wheeling, West Virginia, plant in a consolidation move. Little suggested scrapping most of this equipment or seeking an interested local buyer.

A small satellite operation for machining work to supplement the basic foundry was considered viable and would provide twenty-five to fifty jobs. This would cost approximately $2 million in private funds plus $1 to $1.4 million in public financing.

In total, then, $9 to $13 million in private funds plus $4 to $6.4 million in public funds would be necessary to rejuvenate the foundry. Little also recommended using remaining buildings and space as a business "incubator" for other small companies and parking lots. All this would require perhaps $9 to $11 million in private investment ($4 million for parking lots alone!) and $600,000 in public assistance.

In total, Arthur D. Little's proposals promised three hundred jobs immediately and six hundred within a few years. The total cost would be $20 to $24 million in private capital and $4.6 to $7 million in public assistance. The public costs looked high for a venture that would immediately save less than one-half the existing jobs. Little's public cost-benefit analysis showed, however, that savings in unemployment compensation costs ($1.9 million) plus savings in local public assistance and increased tax revenues plus the ripple effect on the rest of the local economy would generate enough tax savings and collections to almost cover these public expenses. With any grant money from the federal government, the state and local governments would indeed recover their expenditures in less than two years.

The Arthur D. Little report had two unusual recommendations that reflected the public source of much of its funding and the pressure union and community forces had exerted on the firm. First, it recommended that the city and the Blaw-Knox Steering Committee be actively involved in the transfer of ownership of the plant in order to protect the interests of workers and the community:

> The City and Blaw-Knox Steering Committee should play an active role monitoring the negotiations of White Consolidated Industries, Inc.'s disposition of the Blaw-Knox facilities in East Chicago. Efforts should be made to encourage its sale to a company that will reuse the facilities rather than run-out the current tank contract and liquidate the plant (I-3).

Were this recommendation acted upon, there would have been none of the secrecy and privacy normally associated with sales negotiations. The public interest would have been forcefully injected into a supposedly "private" affair within the private sector. Aggressively following such a course of action would have breached the normal business climate approach that is standard economic development practice in northwest Indiana and the rest of the United States. It was for precisely this reason that the city and economic development officials were reluctant to carry out the suggestion.

Second, the report recommended that a public development corporation be set up to buy, manage, and market the plant: "Consideration should be given to setting-up an overall agency to acquire the Blaw-Knox facilities, plan their conversion, undertake marketing, provide financing, oversee operation and eventual disposition of most facilities (excluding the incubator buildings) (VII-4).

This was also a rather unorthodox recommendation, in that it suggested injecting public control into transactions normally considered to be exclusively in the private domain. Mary Kaczka, director of business development for East Chicago, immediately rejected this recommendation: "I think without a buyer we would not want to put ourselves in that position" (*Gary Post-Tribune*, July 20, 1985).

Monitoring by the Steering Committee of any possible sale of the foundry quickly became an issue. At a July 24 committee meeting to discuss implementation of Little's proposals, plant manager Jon J. O'Connor indicated that serious negotiations were under way to sell the company, although he declined to give details. The chair of the committee, an official of a regional economic development agency, then requested that all members of the committee send in "scenarios" of what should be done in the coming months, based on the Arthur D. Little report.

Worried that the plant would be sold to a buyer that was interested only in running out the armor contract and then liquidating, Lynn Feekin, director of the Calumet Project, who was representing the United Citizens Organization on the steering committee, developed a memo that listed four common goals for all possible scenarios and suggestions based on different scenarios. The four goals were as follows:

- New buyer will provide stable business operations in East Chicago for an adequate period of time.
- New buyer will reinvest sufficient monies in the East Chicago Blaw-Knox facility to assure long-term viability.
- New buyer's operations will provide jobs for current Blaw-Knox employees.
- New buyer will recognize the union.

The first scenario assumed that White Consolidated would sell Blaw-Knox. It was recommended that the steering committee contact the (potential) new owner to determine the intended use for the East Chicago plant. If the owner planned to reinvest with financial aid from the city and/or state, the Blaw-Knox Steering Committee could set out the conditions under which the aid would be given, based on the four common goals. If the new owner planned to reinvest without public aid, it was suggested that the steering committee meet with the owner to encourage conversion in line with Little's recommendations.

If the new owner had no reinvestment plan, the Blaw-Knox Steering Committee could push for suitable reinvestment. Failing in this, the memo suggested that the steering committee could possibly propose use of "eminent domain" (involuntary sale to the government at reasonable compensation "for the public good"). Arthur D. Little's "nominal cost" could be the basis for determining what was reasonable compensation.[7]

The memo suggested that if White Consolidated did not sell the plant the steering committee could request that the company establish a reinvestment fund by setting aside a certain amount of money per tank produced, the specific figure to be determined later. This money, plus a newly created public development corporation, could be used to facilitate the eventual transfer of ownership and reinvestment.

On August 26, the board of directors of the United Citizens Organization endorsed the four goals and unanimously passed a motion recommending that "no private deals [be] made on a financial package without the Blaw-Knox Steering Committee or the larger committee's involvement." In a letter (Sept. 5, 1985) to John Artis, the executive director of the East Chicago Department of Redevelopment, Rev. Vincent McCutcheon, the president of the UCO, noted the motion and continued, "UCO is outraged that this union-initiated process, which initially comprised very broad-based representation, has been narrowed down to a select few."

The suggestions from the UCO and the Calumet Project were not acted upon. The regional development official chairing the Blaw-Knox Steering Committee postponed two meetings in a row, deferring to a request from the company to cease meetings temporarily pending an imminent sale. The economic development officials from the city were unwilling to confront White Consolidated to demand or even ask anything regarding the pending sale. Even the leadership of the union local was unwilling to demand a real role in the sale; it was completely passive and gave no overt support to the UCO/Calumet Project's recommendations. Further, the company took a very dim view of any such "meddling" in its "private" affairs; an ex-manager in 1989 told me that he considered the Calumet Project representative "nothing but a godamn Communist" for putting forth such suggestions.

The Blaw-Knox Steering Committee passively awaited word on a new owner. In late September, WCI announced that it had sold seven companies with nine plants to a group of private investors led by Robert J. Tomsich, chairman of Nesco, a Cleveland holding firm. One of the units sold was the East Chicago foundry. The new company was to be called the Blaw-Knox Corporation and was to be headquartered in Pittsburgh. East Chicago manager Jon J. O'Connor stated that the new company planned to keep all nine plants open. "As far as East Chicago specifically, their desire is to follow up on the Arthur D. Little study," he told the press. The union greeted the news positively. Tom Patterson, president of Steelworkers Local 1026, stated that he was "very pleased" with the news: "I'm very optimistic that it's going to be something for the betterment of everybody. White had made it very clear that they don't want to be in the business we do anymore. Maybe the new company will" (*Gary Post-Tribune*, Sept. 28, 1985).

Jack Parton, director of United Steelworkers District 31, also expressed guarded optimism: "Right now, let's just say I'm happy the company has been bought by businessmen who say they want to keep operating the plant. It could have been worse: the facility could have been bought by U.S. Steel" (*Crain's Chicago Business,* Oct. 7, 1985, 69).

The optimism turned out to be misplaced. Although O'Connor claimed the new company would implement Arthur D. Little's recommendations, it never did. The Blaw-Knox Steering Committee did not monitor the sale or meet with the new management to force the company to reveal its intentions toward the plant. In fact, the chair of the steering committee refused to call any more meetings; in effect, the steering committee disbanded. The UCO/Calumet Project's proposals were never allowed to be discussed. With the feasibility study completed and an ownership change accomplished, the chair considered the steering committee's legitimate tasks accomplished.

The new owners stated repeatedly to the press their intention to implement Little's recommendations. When pressed for specifics, however, they backed away from any particular commitments.

Ultimately, the only portion of the study that management energetically acted on was the call for wage concessions. Management demanded that wage cuts take effect on December 1, 1985, for all other plants and on March 1, 1986, for the East Chicago facility (approximately the time the armor contract would run out). The union demanded basic financial information before it would consider concessions; the company refused to provide it.

The union and later the company filed unfair labor practice charges with the National Labor Relations Board (*Hammond Times,* Nov. 10, 1985). The union also took a case to arbitration involving the pensions of workers who took early retirement. The months from November 1985 to February 1986 were thus spent fighting over contractual issues. The contract was repeatedly extended two to three months at a time. Meanwhile, the company made no move to upgrade or consolidate the foundry. Only the remaining tank orders, due to run out around March, were being worked on.

A comparison of the foundry's wages with those of other foundries show them to be about comparable. In October 1986, production workers of ferrous foundries in the Great Lakes region averaged $11.00 per hour, compared with $10.90 at Blaw-Knox. For foundries with 250 or more workers, the average was an even higher $12.15 per hour. These figures are skewed upward, however, because captive foundries producing only for the parent firm are included (average: $13.36 per hour). Purely commercial foundries in the region averaged only $9.42 per hour. Also, the average for the entire United States was only $9.53 per hour. Wages were also lower for *steel* foundries than for all foundries: $9.11 per hour for the region, $9.85 per hour for the larger regional firms, and $8.50 per hour for the United States as a whole. The 20 percent pay cut recommended by Arthur D. Little would have reduced wages at Blaw-Knox to an average of $8.72 per hour—well below any regional standard, and even below comparably large firms (more than 250) in the United States ($9.12 per hour) (U.S. Bureau of Labor Statistics 1988:4, 68).

Whether any wage reduction would have helped make Blaw-Knox's East Chicago foundry competitive was academic; the company never committed to upgrading the facility and never even put an offer to upgrade on the table as a bargaining chip to obtain concessions. Under the circumstances, the union refused to give any.

In early February 1986, the Egyptian government announced that it was canceling a tentative order for M-60 tanks. At this point Blaw-Knox's managers understood that tank production would end by summer or early fall; before, they had counted on work into 1987 or possibly 1988.

In November 1985, O'Connor had become president of the company and had moved to Pittsburgh. His replacement as local manager, Gary Stanklus, announced a meeting of the Blaw-Knox Steering Committee for February 24, 1986. By this time the committee had not met for almost six months.

The steering committee met without representation from the union local or the UCO/Calumet Project. Stanklus's intent was to get help in obtaining more tank orders. Economic development officials and politicians obliged. City and regional economic development personnel flew to Washington, D.C., to plead with the Pentagon for more orders. On March 4 and 5, Indiana senator Richard Lugar and influential Indiana congressman Lee Hamilton wrote letters to the Egyptian ambassador asking that the Egyptian government reconsider its decision to cancel its order. On March 12, Indiana's two senators and Pennsylvania's two senators plus Congressman Visclosky wrote to Army Undersecretary James Ambrose conveying an offer from Blaw-Knox to release the army from certain termination costs in the event of a plant closing (perhaps up to $20 million worth) *if* the army would give the company more tank orders.

Members of Congressman Visclosky's office were upset that union and community representatives had been cut out of the meeting of the revived Blaw-Knox Steering Committee. They insisted that the entire membership of the committee be included in future meetings.

On March 14 and 18, expanded meetings were held; Stanklus chaired. His agenda called for a "public awareness campaign" whereby employees, concerned citizens, and others would write letters and sign petitions begging the Department of Defense for more tank orders. Stanklus even had draft letters prepared (by the company) for people to sign. The model "employee letter" equated job preservation with continued tank orders and relied heavily on patriotism and belief in the "American way":

> I believe in the American dream that if you work hard for a living, the rewards will come. But I feel as if my country is letting me down when the government says thanks for your efforts, but we no longer need you. . . . I need your involvement in helping to keep the doors of Blaw-Knox open with continued production of the M-60 tank. Your sincere efforts with regard to my plea for help may restore my concept of the "American way."

The draft "taxpayer" letter relied on an alleged Soviet threat plus arguments that the M-60 tank was a better buy than the M-1:

> The ever-present military threat of the Soviet Union demands that we maintain our military readiness. It seems that the M-60 tank at one-third the price of the M-1 tank has a real place in this budgetary/military strength dilemma. Does it really make sense to completely eliminate the M-60 as an option to the more expensive, less reliable M-1?

Finally, the petition stated that loss of the facility would harm the economic base of the local economy and have a severe impact on the industrial strength of the country. It claimed that more armor casting work would enable the company to "achieve stability and implement long term programs aimed at future operating and employment goals."

The UCO, which had recently passed a resolution against wasteful military spending, refused to go along with Blaw-Knox's effort to drum up more defense work. The UCO demanded that the company live up to Arthur D. Little's recommendations and convert to commercial casting. The union also indicated that the company had used and abused the steering committee by changing its entire intent. Tom Patterson, president of the local, stated: "The steering committee has become a way for the company to manipulate political people and clout in the steering committee to their own use and has lost sight of what the intent was. The company has really taken it over" (Moberg 1986:32).

The company's public awareness campaign fell apart because of internal dissension within the steering committee. The letter-writing and petition campaign did not materialize.

In March and April 1986, the Blaw-Knox Steering Committee divided into six subcommittees to work on all aspects of saving the plant (obtaining a new government contract, retaining government equipment, transitional operating costs, funding for facility conversion, employee matters, and commercial market plans). The subcommittees were exercises in futility, however, because the company never committed to anything. Even the business-oriented members of the committee began to get disgusted with the company. Richard Griebel, a $90,000+ executive with a northwest Indiana "super-Chamber of Commerce" known as the Northwest Indiana Forum, was upset:

> What is the business plan? What is the alternative? What commercial applications are there? What alternative military applications are there? I found to my surprise and dismay there was nothing like that. There is no business plan there. . . . If the company is lucky and succeeds in getting new orders, it will only put things off a year (Moberg 1986:32).

One by one the subcommittees stopped meeting; the full committee never met again.

The company continued its attack on the union and also used local and state politicians in a vain quest to obtain more tank orders. Stanklus demanded $6 per hour concessions from the union, arguing that the union's participation on the steering committee meant it had agreed to Little's recommendations to cut wages. Other than that it led to an eventual standoff involving a wage freeze and improved language regarding seniority, this attack did nothing but divert attention away from the company's continuing failure to tackle the more fundamental problem of conversion.

Senators and congressmen continued their efforts to obtain further tank orders in exchange for lower "facility termination costs" for the government. These latter efforts led to some amusing moments because the company, in its attempt to manipulate the politicians into pressuring the Defense Department, was occasionally exposed in some misrepresentations. The pleas for more tank orders were ultimately unsuccessful, although they almost succeeded.[8]

The plant completed its last armor castings in the late spring and early summer of 1986. Final finishing work required some employment into the early fall. On October 28, the plant was officially closed.

In fact, the company had never intended to upgrade the facility and convert to commercial castings. All statements to the press expressing a commitment to carry out Little's proposals had been intentionally deceptive. The company intended to milk the plant as long as there were orders for armor castings and then to liquidate.

The Calumet Project, the union, and the UCO charged the company with deception but were unable to prove it. The company could always claim with at least some minimal plausibility that it intended to convert but needed more "breathing space". in the form of more tank orders. Certainly the politicians who were frantically intervening to obtain more orders believed the company's claim.

In the fall of 1989, an ex-manager confided to me that Robert J. Tomsich, chief executive officer of the new company, had told top-level plant managers that "from day one" management had intended to "run the armor work out to the end, and then dump the joint." Tomsich had expected to get two years of armor work; he miscalculated and got only one. It is unlikely that he and his fellow investors lost anything, however. They bought the company for what my informant called "peanuts" and got the Defense Department to pay them for a major share of the pension liabilities they assumed.

Even the pension question ended on a sour note. In January 1992, the Pension Benefit Guarantee Corporation announced that it was forced to terminate the Blaw-Knox pension plan for hourly employees because of an underfunding of $81.6 million. Blaw-Knox had been missing payments to the plan for some time. The government-funded PBGC assumed responsibility for the pension payments; basic benefits were guaranteed, but supplemental plant-closing benefits for those under age sixty-two were discontinued. The former union president, Tom Patterson, was one of those who lost money: $400 a month, one-third of his pension. He expressed concern to the press: " 'It's going to take tightening up and making adjustments,' said Patterson, who said he will probably have to start dipping into savings and his Individual Retirement Account" (*Gary Post-Tribune,* Jan. 31, 1992). While Patterson and other retirees worried about further possible loss of health and life insurance and the taxpayers through the PBGC assumed pension obligations, Blaw-Knox continued operating at Wheeling, West Virginia.

Conclusion

The closing of the Blaw-Knox foundry illustrates many of the forces at work in plant closings in the United States today. Control over investment and production decisions by absentee owners, frequently conglomerates like White Consolidated, makes local work forces and unions and communities vulnerable to job loss and economic disruption. Because major economic decisions are dictated by corporate structures, options, and priorities far removed from the local geographical area, the work force and the community are subjected to a very insecure environment.

White Consolidated had essentially narrowed its local product line in East

Chicago to a defense-related item that was scheduled to become extinct. It had also disinvested in major portions of the facility. At the same time, WCI had further consolidated its position in its "core" business, home appliances, at the expense of its other divisions. None of these business decisions responded to local East Chicago concerns because structurally and economically the corporate decision makers were never required to.

In attempting to deal with decisions detrimental to the local community, local forces are at a distinct disadvantage. One major obstacle is corporate secrecy. Throughout this case, corporate decision makers used the "confidential" nature of their private business affairs to thwart any effective worker or community intervention. There were repeated instances of deception, both large and small. Even when there is no intentional deception, because they lack the necessary information, unions, communities, and local governments are unable to plan effectively or to counter corporate decisions.

There are, however, several sources of power available. One such source is the press. Both White Consolidated and the subsequent owners were forced to respond to press interest and to reveal certain facts that removed to some extent the veil of secrecy surrounding their operations. Publicity also can induce corporations to respond to community interests to some degree simply because the company wishes to maintain a good image with the public.

A second source of leverage is political. Corporations depend on a supportive political environment for their success. If the political goodwill of senators, congressmen, the governor, and mayor can be made to be dependent on the corporation's behaving in a manner that is beneficial to the local community and work force, significant pressure can often be brought to bear.

In this case, political pressure was only partially applied. Tied to a business climate conception of government-business relations, the political community more often was used and dictated to by the business owners than vice versa.[9] This lack of political willpower was evident in the unwillingness of local political figures or their economic development allies to push the corporate owners even minimally. The politicians and their allies were unwilling to insist that they be allowed to interview potential buyers to ascertain their intentions regarding the local plant. Once the foundry was sold, they were afraid to insist that the new owner inform them of its business plan. Fearful of taking even these mild measures, they were definitely unwilling to consider using eminent domain to take possession of the premises. The city's refusal to set up a public development corporation to acquire and broker the plant was yet another example of this lack of political willpower. Despite the limitations in this actual case, political clout could have provided considerable leverage had it been developed.

A third possible source of power is the union. In this case the union engaged in coordinated bargaining for all three plants of the Blaw-Knox Mill and Machinery Company, plus Aetna-Standard. All four plants were represented by the same union, the United Steelworkers. The union therefore had more power in this instance than local unions do in other situations in which nonunion plants, different national union affiliations, or lack of coordinated bargaining hamper effectiveness.

Nevertheless, union power was severely limited. The union focused mostly on labor relations matters, which is only natural, but this meant that it could play only a limited role in the broader struggle to save the plant. At the same time, it is important to emphasize the degree to which the union did play a positive and important role. The initial memo from the president of the local was the catalyst for the entire effort. The district director of the Steelworkers repeatedly took the initiative to call meetings that forced the Blaw-Knox Steering Committee to account for its actions to the press and the local work force. Further, it was mainly union pressure that kept the steering committee from operating in secret.

A narrowness of perspective prevented the union from playing a more aggressive or initiating role. For example, a union officer could have chaired steering committee meetings, developed the agendas, and so on, rather than letting this central role fall to a regional economic development official who deferred to company agendas. Instead of being active, the union was largely reactive. Given this lack of forceful initiative, the Blaw-Knox Steering Committee fell under the sway of the company in the end, at the very time the new owners were bent on deception as they milked the dying facility.

A fourth possible source of leverage is the community itself. The community organization (the United Citizens Organization) and a worker advocacy project (the Calumet Project for Industrial Jobs) definitely exhibited the greatest awareness of the situation and of the power dynamics at play. Unfortunately, these organizations had the least clout of any of the major players. What little clout they did have was well used: the Calumet Project induced the union local to undertake virtually all initiatives it did take, including writing the original memo. The UCO parlayed two community meetings and the organization's own community network into considerable publicity and pressure for accountability. Nevertheless, the power of the Calumet Project and of the UCO was inherently limited in the absence of more hospitable politicians or a union with a broader vision.

Chapter 8
USE OF FEDERAL FUNDS TO SUPPORT RELOCATIONS

Gene Daniels

IN JULY 1984, the city of Wilmington, North Carolina, applied for an Urban Development Action Grant from the Department of Housing and Urban Development to provide debt financing to American Hoist & Derrick Company (Amhoist) of St. Paul, Minnesota. Amhoist said it wanted to produce components for the large industrial cranes in its American Crane Division manufactured in St. Paul rather than continue having them made by outside contractors. Job losses in St. Paul resulting from the decision would amount to only a handful of supervisors. In other words, the project would not lead to "the relocation of an industrial or commercial facility" from St. Paul to Wilmington (General Accounting Office [GAO] 1986:7).

Within a short time the application was approved and the loan agreement signed and delivered. By August 1985, however, at least 750 jobs involving crane production had been lost in St. Paul and 450 new ones created to produce cranes in Wilmington (U.S. Congress 1986:20; *Minneapolis Star and Tribune*, Feb. 16, 1987, 1M, 11M; interview, Scott V. Johnson, Amhoist general counsel, July 2, 1987).

American Crane had flown south on federal tax dollars from what it later said was an inefficient crane operation in Minnesota to a newer, more streamlined plant in North Carolina. Two years later, however, Amhoist was found to have illegally used federal UDAG funds to relocate American Crane Division production jobs to Wilmington.

This chapter reviews the events leading up to the HUD grant and the transfer of production from St. Paul to Wilmington, the subsequent controversy and finding against Amhoist, and the termination of crane operations. In the first section, I discuss the structure and performance of Amhoist and its American Crane Division and the relationship between the company and its St. Paul unions through the 1983 round of contract negotiations; I next describe Amhoist's use of the UDAG grant and other government subsidies to relocate crane production from St. Paul to Wilmington. I conclude by analyzing the American Crane case.

The Company and the Union

The incidents described here began in 1982 when the board of directors of Amhoist brought in forty-one-year-old Robert Nassau, a former executive of Ford Motor Company and vice president of J. I. Case, to develop and carry out a five-year corporate plan to reorganize and revitalize the historically profitable but declining old-line company. The plan included divesting unprofitable and marginally profitable product lines, especially in crane production.

Nassau was made president and chief operating officer. Two years later he advanced to president and CEO. To assist him, William Hobbs was hired away from the conglomerate FMC to head Amhoist's marketing department. A year later, in 1984, at the age of thirty-five, Hobbs was named president of the Amhoist crane division. Scott V. Johnson, an Amhoist staff counsel since 1978, had been promoted to vice president and general counsel in 1982. Nassau, Hobbs, and Johnson made up the management team responsible for the Amhoist consolidation.

During subsequent congressional hearings into the relocation and HUD grant, Johnson explained the team's consolidation and relocation strategy for American Crane.

> In 1982, we experienced a catastrophic collapse of the worldwide crane market. Coincidentally, the value of the dollar rose to record highs, severely hampering foreign sales of U.S. built machines. . . . Basically, all but one of our competitors, American competitors, got out of the business.
>
> Beginning in 1982, Amhoist closed three North American crane producing facilities and moved production to our last remaining plant in St. Paul. The market continued to deteriorate. There simply were not enough crane sales for more than one plant. Competition and the market would not permit inefficient manufacturing operations. Amhoist's choice was between a streamlined U.S. plant or none at all.
>
> In July of 1984, the Amhoist board decided we could not continue with crane manufacturing operations in our St. Paul facility. Our choices were to utilize our Brazilian subsidiary, to enter into expanded license operations with our Korean licensee, to go elsewhere in the United States or go out of business.
>
> This background, plus the inherent limitations on the size of cranes which could be produced at St. Paul resulted in the Wilmington plant decision (U.S. Congress 1986:20).

Johnson left unanswered the question of which cranes Amhoist planned to build in Wilmington. As it turned out, Amhoist would build whatever cranes it had on order, regardless of size and model. These included both those traditionally built in St. Paul and the larger, new-generation cranes that Amhoist hoped to begin building in Wilmington.

Amhoist's corporate headquarters, now in Denver, used to be in downtown St. Paul across the Mississippi River from the now-vacant American Crane plant. Started as a machine repair shop and incorporated in 1928, Amhoist was a well-known manufacturer of industrial booms, hoists, derricks, and related hardware. Crane production generated larger sales and profits than any other Amhoist product line. American Crane operated crane plants in Minnesota, Michigan, and Indiana and also maintained modest production operations in Brazil and South Korea. Like many other major U.S. manufacturers, Amhoist diversified in the 1960s into production of various durable-goods products, and by the end of the decade it boasted an array of forty-three products in twelve product lines and four product groups. The 1970s were growth years for durable-goods industries, and in 1981 the company was still dependent on heavy-lifting and construction equipment for 70 percent of corporate sales and 81 percent of earnings (*Amhoist Annual Report* 1979:4–5).

By the late 1970s, most U.S. companies were abandoning diversification strategies, but Amhoist continued making acquisitions despite the 1981–82 recession, which was especially severe in Amhoist's heavy-product lines. It did this in part because company officials believed President Ronald Reagan's economic program would bring an early end to the downturn and spark a resurgence in capital spending (*Annual Report* 1981:6). The recession was too formidable, however, and Amhoist had to terminate unprofitable and marginally profitable product lines and redistribute assets to try to achieve a more balanced corporate structure. It sold its entire construction equipment division, shut down three other plants, relocated one facility, and closed all of its domestic crane plants except the one in St. Paul. By 1985, the company operated product lines in three product groups—capital equipment, industrial products, and wholesale hardware—and employed 3,139 workers worldwide, down from 7,849 in 1979 (U.S. Securities and Exchange Commission 1985).

Amhoist executives expected the sales and earnings slack created by the slumping crane division and divestiture of the construction equipment division to be taken up by the other product lines. But this did not happen. None of the other three product groups expanded fast enough to offset

Amhoist's overall decline. Wholesale hardware products were the most promising in this regard, but sales were not large enough to make a difference. Performance in both the wire and chain and the water-products divisions remained sluggish. As a result, the capital equipment group, which included crane production, accounted for 45 percent of Amhoist's total sales in 1982 and 42 percent in 1985. Cranes alone represented 32 percent as late as 1986 (*Value Line Ratings and Reports,* May 23, 1986, 1359; *St. Paul Pioneer Press,* Oct. 11, 1984, 11; annual reports 1982–86).

Amhoist was never a household name, but historically it was a profitable company that enjoyed global name recognition for its large, made-to-order cranes (in St. Paul) and its reputation as a solid competitor in standard, medium-sized cranes. As such, its profits and sales performance were steadier than those of most large durable-goods manufacturers. In 1969, it became a Fortune 500 company, and it retained that status until 1983, when the recession slashed sales. In 1981, Amhoist had reported forty years of consecutive earnings. But profits had peaked in 1979 at $20.7 million on sales of nearly half a billion dollars and after 1981 they disappeared altogether. In 1983, the capital equipment group suffered losses of $67 million, more than twice the combined profits of Amhoist's other three groups. During the third quarter of 1984, Amhoist reported $3.7 million in profits after it terminated the defined pension plans of several groups of nonunion salaried and hourly employees for a one-time gain of $8.1 million. Otherwise, corporate net losses continued through 1986 (*St. Paul Pioneer Press,* Oct. 4, 1984, 1B; Oct. 29, 1984, 1A, 11A; June 20, 1986, 7B).

At the beginning of the 1960s, Amhoist had six major domestic competitors in crane manufacturing. But the same global market forces that eventually caused Amhoist to stop producing cranes also forced its rivals to dispose of their crane operations, to enter into Chapter 11 bankruptcy proceedings while continuing to produce at greatly reduced levels, or to relocate production operations overseas, sometimes under license to another country. Thus, by the mid-1980s, only one domestic competitor remained, and by then the market had been scaled down considerably to midsized cranes and was dominated by foreign producers (Johnson interview).

Six unions represented the mostly male work force at the St. Paul crane plant and foundry in 1985. The two largest unions were Local 459 of the International Association of Machinists and Local 63 of the International Molders and Allied Workers' Union. The other unions were traditional craft and white-collar organizations. St. Paul is historically a union town, and union members and officers at Amhoist had a strong sense of this tradition.

Because the company was able to expand in the 1960s and 1970s, mainly as a result of profits made in the crane division, workers there expected to be rewarded at the bargaining table. Amhoist also made heavy-lifting equipment in Michigan, Indiana, and Duluth, Minnesota, but each facility built its own models and each local union negotiated separately, with little communication or cooperation among them. In 1985, St. Paul clearly was Amhoist's flagship crane plant—the first and still the biggest.

The Machinists was one of the strongest unions at the St. Paul plant and foundry. Bargaining between Amhoist and its unions nevertheless was at arm's length and was hard line. With company profits rising steadily during the 1970s, union and management regularly negotiated two-year contracts calling for about 11 percent wage and benefit increases in the first year and 10 percent in the second, including cost-of-living guarantees. By 1983, the average hourly rate in the plant (excluding benefits) was about $12.00. This compared favorably with an average $2.93 for production workers and $4.42 for tool workers in 1970. Since the Machinists had the largest unit and negotiated first in each round of bargaining, contract talks with other unions followed the pattern set by the Machinists. When contract talks stalled, however, the Machinists were quick to strike—six times during 1970–83, for periods ranging from two days to fifteen weeks.

The events leading up to the shutdown in St. Paul in 1985 can be traced to Amhoist's planning and preparation for contract negotiations in late 1982 and early 1983. It was during this time that the company began its retrenchment and reorganization strategy. It appears now that the fate of the crane and foundry operations hung on the outcome of bargaining. But Amhoist negotiators never advised the union of this link. If they had, it is unlikely the union would have initiated or prolonged the 107-day strike that followed.

The dispute centered around noneconomic issues. During contract talks the Machinists had agreed in principle to a two-year wage and COLA freeze with a $.25 per hour raise in the third year of the contract if the company made a profit. It objected to company proposals on health-care containment and also wanted jurisdiction over employees in a new service department.

Under a compromise settlement, the union got jurisdiction of the service department and the company won some changes in the health-care package. The union also negotiated a clause that gave members seniority rights to jobs moved to locations within a fifty-mile radius of their old jobs, as in the case of the disputed service department. In retrospect, however, the striking employees unknowingly may have lost their jobs in the dispute.

The Machinists and other unions also resisted company demands for the elimination of most negotiated work rules and a free hand in all work assignments. Union negotiators knew the crane division was not especially profitable and that it might even be in difficulty. Apparently they were willing to make concessions that did not undermine the union as an effective bargaining agent. Union officials later said that Amhoist negotiators never shared the company's long-term plans with them and never offered to cooperate with the union in restructuring and renovating the St. Paul plant. Significant changes in contract language and terms and in the labor process generally were never linked to future job security. As a result, not knowing what the real choices were, union bargainers naturally refused to give in on both economic standards and protective contract language. When the company did not get what it wanted, however, the die was cast, and a little more than a year into the new contract the plant was closed (interview, Paul Burnquist, shop chairman, Local 459, May 12, 1985).

Relocation to Wilmington

As early as August 1983, local newspapers reported that Amhoist was looking at sites for another crane plant. A company vice president conceded that Amhoist was conducting a six-month feasibility study of possible southern plants, as well as alternative Minnesota locations, but said that no decision had been made.

By mid-1984, the company had neither confirmed nor denied these reports to its unions. Officers of Local 459 expressed concern about the lack of a definite answer and said they hoped to receive official notice from management before a board of directors meeting in late August (*St. Paul Pioneer Press,* Aug. 17, 1984, 1A, 5A). Unknown to the union, news reports in Wilmington already confirmed that Amhoist was doing a "preliminary feasibility study" of that city as a possible site and that Wilmington was applying for UDAG money. Local officials there said they believed that Amhoist was the most promising tenant for a large, vacant Babcock & Wilcox plant near the city's seaport (*Wilmington Morning Star,* July 21, 1984, 1A).

In October, following a meeting of Amhoist's directors, the company announced that it was acquiring the Wilmington plant and had received a $4 million UDAG supporting grant to do so. Amhoist would invest $25 million in capital improvements and equipment, for a total expenditure of $37 million on the project, and would employ seven hundred workers and begin building large cranes by mid-1985. The reasons given for the move included the availability of an existing facility suitable for large-crane manufacturing, including provisions for direct deep-water shipping (the Minnesota plant was not big enough to build components for the larger crane), and the availability of local and federal financing. In addition to the UDAG money, the North Carolina Department of Natural Resources and Community Development gave Wilmington $500,000 from a Small City Community Development Block Grant to be used to help Amhoist move machinery from St. Paul to Wilmington. Meanwhile, in St. Paul, Amhoist's president and chief operating officer would say only that the effect on jobs there was uncertain: "There will be some impact, but we have not determined the extent or the timing yet" (*Wilmington Morning Star,* Oct. 2, 1986, 1A; Oct. 4, 1984, 1B; *St. Paul Pioneer Press,* Oct. 5, 1984, 1A).

Amhoist began advertising for skilled and unskilled workers in Wilmington, and by November 1984 it reported that it had received more than enough applications. Nearly eight hundred résumés had arrived for the advertised managerial openings alone (*Wilmington Morning Star,* Nov. 17, 1984, 17B).

In January the following year, permanent layoff notices began appearing on bulletin boards in the St. Paul plant. Signed by the division president, they said:

> The present market for the traditional products that have been built in St. Paul has shown no improvement, and in fact, is forecasted to be lower than last year. For that reason the division will be undergoing a dramatic layoff. There will be a major impact on structural assembly, shipping, and receiving departments. In reviewing the division's overall manufacturing resources, it has been determined that other locations will most likely absorb the majority of the limited manufacturing requirements (*St. Paul Pioneer Press,* Jan. 12, 1985, 1A).

The workers responded with anger and sadness, but, in view of newspaper reports of the North Carolina project and the UDAG grant, they were not surprised. The workers' main concern, especially those in their late forties, fifties, and early sixties was the difficulty they would have finding comparable $500-a-week jobs in the Twin Cities.

In response to a surge of public criticism in the St. Paul area, an Amhoist vice president repeated the reasons for closing and pointed out that some of the Wilmington work, such as the production of new locomotive cranes, was responsible for there still being small jobs in St. Paul. He admitted, however, that when those orders were completed additional layoffs would occur. Nevertheless, he added, "Only crane manufacturing jobs are being lost. About 560 employees in the American Crane Division in St. Paul will stay on the job—in engineering, marketing, parts and service, the foundry, and management." Assurances that the foundry would not be affected by the transfer of production were not very convincing, however, insofar as Amhoist had laid off 70 of its 165 molders the week before (*Minneapolis Star and Tribune*, Jan. 12, 1985, 1D).

Among those most surprised by the mass layoffs was five-term U.S. congressman Bruce Vento of St. Paul. The plant was in his district, and his father, a retired Machinist, had worked for a company that Amhoist later acquired. Vento was stunned at the inconsistency between Amhoist's words and actions. Back in November 1984 he had arranged for a meeting with Amhoist representatives in response to union concerns about events occurring at that time and their impact on the St. Paul plant. Company officials assured him that the fears were unfounded and followed with a letter promising him that "at least 75 percent of the 763 crane-related jobs traditionally and presently performed in St. Paul will remain here. . . . The Wilmington expansion is obviously not a relocation of our crane operations" (*St. Paul Pioneer Press*, Jan. 15, 1985, 1A).

Of course, Vento wanted to know how the loss of some 500 out of 763 jobs was consistent with an earlier guarantee to retain 572 (75 percent) of those 763 jobs. He called a press conference at which he described the nature and scope of his meetings and correspondence with Amhoist and on that basis accused company officials of having broken their word to him. Clearly angered and frustrated at the turn of events, Vento warned Amhoist that it "damn well better not start producing those cranes built in St. Paul [in Wilmington] or they'll have a tiger by the tail. . . . They'll have a problem with me" (*St. Paul Pioneer Press*, Jan. 15, 1985, 1A).

Vento's bitter remarks brought a response three days later from Amhoist's president and chief operating officer. He explained the apparent inconsistencies in the company's promise and performance as follows:

- "In early 1984, Amhoist commenced a study of crane manufacturing alternatives."
- "Whereas 1,730 persons were employed in St. Paul crane operations in 1981, 763 are presently employed in these same crane functions. Even after Wilmington becomes fully operational in 1985, at least 75 percent of the 763 crane-related jobs traditionally and presently performed in St. Paul will remain."
- The difference was in the way he defined the jobs. By "traditional" jobs, Amhoist excluded work transferred to St. Paul from plants closed elsewhere:

> Last Friday, all employees were advised that our large locomotive crane order is nearing completion. These cranes would have been made in Bay City but, because of the closure of that plant, 350 St. Paul people have had additional employment. The layoff would be occurring whether the cranes were built in Bay City or St. Paul because the project was completed. After the layoff of these 350 persons, approximately 763 persons will remain in traditional jobs (*St. Paul Pioneer Press*, Jan. 18, 1985, 1A).

This response further angered Vento because he saw it as duplicitous. Amhoist now said it had 1,063 employees in the St. Paul crane division, instead of the 763 cited in its November letter. But this time the 763 jobs were identified as "traditional," as distinct from the 300 "temporary" jobs in St. Paul in connection with the one-time order for locomotive cranes. These 300 workers would be laid off as the locomotive work was completed. This was a completely novel way of defining the St. Paul work force. No one else—the union, Vento and his staff, or the HUD officials responsible for handling the UDAG grant—had ever seen these numbers and characterizations (*St. Paul Union Advocate*, Jan. 21, 1985, 2).

Congressman Vento proved to be as good as his word. In January 1985, he sent a letter to Samuel Pierce, Secretary of HUD, charging that Amhoist officials had misled him, the city of Wilmington, and HUD officials and had planned all along to use the Wilmington-UDAG project site to build twenty-seven St. Paul cranes. If this were the case, was the company in violation of the antipirating clause of the 1974 Housing and Commercial Development Act, which prohibits the use of UDAG money to facilitate the relocation of industrial or commercial plants or facilities from one area to another.

In response to Vento's allegation and considerable negative press coverage on the role of UDAG money in the relocation of Amhoist's operations, HUD began to investigate the matter. Both Amhoist and Wilmington expressed confidence in the outcome but admitted that they were concerned how such an investigation would be perceived by the private and public lenders on whom the Wilmington project depended for $10 million in industrial revenue bonds and $5 million in commercial financing (*Minneapolis Star and Tribune*, Feb. 10, 1985, 4B; *St. Paul Pioneer Press*, Jan. 27, 1985, 1A, 6A; *Minneapolis Star and Tribune*, Feb. 11, 1985, 4M).

HUD proceeded slowly, and in mid-March Vento charged the agency with foot-dragging. The investigation, he said, "was incomplete and slanted to produce a final report that would justify its initial approval of the $4 million grant award." He asked the General Accounting Office to look into the matter.

The following month HUD reauthorized the Wilmington grant but with the stipulation that Amhoist neither build nor ship St. Paul cranes from the Wilmington-UDAG site. On the surface this provision appeared to resolve the problem, but when asked for his reaction, the manager of the Wilmington plant predicted that the "additional costs of the restrictions will result in the building somewhere else [in Wilmington] of certain model cranes that fall under the restriction, which Amhoist was 'potentially' thinking about doing here [at the Wilmington-UDAG plant]." In any event, the restrictive covenant issued was too late to halt the shutdown of the St. Paul plant at the end of March 1985 (*Minneapolis Star and Tribune,* March 14, 1985, 1A; March 18, 1985, 1A, 18A; *Wilmington Morning Star,* April 19, 1985, 4B; *St. Paul Union Advocate,* April 22, 1985, 1).

Meanwhile, Amhoist announced that, for the following reasons, it had no practical choice but to relocate to Wilmington:

- its board of directors had approved the shutdown of the St. Paul plant as early as July 1984;
- Amhoist paid wages in Wilmington ranging from $7.00 to $8.20 an hour, compared with about $12.00 in the St. Paul plant;
- it cost half as much to ship cranes overseas from Wilmington as from St. Paul;
- the Private Industry Council in Wilmington had awarded it $100,000 to train low-income workers for jobs at the UDAG site;
- labor relations in the St. Paul plant were "stormy"; and
- workers' compensation and unemployment insurance costs were lower in North Carolina than in Minnesota, although this alone was not a significant consideration in its decision to move to Wilmington.

The St. Paul crane plant closed without fanfare. But, as the media reported, there were bitter negotiations between the company and the Machinists over severance benefits for displaced workers. The company was willing to finance a job-placement program, lump-sum payment for unused vacation, certain pension eligibility modifications, and severance pay. But there was an important sticking point: Amhoist wanted to link the severance package to the UDAG review; if the grant was revoked, there would be no severance package. Further, although the value of the severance package was estimated at $300,000 to $475,000, it applied to only about 275 long-term employees, which meant that it excluded 200 others. For these reasons the workers narrowly voted down the offer (*Minneapolis Star and Tribune,* Feb. 7,

1985, 1M, 5M, 8M; *St. Paul Pioneer Press,* Feb. 4, 1985, 1A; Feb. 7, 1985, 1A, 16A).

Amhoist management expressed displeasure at the results but agreed to improve its offer and to link severance benefits to completion of the crane work being done in St. Paul. Six weeks later, members of the bargaining unit voted on a slightly improved package, causing officers of the Machinists local to label it a productivity bonus rather than severance pay. This time members approved the offer by a slender margin. The agreement provided $115 per year of service for covered employees if they retired early, but as little as $85 if they did not. Some workers received supplemental pension benefits, and a job-placement counseling service was established for others. Employees receiving a combination of workers' compensation and company insurance benefits lost the company insurance portion of their disability benefits (*Minneapolis Star and Tribune,* March 19, 1985, 5B).

During the summer of 1985, five months after the closing of the crane plant, Amhoist quietly closed its St. Paul foundry. The previously announced temporary layoffs became permanent. One-third of the molders took early retirement. The negotiated severance benefit averaged $2,114 per recipient, or about four to six weeks of pay under the old contract. This amounted to $91.50 per year of service and one holiday payment of $91.50. The average outgoing molder had twenty-three years of service with Amhoist. It was reported that none found jobs paying the equivalent of the $11.50 per hour average earned at Amhoist. At least one hundred additional jobs were lost among supervisory and other white-collar workers (*Minneapolis Star and Tribune,* July 30, 1985, 1B).[1]

Three events marked the final chapter in American Crane's flight south. First, the GAO reviewed HUD's grant decision at Congressman Vento's request. Second, Vento, as chairman of the House Subcommittee on Housing and Development, held hearings on the events surrounding the decision, including the role played by North Carolina senator Jesse Helms. Third, a group of displaced workers brought suit against Amhoist for lost wages and benefits as a result of the closing.

The GAO's report in February 1985 supported the charge that Amhoist made bad-faith promises to Vento and that its Wilmington facility was a runaway plant. It concluded that "because Amhoist is now manufacturing the same mid-sized cranes at the Wilmington plant as it traditionally did at the St. Paul plant, it is our opinion that this project is a relocation within the context of section 119(h)." The report also was critical of HUD's handling of the UDAG grant procedure:

> HUD should have been more aggressive and alert to the relocation possibilities that were inherent in the Amhoist matter. . . . Even though HUD has stated that the transfer of equipment is not, in and of itself, a sufficient basis to conclude relocation will or will not occur, the transfer of the equipment in this instance was significant. Without such equipment it would have not been feasible for Amhoist to maintain—in terms of mid-sized crane production—a manufacturing capability in St. Paul. . . . Amhoist is manufacturing the same type of cranes at the Wilmington project that it made in the St. Paul plant. In our view, the amendment does not avoid a relocation compliance (GAO 1986:3).

Vento released the GAO report in a dramatic news conference outside a locked gate at the closed plant. "HUD aided and abetted the stealing away of jobs from our community," he charged. "This conduct from our federal government is not acceptable. This HUD performance needs to be exposed to the light of day." He further announced that his subcommittee was scheduling hearings on the matter (*St. Paul Union Advocate,* March 10, 1986, 1, 2).

A few days later, HUD froze the unused portion of the grant—$1.2 million—at least until HUD completed its antipirating investigation. Amhoist countered that the St. Paul plant had been closed for reasons other than the acquisition of the Wilmington plant and that any problem with the grant was therefore between the GAO and HUD. Amhoist's president and chief operating officer tried to explain to the community why the UDAG grant was immaterial to the closing, but his account contradicted company statements made at the time of the shutdown. First, he claimed that Amhoist had not "moved" to Wilmington but simply had closed a plant in St. Paul and later opened another one in Wilmington and that Amhoist had decided to stop making cranes in St. Paul even before applying for the Wilmington-UDAG grant. Second, Amhoist had to rationalize crane operations in a single plant that enabled it to make and ship a full line of cranes, including made-to-order and midsized products, which it could not do in St. Paul. Third, Amhoist had cooperated fully with HUD and notified the agency that two hundred jobs in crane production would be lost in St. Paul (*St. Paul Pioneer Press,* March 4, 1986, 1A, 2A; *Minneapolis Star and Tribune,* March 4, 1986, 1B, 2B; March 9, 1986, 1B, 2B).

Vento's subcommittee convened on March 20, 1986. The hearing opened with testimony from GAO officials that HUD's procedure in reviewing the Amhoist application was inadequate and that the grant had been used to support an improper relocation under the law. HUD representatives followed with testimony that Amhoist had breached a restrictive covenant in the HUD grant prohibiting the company from doing St. Paul work at the

Wilmington-UDAG site. For that reason HUD had frozen the unallocated portion of the grant and, two weeks before the hearing, had referred the matter to the Justice Department for remedy. According to the latter, HUD had requested that the Justice Department declare Amhoist in default for having breached the terms of the restrictive covenant and seek a permanent injunction against Amhoist to prevent further violations.

Amhoist's general counsel testified for the company. He argued that Amhoist's move to Wilmington was an expansion and not a relocation of production; that Amhoist had decided to terminate manufacturing cranes in St. Paul before the grant was awarded; that only two hundred jobs were lost in St. Paul because of the opening of the plant in Wilmington; that there had been no significant and adverse impact in St. Paul as a result of the closing because unemployment there remained at less than 5 percent, compared with a national average of more than 7 percent; that Amhoist's manufacturing requirements included a bigger on-site production crane and a deep-water port; that Amhoist had complied fully with the HUD restrictive covenant; and that HUD officials had understood Amhoist's intentions fully and at all times in the procedure (U.S. Congress 1986:13–33, 47).

The hearing also delved into the role played, if any, by Senator Jesse Helms in HUD's approval of the grant. Reportedly, a few days before HUD approved Amhoist's grant application in November 1984, Helms's office had arranged a meeting in the office of Samuel Pierce, HUD's Secretary, attended by HUD officials, representatives from Amhoist and the city of Wilmington, and a person from Helms's staff. The purpose was to discuss a company proposal designed to silence critics and justify HUD's approval of Amhoist's application. As a condition for receiving the UDAG grant, Amhoist offered to sign a restrictive covenant prohibiting it from building or shipping St. Paul cranes from the Wilmington-UDAG site. Those present agreed, and the grant application proceeded favorably (*Minneapolis Star and Tribune*, March 9, 1986, 1B, 6B).

The general counsel for HUD testified that he "was not personally aware of contacts from . . . Senator Helms' office or the Senator himself" before February 1985. He said he recalled the senator making "inquiries" of some sort at the department but that none was made directly to him.

Vento later questioned Amhoist's general counsel on this point:

Vento: What was your connection with Senator Helms?
Johnson: To the best of my recollection, either—factually neither I nor any other person from Amhoist had any contact with Senator Helms or anyone from his staff or any other representative of Congress during 1985.

Vento: During 1985.
Johnson: On this issue.

Was the general counsel aware that Helms had received a copy of Amhoist's letter to Vento in November 1984? No, he was not, answered the attorney. Moreover, he added, "There were no meetings held between anyone from Amhoist and any member of Congress prior to the grant." With that, Vento abandoned further inquiry into the alleged Helms connection, although one subcommittee member suggested complicity: "I think the record ought to show that the gentleman from North Carolina . . . does not leave paper trails." Interested parties were left to await the outcome of the Justice Department's legal investigation and possible action (U.S. Congress 1986:40, 47).

Before anything happened at the Justice Department, however, a majority of the displaced St. Paul workers tried unsuccessfully to sue the company on the grounds that they were "injured as a result of Amhoist's deliberate misuse of federal funds to pay for its move to a new plant." They wanted the full value of the wages and benefits they would have earned had the plant remained open until the May 31, 1986, expiration date of the contract in effect at the time of the closing. Each worker who joined in the suit paid $75 to a law firm to handle the case. But at the end of May 1987, they received a letter from their attorney notifying them he was not pursuing the case. Enclosed was a check for $75 plus interest (*Minneapolis Star and Tribune,* April 12, 1985, 7B, 13B).

The final outcome of the controversy was determined by several events that started about a year after the closing of the St. Paul plant and foundry. During the fall of 1986, Insituform Group, Ltd., a Canadian holding company, purchased a substantial number of Amhoist common shares at greatly reduced prices, making Insituform the third largest owner and fueling speculation that Amhoist was going to be acquired and reorganized. Shortly afterward, Amhoist reported reduced sales revenues and a net loss of $70 million for 1986, nearly ten times that for 1985. Part of the loss was due to a pretax charge of $51 million against the crane division. Stockholders' equity was cut by half. Amhoist's capital equipment group and industrial products group had combined operating losses of $59 million, far outweighing small profits in its wholesale hardware and foreign operations (*Minneapolis Star and Tribune,* Nov. 22, 1986, 9B, 12B; Amhoist, proxy statement, April 9, 1987; *Amhoist Annual Report* 1986).

The crane division continued to unhinge Amhoist's retrenchment efforts.

Cranes accounted for nearly 80 percent of the capital equipment group's sales of $108 million. American Crane's revenues were falling but still represented about half the domestic market, indicating the extent to which the U.S. crane market for heavy-lifting equipment had deteriorated—down by 85 percent during 1981–86. The division now employed 558 workers, a little more than one-sixth of Amhoist's total work force, compared with 36 percent earlier. (Overall corporate employment had fallen from about seven thousand to three thousand.) Amhoist therefore continued to phase down its crane division. In early 1987, it sold the marine/energy (large) crane line to the U.S. subsidiary of AMCA International, Ltd., a Canadian holding company. This consisted mainly of the heavy, custom-made cranes previously built in St. Paul and more recently in Wilmington. AMCA consolidated the line into its Clyde off-shore oil-drilling operations in New Orleans. The merged company, Amclyde, would be headquartered in Amhoist's former St. Paul offices and production would occur in both New Orleans and at a former Amhoist site in Pennsylvania. Divestiture of the large-crane line cut Amhoist's crane sales in half and limited production to standard, medium-sized models with the greatest market stability. It also trimmed overhead costs considerably (*Minneapolis Star and Tribune,* Feb. 11, 1987, 1M; *St. Paul Pioneer Press,* Feb. 11, 1987, 7D).

All of this occurred even though Amhoist had said it needed the Wilmington plant to build large, custom cranes and that standard cranes—the disputed "traditional" work discussed above—would not be made there. Now the large-crane business had been sold and Amhoist's standard cranes were to be built exclusively in the Wilmington-UDAG plant. The Justice Department had yet to decide, however, what to do with HUD's request for a declaratory judgment and permanent injunction against Amhoist.

In the end, events other than the snaillike Justice Department investigation determined the outcome and made the public procedure irrelevant. The company posted modest net earnings ($2.7 million) for the first quarter of 1987. Amhoist's management attributed the improvement to its restructuring strategy, including increased efficiency as a result of the move to Wilmington, and to a tax credit for previous operating losses. This was only the third profitable quarter for Amhoist since 1982, when it had lost $157 million. Company officials also said they did not expect to lay off additional employees in the crane division (*Minneapolis Star and Tribune,* April 2, 1987, 1M; April 10, 1987, 10B; *St. Paul Pioneer Press,* April 10, 1987, 7D).

Technically the last statement was true. Amhoist sold its remaining crane operations and new owners ordered the layoffs. In July 1987, Amhoist announced it was ending its 105-year history in the crane business. What was left of the business was being acquired by Ohio Locomotive Crane Company of Bucyrus, Ohio, for $40 million. A privately owned company, Ohio Crane employed 125 workers who manufactured standard cranes for use in rail, construction, and agricultural operations. At the time, American Crane employed 475 workers: 350 in Wilmington and 125 in St. Paul (*St. Paul Pioneer Press,* June 19, 1987, 1A, 4A; *Minneapolis Star and Tribune,* June 19, 1987, 11B, 12B).

Congressman Vento refused to drop the HUD controversy, however. He reminded the company that the Justice Department was still investigating possible misuse of federal grant money and as far as he was concerned selling the crane division did not absolve Amhoist from responsibility for the results of any improper behavior on its part. The company seemed to agree, at least in principle. In an agreement worked out with HUD and the Justice Department, Amhoist denied any wrongdoing but offered to repay, with interest, the $2.8 million it had received from HUD. Repayment was conditional, however, on Amhoist's successful sale of the division to Ohio Crane. If the deal fell through for any reason, Amhoist would not have to make any payments until July 1988 (*Minneapolis Star and Tribune,* July 26, 1987, 1B).

The sale did go as planned, repayment was made, and the migration of American Crane was complete. Some cranes made it back to St. Paul, others landed in familiar King of Prussia, Pennsylvania, and unfamiliar New Orleans, and the Wilmington cranes now belonged to an Ohio employer. Amhoist expressed delight with the results of its five-year corporate restructuring strategy and that it no longer made cranes. Vento still wanted $4 million from the federal government for local economic development and retraining of displaced St. Paul crane workers. Perhaps his summary of the relocation and the controversy surrounding it best echoes the sentiments of the workers, unions, and community that were adversely affected by Amhoist's relocation and subsequent divestiture of the century-old crane works: "This entire episode [is] a hollow monument based on greed and human suffering, and to a slipshod bureaucracy unwilling to follow the law" (*St. Paul Union Advocate,* Aug. 3, 1987, 1).

Amhoist too is now extinct. Its touted five-year plan failed partly because management overloaded the company with debt obligations resulting from corporate expansion. In 1988, Amhoist acquired CoastAmerica Corporation and Globe Distribution, a nationwide hardware chain. The acquisition cost Amhoist $110 million plus the estimated $100 million in CoastAmerica's debt that it had to assume. Amhoist increased sales revenues in the expansion but continued to lose money.

In February 1989, Amhoist changed its name to Amdura. By now it was carrying a dangerously high debt/equity ratio of 2.4, and although it had increased sales and earnings in 1988, it continued to lose money. Purchase of CoastAmerica led Amhoist to abandon its St. Paul headquarters and move to Denver, where CoastAmerica is based.

By the third quarter of 1989, Amdura faced debts of $240 million with only $100 million in equity. Meanwhile, corporate investor Tony Cilluffo had quietly accumulated controlling interest in the company. Under his direction, the Amhoist board fired the president and CEO who had closed the St. Paul plant and planned and executed the ill-fated five-year strategy. This was after the company had posted an $8 million loss in the first six months of 1990 (*Minneapolis Star and Tribune,* Jan. 19, 1989, 2D; Feb. 1, 1989, 1D; Feb. 14, 1989, 1A, 5A).

Analysis and Conclusion

Among labor circles in St. Paul, Amhoist was accused of "union busting" in relocating its crane production to Wilmington. For their part, Amhoist officials said it was necessary to relocate to Wilmington to make its largest division profitable again. They explained the move as a purely business decision to rationalize crane production in the face of industry overcapacity caused by an 85 percent drop in U.S. crane sales. Under these conditions, they argued, it was logical to consolidate crane operations in a single plant. And in view of the vintage of the St. Paul works, it made good sense to take advantage of the opportunity to relocate to a modern, better-situated facility.

Union and community critics concede that Amhoist needed to rationalize its crane operations (i.e., to make them more efficient organizationally), but it was not necessary for it to relocate to Wilmington, since doing so would result in the loss of its experienced production work force. St. Paul had been building high-quality cranes for a century and might have continued to do so with the proper equipment, product line, and leadership. Production rationalization, not relocation, was in order. The critics believe that union labor relations and the company's desire to take advantage of government grants and incentives sent American Crane flying south. To them, Amhoist moved production from St. Paul to flee union wages, benefits, seniority, and work rules; to avoid future strikes; and to make the move as cheaply as possible by financing part of it with federal, state, and local tax dollars. Organized labor's charge against Amhoist, therefore, is union busting by virtue of its being a runaway employer.

Whether or not Amhoist would have relocated production to Wilmington if it had not received government subsidies and if labor relations in St. Paul had not been "stormy" cannot be determined from the record, but certainly the move was facilitated by both considerations. The strategy also depended on a sufficient demand for heavy cranes to support continued production in St. Paul while the new site was being readied and the new work force trained. In the end, however, neither the estimates concerning job losses in its grant application nor its statements about the market for cranes were accurate. Amhoist needed one to two years to phase out production in St. Paul and smoothly ease in production in Wilmington. In Amhoist's grant application, the company estimated that job losses in St. Paul would be limited to the twenty-five supervisory personnel who would constitute the startup management team in Wilmington. A game of semantics followed involving the number of jobs displaced in St. Paul and their classification. Amhoist argued that no "traditional" jobs were lost there as a result of the relocation. Vento and the union, by contrast, insisted that such jobs were lost.

In its application to HUD, especially its request for money to move equipment from St. Paul to Wilmington, Amhoist said that the purpose of the move was to finance the manufacture of large, newly designed cranes and that therefore the Wilmington operation would be different from the one in St. Paul. HUD was aware, however, that some crane lines would be discontinued in St. Paul and perhaps two hundred jobs lost there and that there was some speculation that the St. Paul plant might be closed altogether. The agency nevertheless approved the grant, certainly over the objections of Congressman Vento and possibly at the urging of Senator Jesse Helms.

Even under these conditions events might have progressed favorably for Amhoist. By the time the Wilmington-UDAG site was in operation, publicity over the HUD grant and the St. Paul layoffs should have subsided. Time, however, was not an ally of the company. With crane losses mounting, Amhoist no longer could afford to phase out production gradually, and by the spring of 1985 it had to announce its intention to close the St. Paul plant.

Under the scrutiny of Congressman Vento, whose steady stream of press releases kept the issue in the public eye, Amhoist was thus put in a dilemma. Its explanations for the closing were well publicized and contradictory, but the more openly it debated Vento and the unions, the more unlikely it became that it was going to be able to squelch the controversy and proceed with its strategy to restructure American Crane along low-wage, nonunion, federally subsidized lines. Forced to give contradictory explanations for its actions, Amhoist became hostage to its conflicting public statements. It could not reveal the logic and consistency of its reorganization strategy since the strategy depended in part on receiving improper UDAG funding.

Amhoist did not anticipate that it would have to divulge its crane plans in public or undergo a HUD review, a GAO investigation, and a congressional oversight hearing, all of which revealed contradictions between the company's behavior and its rationale. The St. Paul employees had to be carved into "traditional" and "other" work groups—with the latter subject to dismissal and the former identified with shifting models and sizes of cranes—as Amhoist scrambled to convince outsiders it was not moving St. Paul work to Wilmington. When it was no longer tenable for it to deny that it was building "traditional" cranes in Wilmington, Amhoist drafted and HUD accepted a restrictive covenant to stop such production. But Amhoist complied with the covenant just as its Wilmington plant manager had predicted: by moving the disputed work to another American Crane facility in Wilmington that was not part of the UDAG grant. For purposes of the covenant, Amhoist had to define the words *produce, assemble,* and *prepare for shipping* in new and creative ways (letter, Nassau to Vento, Nov. 15, 1984; U.S. Congress 1986:18–27, 30–31, 43–49, 55–57).

A final objective of Amhoist's restructuring of its crane production was to "streamline" operations through capital investment. Amhoist management considered the St. Paul facility inappropriate for renovation. It was not that the plant's physical condition and layout prohibited retrofitting, but that Amhoist simply did not want to stay there. Although this surely had to do with the influence of the St. Paul unions and collective bargaining, the company could not say as much publicly.

The last straw for Amhoist in this regard probably was the lengthy strike by the Machinists in 1983 over company demands for extensive changes in job descriptions and work-crew practices. Management could have pressed these issues and threatened to shut down if the union did not agree to review the contract and the union-company relationship with an eye toward cooperative efforts to resolve such operating problems as the need for flexible work rules in an up-to-date manufacturing facility. But Amhoist did not make any threats. Instead it chose to streamline its work force in the crane division rather than in its St. Paul plant, to substitute nonunion labor for union labor, and to displace the St. Paul labor force rather than try to establish a cooperative, productive relationship with it. In this way, the company removed its production workers in cranes from negotiated work standards and processes.

Amhoist did not go to Wilmington solely to avoid unions or out of operational necessity. It did so for both reasons. The product market was changing, the St. Paul work force was experienced but high paid, and the plant was aging but serviceable and capable of being upgraded. In response, Amhoist chose a low-wage, relocation strategy. The alternative would have been a strategy based on costly (but essential) research and development, a high-technology production process, and a high-paid high-skilled work force.

Whether such a strategy would have been successful is uncertain. What is certain is that the chosen strategy failed. To be sure, it made Amhoist unaccountable to unions and communities in the short run, but this was not enough to rescue a troubled company from being badly served by its top management and from being broken up in future corporate reshuffling. The best-laid plans go astray, and today American Crane is extinct and Amhoist has joined the other venerable U.S. manufacturers that expired while in the hands of the "go-go" managers of the 1970s and 1980s.

Chapter 9
STRIKE AND RELOCATION IN MEATPACKING

Charles Craypo

THREE EVENTS DOMINATE labor relations in meatpacking in recent years: plant closings and relocations, declining labor standards and bitter labor disputes, and the levying of government fines for job health and safety violations. This chapter identifies and describes the corporate restructuring, intensified product competition, and changes in employer strategies in meatpacking. The purpose is to explain how these trends have interacted to produce the current tensions between large meatpackers and their workers and the communities in which they operate. It focuses on IBP (formerly Iowa Beef Processors), for years the nation's largest beef packer and the industry leader in determining labor standards, production processes, and product marketing. Specifically, it traces labor and community relations during a 1986–88 lockout and strike at IBP's flagship plant in Dakota City, Nebraska.

The first part describes IBP's impact on meatpacking since it was organized in 1960; the second part analyzes IBP's low-cost labor strategy as illustrated by the Dakota City dispute; the third part discusses IBP's corporate relationship with Dakota City and other communities in which its plants are located and with government regulators. The fourth and final part analyzes these events and outcomes from a structural, institutional perspective.

IOWA BEEF AND THE MEATPACKING INDUSTRY

Meatpacking is one of the nation's largest nondurable manufacturing industries.[1] A few large firms have historically dominated the industry.[2] Their identities have changed from time to time, as in the 1960s, when new companies began replacing traditional old-line packers. This shift resulted from several changes occurring inside the industry. First, western cattlemen built local feedlots rather than continue to ship their herds east for fattening, slaughtering, and processing; soon enough, packers were convinced to relocate plants there to take advantage of the economies of scale and the new, more efficient plants. Second, retail supermarkets began making volume purchases of prepacked beef cuts rather than storing and processing carcasses or purchasing small lots from distributors. Third, improved truck refrigeration and warehousing and advances in packaging methods enabled packers to ship partial cuts of meat long distances without spoilage or dehydration. Fourth, and finally, conglomerate acquisition of the leading meatpackers weakened their ability to compete and opened the way for aggressive, well-financed newcomers to gain control of the industry from the old-line producers (Skaggs 1986, chap. 6).

IBP was the first such newcomer. Incorporated as Iowa Beef Packers in 1960, it became Iowa Beef Processors in 1970 and in 1982 was acquired by Occidental Petroleum Corporation, which changed its name to IBP. Iowa Beef exploited the new environment and soon was the lowest-cost, most profitable, and fastest-growing packer in the country. Founded by veteran meatpackers on the strength of a small business loan, IBP followed a production strategy that involved having single-story plants, fully integrated disassembly lines, and generally homogeneous production workers. This strategy ran counter to that of old-line packers, characterized by their multistory plants, separate production departments, and skilled and semiskilled workers. IBP's labor strategy also differed markedly from standard industry practice. Instead of recognizing unions and negotiating labor terms and conditions, it resisted unions as much as possible, imposed standards unilaterally and on a plant-by-plant basis, and, as a precaution, integrated production so as to maintain output even if one out of every three of its plants was on strike.

IBP represented the latest chapter in the competitive history of meatpacking. Large, innovative, and aggressive packers traditionally have put their established rivals at a disadvantage by finding better ways to slaughter and process meat and get it to market (Williams and Stout 1964, chap. 1; Skaggs 1986, chap. 4). IBP simply incorporated all the options offered by the new environment, just as Gustavus Swift and other nineteenth-century packers had done. IBP executives evaluate themselves in terms of traditional American business values: entrepreneurial trepidation, individualism, and hard work. They claim to have replicated the successful strategy of the old-line packers, which was to build large plants, locate them as far west as possible, reduce transportation and labor costs, and satisfy consumer demands (Tinstman and Peterson 1981).

IBP AS INDUSTRY LEADER

From obscure beginnings, Iowa Beef became a Fortune 500 company by 1963, and by the mid-1970s it had overtaken Swift to become the nation's largest beef packer, indeed bigger than the five next largest beef producers combined. At the end of the 1970s, it was the nation's seventy-seventh largest industrial corporation. By 1987, it was also the biggest pork packer even though it had been in the industry just six years, and by 1990, despite competition from industry latecomers ConAgra and Excel, it controlled 32 percent of the nation's beef-packing and 15 percent of the pork market. IBP, ConAgra, and Excel together slaughtered nearly 70 percent of the grain-fed cattle and 40 percent of marketed hogs (*Los Angeles Times,* April 22, 1990, D7).

IBP was also the most profitable packer. Meatpacking, like retail food, is a high-volume business in which sales revenues are high relative to capital investment. Profits on sales therefore are relatively low—at or below 2 percent most of the time. Profits on investment (shareholders' equity) can be quite high, however. Throughout the 1960s and 1970s, for example, IBP regularly reported profit/equity ratios of 20 to 25 percent in an industry that was then averaging 7 percent. As table 9.1 shows, however, IBP's profit ratios fell sharply in the 1980s. Sales for 1984–88 were nearly five times those of 1972–76 and net profits were more than three times as great, whereas profit on sales averaged 0.8 percent compared with 1.04 percent in the earlier period. Moreover, profit on equity for 1986–88 was less than half that for 1972–76. The 1989 figures also were disappointing: IBP's profit–sales ratio was 0.4 percent, half the average during 1984–88 (*Wall Street Journal,* March 1, 1990, C2).

Reasons commonly cited for IBP's decline in profitability are, first, that sales of unbranded red-meat products began to decline as Americans became

Table 9.1. IBP's sales and profits, 1972–76 and 1984–88

Years	Sales (billions)	Net profits (millions)	Profit on sales (percent)	Profit on equity (percent)
1972–76	1.6	17.6	1.04	24.8
1984–88	7.4	59.6	0.80	11.6[a]

Sources: IBP annual report 1976; U.S. Securities and Exchange Commission, 1988.
[a]1986–88.

more health conscious and, second, that ConAgra and Excel were expanding into the industry by acquiring packing plants and operating them the same way as IBP. As a result, excess capacity in the industry was estimated at 25 percent in 1990 and the biggest packers were having to process larger numbers of cattle, reportedly at higher prices, to operate their plants efficiently.

Labor Relations at Iowa Beef

Nineteenth-century packers made money in both the product and the labor market. In the former, they organized producer cartels and devised various price-fixing and market-sharing schemes.[3] In the latter, they hired immigrants and others who often had no choice but to work at the terms offered (see, for example, Barrett 1987).

Unions found it difficult to organize and bargain with multiplant firms using decentralized production processes, a situation further complicated by craft divisions among unions and the setbacks organized labor usually experiences during business downturns. Labor gains in meatpacking therefore were intermittent until the 1930s and 1940s, when two rival unions, the Amalgamated Meat Cutters (AFL) and the United Packinghouse Workers (CIO), separately organized the old-line firms. Each established multiplant contracts and patterned its bargaining demands and settlements after the other. By 1953, they were coordinating their efforts, and by 1968, they had formally merged. In 1979, the combined Amalgamated Meat Cutters merged with the larger Retail Clerks International Union to form the United Food and Commercial Workers International Union (UFCW), at the time the AFL-CIO's largest affiliate. Pattern bargaining soon resulted in nearly uniform increases in wages and benefits among major packers, despite differences among individual plants, and similar but not identical wage and benefit levels across the industry (Brody 1964, chap. 11; Perry and Kegley 1989, chap. 8).

The effect was to take labor out of competition, that is, to prevent one packer from getting a competitive edge over the others by paying substandard wages and benefits, intensifying work effort, or operating unsafe plants. Negotiated standards were high relative to those in other manufacturing industries, and union and job rights were among the strongest in the nation. Union and management maintained an arms'-length, formal bargaining relationship. Unions struck against one or more of the major producers in about half the bargaining rounds over master agreements. Nevertheless, in most situations the parties worked together in areas of common concern, such as job relocation and training assistance for employees displaced by plant closings.

Centralized bargaining and sizable economic settlements continued through the 1970s, even though IBP's market expansion and labor policies had been putting pressure on established packers to abandon their postwar labor relations system and reduce their direct labor costs. Eventually the old-line packers tried to offset the growing labor cost disadvantage between them and IBP by holding the line on wages and benefits and eroding job conditions. Labor thus became a competitive factor again and widespread union concessions followed. Small packers that had patterned their contract settlements after the master agreements negotiated by the major packers began asking for and getting concessions on the grounds that otherwise they would have to close their doors. Now the majors demanded multiplant concessions as well.

In 1981, the UFCW agreed to cut wages industrywide to $10.69 an hour, a concession it hoped would put a floor on wages and stop the downward slide. As it turned out, however, this became the maximum wage individual firms would agree to now that labor was back in competition. The international union soon found it impossible to hold either employers or local unions to the $10.69 figure. The Wilson Company declared bankruptcy and unilaterally cut wages by 40 percent. Armour permanently closed thirteen plants that had been under the master wage agreement and sold three others to SIPCO, a highly leveraged successor to Swift's beef operations; SIPCO promptly reopened the former Armour plants at wages of $5.00 per hour before closing six of its own unionized plants. Meanwhile, John Morrell and Company opened two other nonunion beef plants at $5.00 wages. Altogether, some twenty-three union plants employing nine thousand workers were closed in 1983.

Reeling from plant closings and a free-fall in industry wages, the UFCW tried unsuccessfully to establish a floor with numerous wage freezes and reductions (Moody 1988:179–82, 314–27; Perry and Kegley 1989, chap. 9). This continued until the 1986 round of bargaining, when the union finally established a $10.00 hourly base rate (to become effective in 1988) in most of its multiplant contracts.

Throughout this period IBP was a major source of wage and operating instability. The UFCW had only one IBP plant under contract and therefore was unable to extend master agreements negotiated with other companies to IBP, which by now was the industry leader. Although company negotiators insisted it was a pattern taker, IBP in fact had become the pattern setter in industry wages and working conditions (*Wall Street Journal*, Jan. 23, 1987, 7).

It had inherited a union when it acquired its first plant but decertified the local following an unsuccessful strike. The Amalgamated Meat Cutters organized IBP's Dakota City plant three years after it opened, but neither it nor the United Packinghouse, Food and Allied Workers was able to win another IBP plant. The International Brotherhood of Teamsters, however, was certified at a large new IBP plant in Amarillo, Texas, and a smaller acquired plant in Pasco, Washington. Other unions claimed these were "sweetheart" arrangements insofar as IBP did not resist the Teamsters but then negotiated "substandard" contracts in both plants.[4] Thus, in the 1980s, IBP operated union-free in ten of its thirteen plants, by far the industry's lowest unionization ratio.

IBP also paid lower wages than most old-line packers. It did so on the grounds that wages and benefits were lower in beef than in pork and, unlike other major packers, it was exclusively a beef processor.[5] In addition, it argued that because net profits as a ratio of sales in meatpacking are 2 percent or less, and labor costs are the next largest component of production costs after raw material (livestock), the key to profitability in meatpacking is to minimize direct and indirect labor costs.[6] In 1970, for example, IBP said that if it had paid average industry wages in 1968 it would have earned one-fifth less than it did, although it still realized an 18 percent return on equity that year compared with Swift's 5 percent (*Forbes,* May 1, 1970, 31). As a former IBP vice president for labor relations was quoted as saying during a National Labor Relations Board hearing in 1984, labor productivity "is the alpha and the omega" to making money in meatpacking: "Whether you're going to survive and prosper or whether you're going to fall by the wayside and close your door is dependent upon what you pay and how much you get back. It's not a complicated business from that standpoint" (cited in *Chicago Tribune,* Oct. 25, 1988, sect. 3, 8).

IBP appeared to have a competitive cost advantage in this regard. Its plants reportedly required fewer hours of labor and less labor skill and experience than those of its industrial rivals because boxed beef production methods and strict supervision enabled it to run its disassembly lines, called chains, faster than those of its competitors. Faster chains facilitated a quicker work pace and more repetitive motions on the job as part of a generally more intense labor effort. By the 1980s, however, neither IBP nor any other packer had fundamentally changed its production process. The microelectronic revolution in manufacturing had not yet altered the way animal carcasses were slaughtered and processed, as it had the way cars, machine tools, and tons of steel were produced. Workers still disassembled carcasses using knives and cutting techniques essentially unchanged from those used a half-century earlier. As a Bureau of Labor Statistics bulletin notes: "In meatpacking and poultry processing plants, new technologies were introduced in the 1960s that mechanized processing to some extent and reduced unit labor requirements. However, most cutting tasks must still be performed manually, and the industry remains relatively labor intensive" (U.S. Department of Labor Bureau of Labor Statistics 1982:1).

DAKOTA CITY STRIKE

With some twenty-eight hundred production workers in the mid-1980s, the Dakota City plant was IBP's largest fresh-beef operation. The company processed thousands of cattle a day, mostly its own but also some it purchased from other packers. Workers there had been represented by UFCW Local 222 since 1969. In five rounds of contract bargaining between 1969 and 1986, the union and the company had never renegotiated a contract without a work stoppage. Each time Local 222 extended the contract when talks broke down, and each time the company either locked out the workers or the workers struck and were replaced by strikebreakers. IBP's use of replacements invariably resulted in picket-line violence, the worst of which occurred in the 1969–70 stoppage, when two persons were killed—a relative of a company informant and a striking worker—and IBP property in Dakota City and elsewhere was destroyed.

In each round of bargaining, IBP refused to match the industry pattern and instead demanded union concessions on the grounds that it needed them to be cost-competitive.[7] But the union neither accepted these demands nor initiated a confrontation with the company, in view of IBP's strength and antiunion philosophy and because union leaders knew that an extended strike could end in union decertification.

Local 222 nevertheless made modest gains in its first three contracts with IBP, although it had to take wage freezes and reductions in the next two rounds of bargaining. Basic wages tripled between 1969 and 1982, in large part due to the combination of rapid increases in the consumer price index and escalator clauses in the contract. After that base wages were reduced by 12 percent and then frozen at $8.20 in slaughtering and $7.90 in processing. In the 1986 negotiations, IBP wanted to freeze these rates for four more years.

The company also refused to extend the contract while negotiations continued on the grounds that doing so in the past had led to bargaining misunderstandings and lengthy strikes. Besides, said company officials, the union planned to conduct "in-plant" disruptions while negotiations continued (*Sioux City Journal,* Dec. 7, 1986, A16; *Omaha World Herald,* Dec. 10, 1986, 2). So, in December 1986, when workers rejected its final offer by a forty-five-to-one margin, IBP locked them out and unilaterally lowered wages to between $7.45 and $7.60 per hour. In addition, IBP wanted a two-tier wage system whereby new hires would permanently earn less than current employees doing the same work, a profit-sharing formula in place of the existing pension plan, worker copayment of medical plan premiums, and the elimination of daily overtime pay after eight hours. The last item was a major concession for the union because workers had come to depend on extra earnings from work shifts that typically ran beyond eight hours.

The union had its own demands, but local officers refused to hold a strike vote or take other action preliminary to striking because they feared IBP would try to break the union with nonstrikers. (Employers cannot legally hire *permanent* replacement workers during a lockout). Chief among the union's demands were wage and benefit increases and improvements in job safety.

Job safety was becoming increasingly controversial in IBP and the industry. Since 1983, according to congressional sources, meatpacking had had the highest number of injuries and illnesses of any industry in America, higher even than coal mining and construction, and nearly three times that for all manufacturing. The average number of workdays lost because of injuries had risen in meatpacking from 137 per 100 workers in 1973 to 238 in 1986, a period in which production employment fell and labor productivity rose in the industry (*Chicago Tribune,* Oct. 23, 1988, sec. 3, p. 5). Table 9.2 shows injury rates in meatpacking compared with those in other manufacturing industries.

IBP's thirty-five to forty injuries a year per hundred workers was above the average even for meatpacking and second highest in the industry after Morrell

Table 9.2. Injury and illness rates per 100 full-time workers, by industry, 1975–87

Industry	1975–79 Total injuries	1975–79 Lost workdays	1982–87 Total injuries	1982–87 Lost workdays
Total private sector	9.3	62	7.9	64
All manufacturing	13.2	83	10.6	81
Meatpacking plants	33.8	204	33.0	253

Source: U.S. Department of Labor, Bureau of Labor Statistics, *Occupational Injury and Illness Incident Rates by Industry,* various years.

(U.S. Congress 1988:8–9). A former worker and union official at Dakota City described plant conditions:

> Workers stand in a sea of blood. Others work in cold temperatures of 25 to 35 degrees with powerful fans blowing cold air down on them. Nearly all the workers stand on treacherously slippery floors covered with animal fat buildup which provides a situation where workers slip frequently. The working conditions are cramped. Lines of people stand side-by-side with approximately 48 inches of working space between them.
>
> Nearly all of the workers . . . wield razor-sharp knives and power tools, frantically working at a pace, trying to keep up with a relentless chain bringing production to the work station. Because of the breakneck chain speeds and close working conditions, workers frequently are accidentally stabbed by their neighbors who are also trying to keep up with the chain speed and tolerate the close working conditions (U.S. Congress 1987, pt. 1:9–10).

According to testimony from injured workers and outside safety experts, IBP plants were accident-prone because of their accelerated line speeds and the constant pressure on workers to meet arbitrary production quotas; their use of untrained, inexperienced, and often young workers; and the company's failure to maintain equipment properly, to identify hazardous machinery and other dangerous conditions, to give workers proper safety equipment and clothing, and to prepare and train employees in safe work practices.

Following the December lockout, the parties did not discuss plant safety or any other issues for more than a month. IBP then announced it would withdraw its final offer. It also reminded the union that the last time workers had struck over a wage freeze they had lost the strike and had had to settle for a pay cut. Union members nevertheless rejected the offer by the same wide margin. At the next bargaining session, two months later, the union again turned down IBP's December offer.

STRIKE SETTLEMENT AND OSHA VIOLATIONS

Two weeks later, IBP reopened the plant and offered the workers their jobs under new terms. Included among the offers was an annual cash bonus to compensate for the wage cuts IBP made after locking them out in December. Plant officials said they no longer feared worker support for in-plant actions by the union.

When few union members reported to work, IBP began hiring workers from other parts of the country, many of them laid-off and displaced factory workers and immigrants, especially Cambodians, Laotians, and Vietnamese.[8] At that point, apparently feeling it had little more to lose, the local went out on strike. It asked to continue bargaining, but IBP refused to revise its last offer.

The lockout/strike had lasted more than seven months in July 1988 when IBP made a settlement offer to the union. The offer was more favorable than might have been expected given that IBP was able to get limited production in Dakota City by using supervisors and replacement workers and may have been able to make up any difference in output from its nonunion plants. Not only did IBP drop its most objectionable demands, but in doing so it meant the company also abandoned any plans it might have had of letting the strike run for a year and then trying to oust the union in a decertification election. Union decertification would have been a logical strategy for IBP because only replacement workers would have been eligible to vote. (On the importance of this requirement, see chapter 3 in this volume.)

Why did the company make an offer that virtually assured it continued union representation? Apparently it was in response to a developing crisis involving allegations that IBP had violated federal job safety laws and the possibility that corporate officials could go to jail for having given false testimony at congressional hearings into the latter (*Sioux City Journal*, July 22, 1987, A1). Employers must record and keep for statistical and inspection purposes a log of all occupational illnesses and injuries that occur in the workplace and that result in lost time or restricted work duty. This record is called the OSHA 200 form. Beginning in 1981, OSHA policy was to exempt specific plants from comprehensive or "wall-to-wall" inspections by agency officials if their self-maintained logs showed that their injury rates were lower than the national average for all manufacturing. Thus, if an inspector came into a plant prepared to do a full-scale investigation but was shown an OSHA 200 form with below-average injury rates, he or she normally terminated the visit. This arrangement naturally provided an incentive for employers to underreport injuries so as to avoid close plant inspections.[9]

In August 1985, Local 222 requested OSHA-related data from IBP in connection with grievance bargaining at the Dakota City plant, a right it had under federal labor law. IBP responded with a list of some 1,800 injuries sustained in the plant during a three-month period earlier that year. The following March, an OSHA inspector appeared at the plant to investigate a specific complaint and was shown an OSHA 200 form listing 160 recordable injuries for the same time period. The significance of this difference is that a rate of 160 cases is below the national average and the plant would therefore have been excluded from a comprehensive OSHA inspection, whereas a rate of 1,800 cases is above the average and the plant would therefore have been eligible for a "wall-to-wall" inspection. Confronted with the below-average numbers in March, the OSHA inspector had confined his investigation to the original safety complaint—a minor mechanical problem that the company already had remedied.

Area OSHA officials had not made a comprehensive inspection of the Dakota City plant since 1983, although they had visited occasionally in response to specific union and employee complaints. One such visit had occurred in December 1986 (the month IBP locked out union workers) following complaints concerning plant accidents in November. At that time, IBP had denied OSHA access to the plant and its safety records, however, on the grounds that the OSHA officer had said he wanted to conduct an open-ended investigation rather than one restricted to the areas cited in the UFCW's complaint. In addition, company officials later said they believed the union was trying "to use OSHA to put pressure on IBP to reach an agreement in the labor dispute" (U.S. Congress 1987, pt. III:35).

In October 1986, the union again requested data on plant safety, this time in connection with upcoming contract negotiations. The company, apparently unwittingly, gave the union the data sheets on which 160 injuries were reported, which, of course, contradicted the logs it had given the union in 1985, listing 1,800 injuries. Union officials said nothing publicly about the difference until the lockout occurred, at which time they charged IBP with keeping and submitting false OSHA 200 records. The company denied the charges and insisted its injury levels were below average for the nation and the industry.

In January 1987, the union followed up its accusation with a formal complaint to OSHA in which it documented the wide discrepancies in IBP's data sheets and indicated that IBP was keeping two sets of OSHA logs, one that accurately recorded legally reportable injuries in the Dakota City plant and another that omitted all but a fraction of them. Injuries not recorded in the second log included knife cuts and others requiring surgery, especially several involving workers' hands and backs. When questioned, IBP rejected the union's charges, calling them "a blatant lie" (BNA 1987a:73).

OSHA meanwhile had subpoenaed IBP and was able to gain access to the plant the same day the union filed its complaint. Two weeks earlier, however, IBP had assembled a team of up to fifty regular and temporary employees who worked almost nonstop revising the safety records at the Dakota City plant, going back several years. Some of these employees later gave uncontested affidavits that they worked twelve-hour days transposing information from dispensary logs to official OSHA 200 logs. A former custodian said he had been told to dispose of "garbage bags full of employee medical records" that had been culled from one of the plant's two dispensaries by the special work team, which included company nurses (complaint affidavit 6, William J. Schmitz, business agent and CEO, Local 222, to John Pendergrass, assistant secretary for occupational safety and health, U.S. Department of Labor, May 6, 1987).

Thus, when OSHA officials examined the plant records on January 22, they found yet a third OSHA 200 log, this one listing 992 injuries. The next day Senator Edward Kennedy, chairman of the Senate Committee on Labor and Human Resources, called a press conference to publicize apparent widespread underreporting of plant accidents by large corporations, including IBP. This was a few days before striking Dakota City workers rejected the demand by IBP that they accept a pay cut rather than a wage freeze. A week later some four hundred strikers marched on the plant to demand that the company release its medical records. The request was denied, perhaps because the special team was busy at the time reconstructing the plant's injury records.

The IBP case also came to the attention of Congressman Tom Lantos (D-Calif.), chairman of the House Government Operations Subcommittee on Manpower and Housing. Lantos scheduled a committee hearing on the case for March 19, 1987, which as it turned out was four days after the union struck the Dakota City plant and one day after it filed a second complaint with OSHA. This time Local 222 alleged that IBP was systematically "ignoring basic safety precautions" in its efforts to increase productivity and asked the agency to make a comprehensive inspection of the plant. Again IBP dismissed the union's request as being part of its "media blitz" to improve its strike position. A company spokesperson emphasized that IBP's superior productivity did not come "at the expense of worker injuries" (BNA 1987b:253).

Company officials declined to appear at the Lantos committee hearing in March. It was "inappropriate" to do so, they said, because OSHA already was investigating company records and the UFCW simply wanted "to advance its collective bargaining and nationwide organizing strategy by involving OSHA in the UFCW's labor dispute with IBP" (U.S. Congress 1987, pt. 1:4). Nevertheless, committee members heard former IBP employees describe the unsafe working conditions in the Dakota City plant and the gory injuries they had sustained while working there. They also heard testimony and saw evidence that employee turnover rates in the plant were as high as 100 percent annually (IBP later conceded that the rate was at least

65 to 75 percent); that IBP did not maintain a safe plant and equipment or train and prepare workers for the high-speed, dangerous jobs to which it assigned them; and that the company tolerated continually high rates of apparently preventable illnesses and injuries.

Even more relevant to the committee's mandate to oversee government operations was union evidence that IBP had illegally kept two sets of health and safety records during 1982–86. Union officials showed that IBP had reported that the lost-time injury rate at its Dakota City plant was 20 percent during 1982, well above the national average and high enough to have triggered a comprehensive safety inspection. In 1985, however, IBP had reported that the rate was 8 percent, well below average, despite faster chain speeds and an estimated 23 percent increase in the total number of injuries and illnesses—recordable and nonrecordable. The union also submitted copies of the complaint and affidavits it had filed with OSHA regarding IBP's alleged underreporting on OSHA's 200 forms (U.S. Congress 1987, pt. 1:18–38). After receiving this evidence and hearing the grisly testimony from injured IBP workers, and in view of IBP's refusal to appear that day, the committee scheduled a second day of hearings in May and subpoenaed Robert Peterson, chairman and CEO of IBP, to appear.

Meanwhile, IBP increased its demands for concessions from the union at Dakota City. The parties met for the third time since the lockout but were unable to make any progress toward ending the stoppage. A few weeks later, management added a second shift to the processing line, a signal to the strikers that it was getting enough replacement workers to operate the plant and, by implication, that it was under no pressure to settle the dispute.[10]

On the day of the second committee hearing, the union publicly disclosed its evidence that IBP had underreported OSHA injuries at Dakota City and two other plants. Peterson labeled these charges "sensational and blatantly untrue." Further, he and other company officials steadfastly denied that IBP kept dual records. They admitted the firm had prepared a second OSHA log during the fall of 1985, but, they explained, this was only because the union's August 1985 request for data had alerted safety officers to the fact that the company had been recording all visits to the Dakota City plant's two dispensaries, including hundreds of minor cases that required only first aid or observation, instead of just those resulting in lost time or light duty, as required under OSHA regulations. Thus, they explained, the list of 1,800 injuries given to the union in 1985 was not an OSHA log but a dispensary list, and any discrepancies between the second and third lists, showing 160 and 992 injuries respectively, were caused by confusion among company officers, supervisors, and health-care professionals about OSHA's reporting requirements (U.S. Congress 1987, pt. 2:25–32).[11] Given IBP's adamant denial, the committee adjourned without resolving the matter.

Two weeks later, Peterson and the others followed up their testimony with sworn statements reiterating their denials and further explaining the ambiguous events. That seemed to settle the question. The union meanwhile filed its third complaint with OSHA, this one over IBP's refusal to release the medical records requested by the locked-out employees in February. It also filed charges with the state of Nebraska alleging that IBP knowingly failed to file "first-injury" reports in compliance with state workers' compensation law, which at the time was a criminal misdemeanor in Nebraska.

On June 19, a few days before IBP announced that production at the struck Dakota City plant was back to normal, the Lantos committee received a letter in which the union presented further evidence that IBP gave false testimony at the May hearing. The committee did not include that letter in its published proceedings or its final report, but presumably it consisted of affidavits and documents contradicting company statements. Lantos scheduled a third committee hearing for September 21, 1987, and again subpoenaed company officials to appear.

IBP and the union met twice more in early July but resolved nothing. A few days later, the Lantos committee contacted OSHA regarding the charges against IBP. Then, on July 10, several weeks before the committee's third hearing, Peterson wrote to Lantos and disclosed that IBP representatives had in fact given false testimony at the May hearing and had made false statements in their follow-up declarations. He insisted that they had done so unintentionally and unknowingly. He admitted, however, that he and the others had told the committee the company kept only dispensary records during 1982–86 but noted that at the time they did not know this was true of only the "north" dispensary—and not the "south"—and then only during 1984 and 1986. "I now understand that for at least some of the years in question," he wrote, "separate OSHA No. 200 Logs did exist" (U.S. Congress 1987, pt. 3:12). There was no intention to deceive, he assured Lantos, and both sets of logs had been available to OSHA inspectors if they had recognized the difference and requested to see both.

Peterson also explained why the company gave conflicting data sets to the union. He claimed that in 1985 IBP gave the union daily logs from the Dakota City plant's north dispensary for an earlier three-month period. Then, in October 1986, the union asked for data covering 1982–86. Because the only north dispensary records available for 1984 and 1986 were daily logs, a company task force, under the direction of the medical supervisor, prepared "new OSHA No. 200 Logs which listed only OSHA recordables for 1984 and for year-to-date 1986" (U.S. Congress 1987, pt. 3:13). The company also gave the union existing OSHA 200 logs for 1982, 1983, and 1985, as well as OSHA recordable injury logs from the plant's south dispensary for the years 1982–86.

The confusion leading to the false statements arose, he said, because IBP employees who prepared the information for the company's presentation before the committee "thought we were being asked to testify only about logs existing for the year 1986 at the North Dispensary, the dispensary which was the focus of the UFCW allegations, when they advised me that a separate OSHA No. 200 Log was created only after the UFCW requested access to such a log on October 14, 1986" (U.S. Congress 1987, pt. 3:14). As soon as the mistake was discovered, he wrote, the correct information was compiled and the committee advised.

Less than two weeks after Peterson's admission, OSHA proposed a record $2.6 million fine against IBP for willfully underreporting some 1,038 job-related injuries and illnesses at the Dakota City plant during 1985–86. IBP representatives continued to minimize the importance and severity of the charges, dismissing them as "paper work issues" between it and OSHA and as an "indication of inconsistent enforcement by OSHA and the Labor Department, and of unclear legal requirements." But OSHA's director, who at the committee hearing in March had defended the agency's policy of basing plant inspections on self-maintained employer OSHA safety logs, now called the case "the worst example of underreporting of injuries and illnesses to workers ever encountered by OSHA is its 16-year history" (*Los Angeles Times,* July 22, 1987).

These events put IBP executives in danger of going to jail. Willful underreporting is one of three offenses punishable under the federal safety and health law by both fines and imprisonment, and in fact OSHA was said to be studying the possibility of pursuing criminal proceedings in connection with IBP's violations. In addition, the day that OSHA announced its finding against IBP, Congressman Lantos threatened to charge company officials with perjury for giving false testimony to his committee. Citing Peterson's letter of July 10, Lantos said he was skeptical of IBP's explanation of the events. "Considering the time and the effort that IBP devoted to preparing for the May hearings as well as reviewing the hearing transcript afterwards, it boggles the mind to believe that IBP officials did not know that there was a second log presented to OSHA inspectors for review," he said. "This ominous sequence of events strongly suggests the possibility of perjury" (*Sioux City Journal,* July 22, 1987, A1). Lantos later dropped the perjury charge, although he sternly rebuked IBP executives in the committee's final report for permitting the conditions that led to IBP's inaccurate recordkeeping and reporting (U.S. Congress 1988:14–22).

The matter of government intervention was settled when IBP signed an agreement with OSHA and the UFCW to establish a comprehensive ergonomic program of accident prevention in all its plants (U.S. Occupational Safety and Health Review Commission, *McLaughlin* v. *IBP,* Stipulation and Settlement Agreement, Docket no. 87-1242, Nov. 23, 1988). Under the agreement, IBP did not admit violating federal safety laws but for the first time acknowledged ergonomic stress in its disassembly processes and vowed to attack the problem with union cooperation and participation. Specifically, it promised to maintain accurate OSHA records, to redesign jobs and track workers to minimize cumulative trauma disorders (CTDs), and to detect and treat such injuries in all its plants. It further agreed to complete the experimental program in two years at Dakota City and have it implemented elsewhere. Some fifteen union members were to monitor the program and a joint plantwide committee resolve disputes. Finally, new workers would be trained to recognize job hazards and avoid injuries common to the industry, especially CTDs (IBP Health and Safety Agreement 1988).[12]

The striking Dakota City workers meanwhile had voted to accept the company's contract offer even though it contained givebacks and other objectionable features. It called for a two-tier pay structure in which wages for returning union members would remain frozen until April 1990 and then be raised $.15 an hour. New hires would start at $6.00 an hour and receive $.15 increases every three months up to a maximum wage level well below the average for regular workers, thus making wage differentials among workers doing the same jobs a fixture in the Dakota City plant. The union did retain daily overtime pay after eight hours, secure a pension plan to begin in the final year of a four-year contract, and win improvements in medical benefits.

Government and Community

As a corporation grows and prospers it interacts constantly with community and public officials. IBP's relations in this regard have been heated and controversial. These tensions reflect a conviction among IBP executives that their work is hampered by unions, citizens groups, and government regulators on the one hand and by worker and public mistrust of IBP on the other.[13] IBP plants and offices bring jobs, payrolls, and tax revenues to communities and states and its manufacturing operations vitalize local and regional economies, but they also bring structural and economic problems associated with "boom-town" expansion (Bluestone and Harrison 1982, chap. 4). Several years after IBP reopened a closed Rath Packing plant in rural Iowa, for example, the town remained divided over the relative costs and benefits of the thirteen hundred new jobs in a community of fourteen hundred. Some people, such as a local banker who pointed to the new businesses, residents, and roads, supported the expansion. Others—dismayed by the increased crime, housing shortages, racial incidents, environmental hazards, and social welfare problems stemming from IBP's transient (almost 100 percent annual turnover) and low-wage ($5.00 to $10.00 an hour) work force—regretted the change (*Wall Street Journal,* April 3, 1990, A1).

DECISION TO LOCATE A NEW PLANT

IBP has been criticized for getting states and communities into bidding wars for its plants. Indeed, by 1987, it had received $9.1 million in state of Iowa grants and low-interest loans, more than any other company doing business in the state. Now it was asking for $2.1 million more to build a 1,200-employee pork plant in Manchester, Iowa (population 4,900). But business leaders, community groups, and elected representatives were divided. Economic developers and some government officials supported the incentives as a way of generating new payrolls of up to $20 million a year. They noted that IBP had already used three state subsidies to create jobs and doubtless would do so again.

A statewide activist group and residents in areas adjacent to and down river from the proposed site opposed the new plant. IBP, they revealed, had been fined the maximum amount by state authorities for sewage disposal violations at the former Rath plant and was the state's most frequent and heavily fined violator of truck-weight and speed laws. They also charged that replacement workers at the Dakota City plant were burdening social service agencies in Sioux City, Iowa, which were already strained by high unemployment and the cost of thirty to thirty-five new cases daily from among IBP's workers (*Sioux City Journal,* April 11, 1987, B1).[14]

The economic case against IBP was that it generated uneven, negative-sum growth. Specifically, critics charged that it contributed to excess industry capacity in Iowa and decreased net jobs and payrolls. Further, they claimed, it bought available livestock and forced established packers to close plants that paid farmers higher prices and workers better wages and benefits than IBP. They said its low wages and unsafe job conditions discouraged residents from taking (or keeping) the new jobs. IBP plants instead attracted disadvantaged workers who often arrived in town without resources and later had to apply for public or private welfare assistance because IBP's wages were low and rents and other costs in the area were high. These workers would then quit working for the company and ask for assistance to leave town. In addition, unsafe conditions in IBP plants strained Iowa's workers' compensation system.[15]

Democratic legislators sided with the opponents as part of their own campaign against the Republican governor's business incentive program. They claimed that payrolls from one thousand jobs at the former Rath plant—which IBP had reopened nonunion at a base wage of $5.50 an hour—were offset by the related shutdown shortly afterward of a nearby Hormel pork plant that had employed the same number of workers at a base wage of $10.00 an hour. They predicted that the Manchester plant would give IBP more than 60 percent of the state's hog market and eventually force the shutdown of two remaining union plants in eastern Iowa (*Des Moines Register,* March 15, 1987, A1, A12; June 14, 1987, F1; *Sioux City Journal,* May 28, 1987, A1). These concerns were reinforced by simultaneous plant shutdowns and construction throughout the region. At least twenty-one beef plants had been closed in Iowa and Nebraska during 1969–89, displacing an estimated seven thousand workers, while IBP and other major packers continued to build new ones (*Los Angeles Times,* April 22, 1990).

The community controversy appeared to influence IBP's plant location decisions. For example, in response to what a company press release called "Iowa's negative business environment," IBP chose to build a $9 million hide tannery in Illinois rather than refurbish an abandoned tannery across the river in Iowa, as originally announced. Now IBP said it was considering putting its new pork plant in Illinois rather than Manchester. This prompted accusations by Iowa's economic development advocates that the Democratic legislature and opposition citizens groups were jeopardizing the state's efforts to attract industry. The controversy also polarized pro and con forces in Illinois, raising the same arguments for and against IBP that were being made in Iowa.

IBP eventually announced that it was suspending plans to build the plant in Manchester, citing the actions of opposition groups. "Misleading statements and outright lies spread by these people have created an unpleasant environment and damaged relations in the Delaware County community that may never be repaired," a company official explained. IBP had not abandoned the possibility of locating in Manchester entirely, he added, but warned that "given the cost of continuous delays at Manchester, we must seriously examine some of the alternative proposals presented to us." Among others, Waterloo, Iowa, officials wanted IBP to locate there. Altogether, seven thousand workers had lost jobs in Waterloo when Rath declared bankruptcy, and ten thousand more had been displaced when John Deere closed a local farm machinery plant. IBP located the pork plant in Waterloo (*Des Moines Register,* Jan. 8 and 24, 1988).

THE COMMUNITY AND THE STRIKE

Before bargaining in Dakota City in 1986, the UFCW tried to exploit public mistrust of IBP. Sensing the union needed community support to win a strike against IBP, officers of Local 222 prepared far differently for bargaining than they had in the past. First, they were determined to avoid the violence that had marred earlier disputes and may have turned public opinion against the union. Second, they wanted a better-informed and trained union leadership this time. Thus, long before the contract expired, they began offering steward training programs and sessions sponsored by their national union on "how to deal with the media." And with help from the Food and Allied Service Trades Department of the AFL-CIO, they researched IBP's corporate structure, performance, and behavior. Third, and finally, they tried to raise the local's visibility in the community through frequent contacts and involvement with other unions, the United Way, schools, churches, and farm and minority groups.[16]

Local actions during the subsequent lockout and strike reflected the benefits of this preparation. Union officials organized weekly rank-and-file rallies and press conferences, produced videotapes and interviews for the news media, opened regular membership meetings to the press, effectively exposed IBP's plant safety and environmental violations, and staged well-publicized demonstrations at corporate meetings, testimonials, and other formal events involving IBP officers and board members and those of Occidental Petroleum, its parent company. Rank-and-file members formed local and traveling "truth squads" to present the union's case to the media, public officials, and citizens groups such as environmentalists that otherwise might have been at odds with organized labor. A major objective of all these activities was to discredit IBP's corporate reputation at a time when it was deciding whether or not to put substantial resources into consumer-branded products to offset the declining sales of red meat (*Sioux City Journal,* Dec. 7, 1986, A16).

Local 222's strategy seemed to improve its tactical position. Local politicians and churches claimed neutrality in the dispute, but as time passed and the union effectively portrayed the company as unwilling to settle, they became more critical of IBP and publicly asked it to bargain in good faith. Shortly after the lockout, the Sioux City Council narrowly rejected a motion requesting that IBP reopen the plant and continue bargaining, but at a later meeting packed with striking workers, the council reversed itself and sided with the union (*Sioux City Journal*, April 14, 1987, A16). Local churches also supported the workers implicitly by calling on IBP to show moderation in the dispute; during the lockout, for example, a well-known Nebraska minister challenged IBP to reopen the plant and resume negotiations with the union while she and other ministers took up positions inside to ensure that workers did not damage equipment or sabotage production. An IBP spokesperson "respectfully declined" her offer as "simplistic" (*Sioux City Journal*, Jan. 6, 1987, A1).

The local also received direct help from other unions and UFCW locals. Rank-and-file unionists joined demonstrations and marches in Sioux City and Dakota City. Elsewhere around the nation they supported Local 222's traveling "truth squads," especially when IBP representatives tried to recruit replacement workers in out-of-state communities. They also kept the local in contact with opposition citizens groups in cities where IBP was considering locating plants. More generally, they made the lockout and strike at Dakota City symbolic of the defeats organized labor was experiencing across the country, thereby making Local 222's struggle that of every union activist. But the most successful and important part of the UFCW's community effort was in the area of plant safety. It was this issue that appears to have forced IBP to settle the strike, implement a companywide safety program, and recognize the union voluntarily at other plants—all of which would have been unimaginable at the outset of the strike.[17]

Institutional Interpretation of the IBP-UFCW Confrontation

Labor and community relations in meatpacking changed when powerful firms introduced innovative strategies aimed at reducing their operating costs through the use of cheap labor, intensified production methods, and public subsidies they could use to locate and relocate their slaughter and processing operations. IBP was the industry innovator in this regard. It initiated the low-wage, boxed-beef strategy that came to dominate meatpacking. Beginning in the 1960s, it pursued a corporate strategy that differed fundamentally from the postwar "grand design" of the industry's lead firms. IBP reduced labor standards, curbed unions, and developed production methods that enabled it to intensify work effort in the disassembly process and save on packaging and shipping costs. The low-wage option was especially strategic because of the relatively low-tech, labor-intensive production technology of meatpacking. IBP expanded operations rapidly on the strength of this strategy and soon became the nation's largest beef packer.

The excess production capacity in beef packing that resulted forced many old-line firms out of slaughtering and others to imitate IBP if they hoped to survive. Formidable rivals such as ConAgra and Excel also emerged. They too organized high-volume, low-cost production operations; shipped boxed-beef products directly to major retail and wholesale buyers; and tried to hold down direct labor costs and increase labor productivity by weakening and curtailing unions. In some respects they appeared to beat IBP at its own game. In any event, the overall effect of industrial restructuring and of the social and political changes sweeping the country in the 1980s was that it brought hourly labor back into competition in meatpacking after decades of union and government regulation. Under these conditions, it was not long before the bad labor standards drove out the good.

High labor costs had not been a source of operating difficulties for packers before IBP's entry into the industry. Foreign competition was virtually nonexistent, and consumers were not yet aware of the health dangers of eating too much red meat. IBP talked forever about the low-wage competition, but, in fact, it was the competition. Wage reductions were not forced on it by low-wage competitors and falling product demand but were integral to its corporate strategy. As it came to dominate larger and larger market shares in the industry, its wage policy created competitive labor pressures that, combined with the weakening effects of conglomerate takeovers on the industry's traditional leaders, gave the old-line firms no choice but to abandon the postwar system of union recognition and bargaining. High labor costs had not driven up the cost of beef production and, hence, of beef prices and consumption, thus reducing the demand for production labor. Instead, IBP had made high-wage union labor both a target and a casualty of its competitive strategy to dominate the industry. The erosion of jobs and standards in meatpacking therefore was less the result of downward-sloping labor demand curves than of one firm's pursuit of market shares through, among other strategies, the use of cheap labor.

Werner Sengenberger (1990) argues that industrial restructuring that erodes previously high labor standards produces uneven economic growth and benefits some groups at the expense of others. In this case, intensified competition favored consumers and large producers at the expense of production workers and small firms. Consumers gained from the greater variety and convenience of the new beef products and perhaps also from the reduced costs of production, depending, of course, on the extent to which product innovation and lower production costs enabled new industry leaders such as IBP to increase profit margins.

The gains to consumers and large firms came at the expense, however, of those who disassemble, package, and distribute red-meat products, those caught between powerful, demanding employers on one side and adverse political trends and economic conditions on the other. Hourly workers who stayed in the industry lost real earnings, job security, and good working conditions; those who were forced out may have lost even more, given that traditionally good jobs in durable manufacturing were being replaced by less desirable ones in services, retail trade, and light manufacturing. Finally, the new job holders in meatpacking, especially displaced factory workers, inexperienced youths, and immigrants, had few employment alternatives and therefore had to accept meatpacking jobs at whatever terms were offered. Under these conditions, such workers were undoubtedly the least committed to the company and the community—and in turn were the least valued and rewarded by them. Whether individual communities were net gainers or losers in this transformation is a subjective judgment that would have to be made by the residents themselves.

Like labor, midwestern communities have been vulnerable to corporate demands because they need jobs, especially in manufacturing. They can be made to give financial subsidies in return for corporate promises to locate (or relocate) production operations to their communities. These subsidies often are supplemented by state-government tax abatements, job-training grants, and other incentives. Controversial business-community relations can occur as a result. Corporations may demand too much, fail to honor previous commitments, or bring undesirable practices, such as environmental offenses, with them. Sometimes they get into bitter labor disputes and then try to enlist the support of citizens and public officials on the grounds that the other side is jeopardizing local payrolls and revenues.

IBP's community relations have been heated. Its plants bring jobs and industry to midwestern towns but also social, environmental, and labor problems. Consequently, many residents in meatpacking states such as Iowa, Kansas, and Nebraska question whether economic growth has been more even and positive as a result of IBP's various plant locations and relocations than it would be in their absence. Thus, the residents of Manchester, Iowa, voiced enough concerns about the net cost of having an IBP plant that the company decided not to go ahead and locate there; those of Waterloo, Iowa, by contrast, put aside such reservations and offered IBP an attractive incentive package, perhaps because Waterloo was more determined to replace the production jobs that had been lost when Rath Packing closed its plant there than Manchester was to acquire meatpacking jobs.

During the Dakota City lockout/strike, the union exploited the public animosity toward IBP. Local sentiment appeared to favor the strikers and their union, apparently in response to IBP's aggressive, uncompromising behavior in the dispute and to a disturbing history of company-union confrontation at the plant. The union's "truth teams" were reportedly successful in minimizing IBP's recruiting efforts in cities outside the Midwest, and once the stoppage became widely publicized, impressive demonstrations of union solidarity occurred in Dakota City and elsewhere. It was as if union workers and the public concluded simultaneously by the late 1980s that organized labor was not a primary source of the country's economic problems as previously perceived. Even so, it is questionable whether improved community relations and union solidarity in the absence of the OSHA controversy would have been enough for the union to win the strike.

Health and safety became a key issue once labor became competitive again. When packing plants began competing on the basis of labor costs and work intensity, job safety was bound to deteriorate, especially under the lax enforcement policies of the federal government during the 1980s. And with high unemployment rates in midwestern manufacturing during the first half of the decade, replacement workers became plentiful during strikes. IBP took advantage of the new environment. It got the Dakota City union into a lockout/strike situation and then hired replacements whom it could use to defeat or even destroy the bargaining unit. The company could do this because a sizable and segmented labor force was available, that is, large numbers of disadvantaged workers who were willing to work at low wages regardless of their job skills and experience. Segmented labor markets generate pools of labor willing to work at any wage, especially during economic downturns when there is no alternative employment or private or state-provided means of support (Wilkinson 1983a).

Events in meatpacking and specifically at IBP demonstrate the importance of new employer strategies in product and labor markets. IBP rose to the top in the 1960s and 1970s in part because it was able to avoid and weaken union standards and gain access to disadvantaged workers in segmented labor markets. Having cut labor costs below industry averages in the 1960s and battled unions to a standstill in the 1970s, IBP naturally looked to labor as a source of further cost reductions in the 1980s when it experienced product market difficulties and the presence of formidable rivals. It was a sound business strategy insofar as labor market conditions gave IBP greater leverage with its workers than the company had with any other factor of production or any other buyers and sellers involved in its operations. IBP might have achieved all of its objectives in the labor market had it not invited government surveillance of its plants by mishandling its safety records and not alienated community opinion through its location decisions. In this regard the IBP case illustrates the interaction between corporate strategies and the decline of unions and labor market standards in the 1980s.

Chapter 10
SUCCESSFUL LABOR-COMMUNITY COALITION BUILDING

Bruce Nissen

WHEN CORPORATIONS ENGAGE IN behavior that is disadvantageous to the interests of workers, unions, or communities, the latter frequently are unable to defend their interests. Both the legal system and the collective bargaining system in the United States are structured so that corporations, and only corporations, have the legal and "legitimate" right to make decisions regarding plant closings or product relocations. Further, there are few regulations concerning the terms under which companies may receive public subsidies or governing their labor relations, and these are weakly enforced.

It appears, therefore, that corporations have the upper hand in their dealings with employees, unions, and local communities. The cases discussed in this book further confirm this impression. Given this power imbalance, and the global nature of many of the economic forces encouraging companies to close plants, break unions, and abuse public subsidies, one might conclude that local unions and communities are powerless to take effective measures in self-defense.

Such a conclusion is an exaggeration, however, and reflects a partial misunderstanding of the forces at work. It is true that unions and local communities are disadvantaged in the competitive struggle to ensure their interests. But it is not true that they are powerless. Furthermore, the changes in national public policy needed to correct the imbalance are not likely to occur unless widespread nationwide labor and community activism at the local level forces the issues onto the national agenda.

The following two sections of this chapter detail two victorious local-level campaigns in which a labor-community coalition, the Calumet Project for Industrial Jobs, won clear-cut victories in challenging corporate behavior that was harmful to a local community's interests. One campaign involved an issue normally considered primarily a union concern—loss of jobs caused by a department relocation. The other involved an issue usually considered a community concern—abuse of the local tax-abatement program. In both cases victory was possible only because an effective alliance was formed between union and community forces. Following the case studies, I draw some conclusions about both the importance and limitations of labor-community coalitions such as the Calument Project for Industrial Jobs.

LaSalle Steel Campaign

LaSalle Steel Corporation is a subsidiary of the Quanex Corporation, a producer of steel specialty products in Houston. LaSalle's main facility is located in Hammond, Indiana, in the northwest corner of the state, next to Gary. Employment in 1990 was approximately 350; the workers were represented by the Progressive Steelworkers of Hammond, an independent union based in this one mill.

In early 1990, the union struck over pension issues and company demands to retain a two-tier wage scale. The strike lasted thirty-two days and ended with neither side claiming victory.

In the summer, rumors spread throughout the mill that the turning and grinding department might be relocated to an unknown destination. Since the grinding department was a high value-added part of the mill, the rumors were unsettling to the union. Approximately fifty direct jobs were at stake, but the union feared that if the "heart of the mill" was removed, the remaining three hundred jobs would probably follow, jeopardizing the entire mill.

In late October, the Calumet Project for Industrial Jobs (see chapters 1 and 7) held a training session for northwest Indiana trade unionists to assist them in spotting the "early warning signs" that a plant shutdown may be imminent. (Feekin and Nissen 1991). Five leaders and activists from the Progressive Steelworkers attended this session, at which the rumors were brought out and discussed.

In early November, the union joined the Calumet Project and began joint strategy meetings to develop a campaign to save the department and possibly the plant. Three union committees were quickly formed to carry out the campaign. A corporate research committee conducted research into both the parent and subsidiary to discern company strategy and identify points of corporate vulnerability. A work force committee developed and distributed a survey to the entire membership to collect information about the members' community and religious ties, for outreach purposes. Finally, a workplace committee collected information on suppliers, customers, products and product mix, workflow, and so on for use in the campaign. These three committees functioned well for the duration of the campaign.

Repeated union inquiries prompted Richard W. Treder, a vice president of Quanex and the plant manager of LaSalle, to write a letter to union president Zed Rixie confirming rumors that a relocation of the department was being considered. The letter emphasized that no final decision had been made; its main request was that the union cease all further agitation and minimize its concern until a final decision was reached.

On November 26, Rixie responded with a letter requesting that the union be integrally involved in all future meetings and consultations on the potential move because "the union has information, expertise and opinions which would be of value to the company in making the decision." At approximately the same time, the union gave a practical example of such information and expertise. Going over Treder's head, union representatives wrote a letter to Carl Pfeiffer, the CEO of Quanex, in which they exposed bogus quality records Treder had been using to discredit the grinding department: work of poor quality, which had been contracted to an outside contractor, was erroneously being charged to the grinding department.

These two letters began a pattern that was to characterize the entire campaign: union insistence on involvement in all company deliberations, coupled with circumvention of Treder to the highest levels of the corporation whenever Treder took an action detrimental to the workers. A third element, intense publicity, was soon to be introduced.

On November 30, as required by the union contract, Treder sent an official notice to the union indicating that a tentative decision had been made to close and relocate the grinding department. He said a final decision would be made within thirty days.

On December 5, the union called a press conference that was widely covered by the media; the threat of job loss from the proposed move was detailed. An angry Treder accused the union of "sensationalizing the situation by going public before a meeting between the company and the union could be arranged" (Viani 1990:2). "I'm a little disappointed they've gone public with this," he told the press (*Gary Post-Tribune*, Dec. 7, 1990).

At a private meeting held subsequently with the union's leaders, Treder berated them for applying public pressure on him, claiming that it was a big mistake. He disclosed that the alternative site being considered for the grinding department was in Frankfort, Indiana, approximately 110 miles to the south. A $2 million piece of equipment was scheduled for delivery in August and would augment the department, wherever it was located. Treder refused to share with the union a cost-comparison study of Frankfort and Hammond. More significant, he withdrew the thirty-day notice, claiming more time was needed (*Hammond Times,* Dec. 9, 1990).

On December 10, the union and the Calumet Project held a public meeting that was attended by more than eighty workers and community supporters. The mayor of Hammond, city councilmen, a state senator, and the local congressman's aide all attended and pledged full support for efforts to save jobs. There were differences in approach, however: the congressman's aide and the state senator vowed to intervene to prevent state money from being used to entice the grinding department to Frankfort, but the mayor tried to outbid Frankfort by offering tax abatements and subsidies without conditions. In letters to each of the political figures involved, the union set out a series of conditions, or "strings," to be attached to any public subsidies LaSalle might receive in connection with new capital investment. Both the union and the Calumet Project wanted to emphasize that a "bidding war" was unacceptable.

At this point the union chose to take no further public action, despite urging by the Calumet Project to press forward. Several members of the union's executive board feared that "pushing too hard" would be "going too far" and lead to counterproductive results. Membership involvement activities, such as sending a plantwide "Christmas card to Treder with a message," were also rejected. The three union committees continued to meet, although the union had lost its initiative.

The union was pushed back into action on January 25, 1991, when Treder sent another official notification of a tentative decision to move the grinding department. This time, the new "short-cuts" line was also included in the moving plans. A final decision would be made within thirty days.

At a subsequent private meeting with the union leadership, Treder supplied data purporting to show that LaSalle would save a net $600,000 to $700,000 if the grinding department was moved to Frankfort. Even though transportation costs, installation costs, initial capital costs, and the like were much higher at Frankfort, he claimed a large savings from the use of nonunion labor at approximately half the wages at Hammond. Treder told the union leaders it was up to them to come up with ways to save the equivalent of the $600,000 to $700,000 savings if they wished to keep the department. The union interpreted this as a call for massive concessions, backed by the threat of relocation.

The union immediately went into action; plantwide educational sessions for all three shifts drew more than two hundred workers, many of whom signed up to work on a job-preservation campaign. Next, the union and the Calumet Project developed a six-point strategy: (1) reject all concessions; (2) expose glaring errors and inadequacies in Treder's figures; (3) develop a counteranalysis, based on available information; (4) call for a neutral party to do a feasibility study of how jobs could be retained in Hammond; (5) "persuade" or induce LaSalle to cooperate with those doing the feasibility study and postpone making a final decision until the study is completed and studied; and (6) put unrelenting pressure on Treder through media exposure, political pressure, and religious community support.

This strategy was carried out with a perfectly orchestrated series of actions during the month of February. At least two to three times each week of that month, Treder was hit with entreaties from community and religious figures, interventions from public officials, widespread media coverage, and communiqués to people over his head.

The entire series of events is too detailed to relate here, but three incidents were especially significant. The first such incident was that one of the two major daily newspapers in the region printed an editorial in favor of the union–Calumet Project proposals and chided the company for its lack of loyalty. Entitled "Big Pay Cuts Aren't the Best Way," the editorial stated:

> The company has told the Progressive Steelworkers Union the company could save $600,000 to $700,000 a year by moving its grinding operation, which employs 54 people when operating at full capacity, to Frankfort, in central Indiana.
>
> LaSalle said it will keep the grinding operation in Hammond only if union concessions make up the money the move would save.
>
> Union members fear if the grinding operation is moved, the rest of the Hammond plant's operations may follow suit. Then about 340 jobs, not 50, would be at stake.
>
> LaSalle apparently has forgotten loyalty is a two-way street.
>
> The employees have been loyal to the company, but the company is ready to run off to Frankfort and leave its Hammond workers in the dust. . . .
>
> The company should consider a feasibility study for expanding operations at the Hammond plant. The Calumet Project for Industrial Jobs, a grass-roots labor group, and the union want a third party to examine ways to keep jobs at LaSalle's Hammond plant. . . .
>
> LaSalle should be loyal to the workers who have worked hard and been loyal to the company. LaSalle should be eager to help its workers by agreeing to further study of how its goals can be achieved (*Hammond Times,* Feb. 14, 1991).

The second blow to the company's public image occurred when the Calumet Project charged, through major stories in the local media, that

LaSalle had applied for and received a $97,500 tax abatement in 1989 *for the "short-cuts" equipment it was now planning to move to Frankfort.* A Calumet Project spokesperson called this a "clear betrayal of public trust": "They took tax abatement money for installing equipment and now they're threatening to pull it out. This is not a show of good faith to the community. . . . They promised to retain jobs and these are the very same jobs they're moving" (*Hammond Times,* Feb. 15, 1991). Treder was so angry at the press coverage at this point that he refused to speak to reporters anymore.

Finally, a third event further thwarted the moving plan. Robert Markovich, the president of the Hammond City Council, under pressure from the union, the Calumet Project, and community allies, wrote a letter to the Frankfort City Council requesting that LaSalle not be given public subsidies "in an attempt to lure jobs from one Indiana community to another" (Feb. 25, 1991). The same letter stated that "any sort of 'bidding war' between our two communities would not be fruitful."

Thomas McDermott, the mayor of Hammond, wrote a similar letter to the mayor of Frankfort, Don Snyder. Snyder told the press he "sympathized with the Hammond officials": " 'We're certainly not going to keep anybody out that wants to come here,' he said. 'But I can't see us offering incentives for them to come here because I wouldn't want that to happen to any of our companies,' " (*Frankfort Times,* March 2, 1991).

In addition to these three major developments, a whole series of smaller events occurred. The union sent documents to all public officials in the area detailing the situation, calling for an impartial third-party feasibility study, and inviting each official to meet with the union and, they hoped, endorse its position. Letters from the Calumet Project went to all the top officials of Quanex and to the president of its bar group (which included LaSalle) detailing the case for a feasibility study and inviting their endorsement of the union plan.

Treder attempted to counterattack through a letter to all employees, retirees, and others in which he made the case that relocation could actually be in the overall best interests of remaining employees and the company. He also wrote a letter to the editor of a local newspaper replying to a critical editorial, but he clearly was losing the battle for public opinion. Virtually all interested parties were now aligned against him.

The original plan to relocate the grinding department was now facing serious obstacles, including the following:

- strong union hostility and opposition; labor relations in the plant were poor, and the union was actively campaigning against the proposed move;

- community opposition, spearheaded by the Calumet Project and including all public expressions of community will;
- active intervention and opposition from all concerned public officials at all levels of government;
- prolonged and unfavorable publicity, with the near certainty of more unfavorable publicity should the plan be carried out;
- doubts about LaSalle's motives and behavior by the public officials at the intended site in Frankfort; and
- repeated circumvention of Treder and communiqués to higher corporate officials, alerting them to scrutinize his conduct closely on this matter.

Any plan to implement the relocation was problematic at this point. The plan had contained several risks from the start; now it faced added problems that were certain as a result of the union–Calumet Project campaign.

On March 5, Treder released a written statement to the press reversing LaSalle's previous plan. His prepared statement cited a worsening economy and lower corporate profits as the reason for the change:

> While the new turning equipment we have purchased is scheduled for delivery in August, we are not at present making plans to install it anywhere, because demand for the product has dropped and prices are soft. . . . If the situation improves and the decision is made at some later date to install the new equipment, we would prefer that it be located in Hammond (*Hammond Times,* March 6, 1991).

Clearly, this change in plans was a face-saving gesture. The new equipment would be installed somewhere; *where* had nothing to do with the stated reasons. Local news reporters were unable to get an explanation from Treder, who refused all contact with the press.

Lynn Feekin, director of the Calumet Project, expressed to the press the sentiments of those active in the campaign: " 'It shows that workers doing outreach to public officials and the community can have an impact,' said Feekin. . . . 'I think the union can be proud they were active in this, instead of passively reacting to whatever happened' " (*Gary Post-Tribune,* March 6, 1991).

A few months later Treder quietly retired. He was replaced by a plant manager who went out of his way to emphasize his desire for cooperative relations with the union, the press, and the community. In the fall and winter of 1991, the new equipment was delivered and installed in the Hammond plant. Employment expanded.

The union won on all fronts. Not only were the jobs of the fifty workers saved, but the entire plant was made more secure through new investment. And the source of the antiworker and antiunion behavior, Richard Treder, had been deposed.

Tax-Abatement Victories

In the 1980s, property tax abatements were used increasingly in Indiana as economic development tools. In northwest Indiana, it appeared that virtually all investment projects undertaken by existing companies and all plants in new locations were being granted tax abatements as a matter of course, regardless of need or of benefits back to the communities. Since the taxes thus abated were shifted onto local homeowners and other property holders, they represented a "hidden" subsidy from the public to the favored businesses over which there was little oversight regarding either the process or the outcome.

In the late fall of 1989, the Calumet Project began investigating how well the program was working in the city of Hammond. Research revealed that the program was being grossly abused: in 1988, Hammond had granted tax abatements totaling more than $15 million (given out over the life of the abatements) to sixteen companies. On the "statement of benefits" application, the recipient companies had promised to create 804 new jobs but had actually created only 74. Furthermore, there had been no public participation in the tax-abatement process before the abatements were granted and no oversight or accountability once the abatements were given.

The Calumet Project released the results of its study and began a public campaign to demand accountability in the tax-abatement system. Working together with a Hammond church-based community organization, the Interfaith Citizens Organization, the Calumet Project held public meetings, canvassed Hammond neighborhoods, obtained union endorsements, appeared on the local radio station, brought residents to city council meetings, and engaged in similar actions to bring about a change.

An ordinance was drafted requiring fuller information from companies requesting abatements, public hearings on all such requests, annual reports from recipient companies to the city on their compliance with their job-creation promises, and hearings or possibly fines for companies that failed to keep their promises. The city's Department of Economic Development and the Hammond Chamber of Commerce lobbied heavily against the ordinance. Opposition by the Chamber of Commerce was decisive for a majority of the city council, which did not want to antagonize the city's business community. At the same time, numerous small businesses in the city supported the measure because they perceived both the tax-abatement program and the chamber to be under the thumb of a few large businesses that received virtually all the abatements.

A stalemate throughout the spring of 1990 was broken when a compromise was written that modified the requirement that a company had to provide detailed and "private" financial information as part of the application process. All the other provisions remained intact. With the Chamber of Commerce opposition neutralized, the Hammond City Council passed the measure on June 27, 1990. The Republican mayor of Hammond subsequently vetoed the ordinance, however, labeling the requirement of corporate accountability in exchange for public subsidies a "police state" measure. He was overriden eight to one in the city council along straight Democrat-Republican party lines.

This was a significant victory for the Calumet Project and its allies, but the ordinance fell far short of the ultimate objective: effective sanctions against companies abusing the system. The ordinance could not be stronger because state law did not allow municipalities to rescind tax abatements or fine noncomplying companies.

The Calumet Project therefore convinced legislators to sponsor state legislation that would (1) require applying companies to provide more information, (2) require annual reports on job-creation performance, and (3) allow local governments to terminate abatements for noncomplying companies and reclaim lost revenues from companies that severely abused the system by shutting down operations or removing abated equipment.

As a regional group, the Calumet Project was limited in its ability to influence state legislation. Nevertheless, it lined up solid support from northwest Indiana legislators and marshalled a coalition of the state AFL-CIO, the Indiana Citizens Action Coalition, the two districts of the United Steelworkers of America, and the United Auto Workers in the state in support of the bill. All of these groups had full-time lobbyists who were in charge of shepherding the bill through both houses of the legislature. The bill passed the Democrat-dominated House but was unable to get a committee hearing in the Republican-controlled state Senate. A key provision was added to a bill on enterprise zones, however, which the Republicans wanted passed, mandating that municipalities rescind a tax abatement if companies do not deliver the jobs they have promised. This bill, House Enrolled Act no. 1155, was passed and became law.

In the fall of 1990, the Calumet Project began a study of northwest Indiana tax-abatement programs for cities other than Hammond; it showed that the program had achieved dismal results in them as well. Gary, Indiana, was chosen as the target city for a model ordinance.

In the early spring of 1991, a concerted drive was begun in Gary to pass such an ordinance. From the beginning, leading trade unionists from union locals operating in Gary, community activists, retirees, academics from the local branch campus of Indiana University, and church leaders were contacted for their input on the ordinance and their help in conducting a campaign to pass it. Strategy meetings were held every two to three weeks in the Gary public library throughout the spring and early summer.

The campaign that evolved had many facets to it. Church outreach centered on five of the most active and/or important churches in the city. An insert for Sunday church bulletins informed congregations of the issue and invited participation. A petition of support also received limited distribution through church networks. Despite these efforts, however, the churches did not play a leading or important role in the campaign, only a passive and mildly supportive one.

Senior citizens were another target audience, and several retirees ended up playing important roles in the committee guiding the campaign. Retirees' clubs at a local synagogue and a union local had speakers at their meetings; support for the campaign was nearly 100 percent.

Union outreach was uneven but effective in that several union leaders became actively involved. Leading union officers in the Hospital Workers Union and a large United Steelworkers local at U.S. Steel took important leadership roles in the campaign and were able to use their institutional affiliations to good effect with the Gary City Council.

Outreach was also attempted to community groups, but for the most part little effective contact was made despite attempts to include local block clubs, the Urban League, and so on. Individuals affiliated with various community groups did participate, but the organizations did not do so formally.

Two neighborhoods in Gary were canvassed, and hundreds of signatures were obtained in support of proposed changes. Calumet Project spokespersons and concerned union officials and community residents appeared on a local radio talk show with a wide audience in the black community. A public meeting on April 11 began the process of putting direct pressure on the city council and the mayor to support changes. Although all these public officials were invited to the April meeting, only one city councilman and a representative from the mayor's office attended. The issue was not considered seriously by most city councilpersons at this time.

The outreach and publicity, though limited, were having an effect, however. A meeting on May 22 drew five city councilpersons and the director of the mayor's Office of Economic Development. At the meeting, the president of the city council expressed his anger with the Calumet Project and its allies for using public approaches to attain their goal; he heatedly proclaimed that they should have dealt privately with the city council. Nevertheless, he indicated that he felt pressure from his constituents to support the ordinance.

At the same meeting, the director of the Gary Office of Economic Development attempted to derail the drive for the ordinance by claiming that everything being asked for was already standard operating procedure. When challenged on this, he was unable to substantiate his claims, but he did try to confuse the Gary citizens in the room by continually talking off the subject and claiming that all the requested procedures were already being followed.

In June, a delegation of Gary citizens and Calumet Project representatives met with the mayor of Gary. He was completely noncommittal but promised to study the matter of the ordinance further and get an opinion from the city's attorney. At this point, the outcome of the campaign was still uncertain. Public sentiment, as evidenced by call-ins to the city's radio talk show, public willingness to sign petitions of support, phone calls and talks with councilpersons, and so on, was clearly in favor of the ordinance. But support was "soft": churches were only passively, not actively, involved; the number of petition signatures had not reached a thousand because the number of canvassers and circulators of the petition was confined to an activist core; citizens supported the idea, but public meetings drew considerably fewer than one hundred.

Reaction from the city administration was cool. City council members were still split despite definite gains since the days when there was almost universal skepticism. At least three members of the nine-member council were now supportive, but many others had not been forced by citizen pressure to commit themselves unequivocally.

In the meantime, the Calumet Project had been meeting with community activists to clarify the exact provisions of the ordinance. Through a process involving four or five meetings, the members of the Calumet Project and its allies came up with the following provisions:

- a "sunshine provision," whereby companies applying for a tax break must notify their employees (and union if there is one) that they are applying;

- a requirement that both the applicant and any parent company provide detailed financial information (sales, profits, net assets, capital investments, debts, capacity utilization, and so on);
- a requirement that the applicant list all previous public subsidies received, together with the benefits promised and the benefits actually delivered in exchange for the subsidy;
- a requirement that the applicant list and describe construction jobs created, permanent jobs gained and permanent jobs lost, and changes in job conditions and wages for existing employees as a result of the proposed development;
- a requirement that abatement be denied unless the jobs created are at or above the prevailing wage for that job category, as defined by U.S. Department of Labor statistics (minor exemptions for up to two years for new business startups with fewer than fifty employees);
- a requirement that tax abatement be denied unless the company provides a full health-care package to all employees working more than twenty-five hours per week (exemption for up to two years for employers with fewer than ten workers);
- a requirement that no abatement be granted for the mere *relocation* of jobs, rather than their creation;
- a fine of up to $2,500 for falsification of information in applying for or reporting about a tax abatement;
- termination of the abatement if the recipient company fails to create the promised jobs, moves the equipment, or does not live up to its commitments made in the process of obtaining the abatement.

These are very strong provisions, probably unequaled anywhere else in the nation. Yet they were eminently sensible to the unionists and Gary citizens who formulated them. They were simply requirements for proof of need for a public subsidy; public return (net job gain, well-paying jobs, and health care) for a public investment; and measures to stem the loss if the public gain did not materialize. As Calumet Project vice president (and United Steelworkers Local 1014 vice president) Willie Moore told the press: " 'There have been a lot of companies that have promised a lot of jobs, but they've come back (after receiving the tax break) with four or five jobs. Once they get the money, there was no way you could make them do anything' " (*Gary Post-Tribune*, Aug. 21, 1991).

Although sensible from a citizen's point of view, such strong conditions for public subsidies violate the conventional business climate–oriented wisdom of economic development officials. Desperate for jobs, such officials tend to take a completely subservient attitude toward businesses seeking a public subsidy. To them, a "good business climate" means maximum public assistance and few questions for, and even fewer regulations concerning, businesses asking for tax abatements. This is undoubtedly the reason the mayor and the Gary Office of Economic Development were so cool about the ordinance. The desperation and subservience to potential corporate recipients of public aid that underly the business climate approach are especially apparent in a city like Gary, which has chronic high unemployment and an inadequate tax base to fund its social services.

Nevertheless, the city council ultimately passed the ordinance. Supporters consistently attended city council meetings and spoke in favor of it. No organized vocal opposition materialized; tales of past abuses of the tax-abatement system made it hard even for businesses to oppose the ordinance for fear of appearing to be in favor of corporate irresponsibility. First and second votes in July and August were followed by a unanimous 9–0 vote in favor at the September 3, 1991, city council meeting. The mayor signed the ordinance into law on September 16.

It remains to be seen how well the ordinance will be enforced. Preliminary indications are that the Gary Office of Economic Development is unlikely to implement the full provisions unless pressured to do so by the labor-community coalition, which won passage in the first place.

Analysis of this extraordinary feat should include at least two more points. First, victory probably would not have been possible if there had been major organized opposition from business. Unlike the Hammond Chamber of Commerce, the Gary chamber does not play an active role in political affairs; it generally confines itself to social and ceremonial matters. To some degree this is a reflection of the weakness of the business community in the city. In this case, the biggest corporate powers in Gary—U.S. Steel and the local public utility—stayed out of the matter, for whatever reason.

Second, mobilization of the community and union forces necessary to win was possible only because there was well-conducted research exposing the problem, careful framing of the issue, and careful timing of the campaign; the Calumet Project had credibility in the region; and community leaders surfaced who were willing to lead the fight in the black community of Gary. Significant problems in any of these areas could have killed the campaign.

Conclusion and Analysis

The main lesson from these cases is that victories *are* possible for unions and local communities struggling with large corporate entities, even in today's changing environment. This is true in struggles over such traditionally union concerns as job loss (LaSalle Steel) and such traditionally community concerns as the abuse of public subsidies to corporations (Gary tax-abatement system).

Labor-community coalitions at the local level are both powerless and powerful, depending on the issue and the circumstances. They have very little power over the global economic forces leading to increased capital mobility. They also have extremely limited power to influence national public policy or even public policy in a neighboring state or region. Since many of the forces subjecting local unions and communities to economic insecurity and potential corporate abuse originate far beyond the locale of the union local or the community, they have many limitations on their power to respond.

Workers, unions, and communities are completely powerless, however, only if they fail to organize themselves to exert power in those areas where they do have influence. Most unions and communities are relatively powerless because they do not have an equivalent to the Calumet Project organizing in their midst.

Local labor-community coalitions can exert power when certain conditions are present. First, the issue must be such that the market forces on the corporation are not so overwhelming as to mean there are virtually no alternative courses of action. Despite the usual claim of companies that their actions are simply necessary responses to pure market conditions, there are frequently alternatives. In the LaSalle Steel case, both retaining and relocating the grinding department were possibilities; the savings from the relocation were uncertain, so that the move was loaded with risk. Further, the savings were not of such a magnitude that they meant overall success or failure for the entire company. In the case of the Gary tax-abatement system, the magnitude of the taxes abated was not so great that massive responses in the form of changed investment behavior occurred. Thus, there was a lot of room for maneuvering by the municipality in attaching conditions to its public subsidies without any large apparent harm to its economic development.

Second, the corporation (or corporations) whose behavior is being challenged must be susceptible to influences that can be controlled by a local labor-community coalition. This usually means that in some way the corporation must be dependent on the goodwill of local public officials or the local congressperson, on its good relations locally with the press, on its nonantagonistic relation with its local employees, or on its positive relations with the local community and/or the public. Clearly, LaSalle Steel was dependent on several of these groups, making it vulnerable to a well-run campaign by a labor-community coalition. Likewise, companies desiring tax abatements need the approval of more than one of the above groups; they can therefore be made subject to requirements of good "corporate citizen" behavior if they wish to feed at the public trough. The Gary tax-abatement ordinance shows how direct and powerful such requirements can be.

Third, the union and the community must overcome any existing divisions within their ranks and organize to struggle for their common interests. Only rarely can this be accomplished. The existence of the Calumet Project, with its history of organizing and struggling against plant closings and for labor-community influence in economic development decisions, made a critical difference in northwest Indiana. Had it not existed, neither of the victories related in this chapter would have been possible. The cumulative impact of past Calumet Project campaigns now means that public officials and other important players quickly side with popular struggles against corporate abuses. This is not absolute, of course: politicians in northwest Indiana, as elsewhere, still follow the corporate business climate agenda in their daily conduct, *but* they do have to deal with new items on the agenda because of sustained pressure from labor and community forces. The behavior of public officials in both the LaSalle Steel campaign and the Gary tax-abatement campaign illustrates this.

Absent these three conditions, corporate interests will inevitably win out in any clash with labor and community interests. Nonetheless, local labor-community coalitions can win important victories and can play an important part in revising the terms of the national debate over public policy on labor and economic issues.

Chapter 11
THE IMPACT OF CORPORATE STRATEGIES

Charles Craypo and Bruce Nissen

THIS CHAPTER REVIEWS THE significance of the case studies described in this book in an effort to interpret the impact of corporate strategies in response to changed industrial environments on jobs, labor relations, and competition among communities. In the first part, we summarize the themes that emerge from the cases and identify the dominant patterns of interaction among corporations, unions, and communities that result. In the second part, we consider alternative explanations of the decline of industrial unions and communities. We accept as the most realistic approach the corporate hegemony interpretation that national and global corporations control local situations. Corporations do this through their ability to grant or deny production activity, that is, jobs and revenues, and in this way determine labor relations, manufacturing operations, and the outcomes of community economic development activities.

The conditions within which corporate hegemony arose in these cases included the identification of corporate interests with the "common good" of communities; overcapacity in manufacturing, both nationally and globally; the misplaced self-confidence of unions and union workers following years of successful bargaining and strike experiences; and the secrecy of operations and centralization of administrative authority that characterize large corporations.

In the third part, we describe the erosion of the post–World War II industrial and labor relations system as illustrated in these cases and the responses of unions and communities to the failure of their postwar grand designs to prevent the loss of good manufacturing jobs, declines in living standards and working conditions, and threats to community prosperity, stability, and quality of life. Union-management cooperation is broadly advocated as a way of preserving unions and making employers more competitive, but the employers in these cases showed little interest in genuine cooperation even after they had reduced union power to the point that workers and officers were prepared to do whatever was necessary to save jobs. The cases also show that a business climate approach to community economic development carries hazards and uncertainties and cannot be relied on alone to restore previous levels of manufacturing employment and fiscal stability. Current and future scenarios of relative union-management power project further erosion in the ability of unions and collective bargaining to determine labor processes and labor standards.

The chapter concludes with an exploration of the new forms of institutional power without which unions will not regain the ability to protect their members' economic and job interests and without which communities cannot ensure their inhabitants adequate services and social amenities. These forms of institutional power involve fundamentally new approaches to understanding and managing industrial change; new tactical responses to aggressive corporate behavior that threatens established local conditions and standards; and combined efforts to combat mutually damaging trends and outcomes. This section cites examples of each of these new forms of power: "stakeholder power," to oppose corporate hegemony through the use of productive capital assets; union "corporate campaigns," to oppose local actions by otherwise unaccountable and unapproachable authorities at national and international corporate levels; and union-community "coalitions," to oppose the damaging consequences of absentee corporate ownership.

THEMES AND PATTERNS

Several themes emerge from these cases that reflect the industrial experiences that took place in the Midwest during the period of the 1970s and 1980s. Arranged roughly in the order in which they occurred, they are as follows:

1. During the Golden Age of midwestern manufacturing, labor and management accepted the institutional legitimacy of each other and settled their immediate differences over terms and conditions of employment at the bargaining table. This was possible because negotiations were confined to narrowly defined economic issues and job conditions and involved generally stable shares of a constantly growing pie, rather than such fundamental operating decisions as the location of the plant, competitive strategies and labor's stake in the enterprise, and who would suffer the consequences of a shrinking pie. For a period of time, therefore, manufacturers and communi-

ties grew and prospered side by side, secure in an implicit understanding that neither would directly challenge or damage the other.

2. Manufacturing firms found themselves in a changed environment in the 1970s. Competition was becoming more intense, and the threat of permanent job losses from nonunion operations and foreign imports had made unions ineffective at the bargaining table and in strike situations. Competition created two kinds of firms: the disadvantaged and the opportunist. The former responded defensively; they tried to cut operating costs to recover or offset declining market shares, especially direct labor costs because labor was the most vulnerable factor of production, or they tried to divest out of existing product lines and into new ones. Or, as in the case of U.S. Steel in the early and mid-1980s, they did both (Nader and Taylor 1986: 3–61). Opportunist firms responded proactively by taking advantage of the changed environments to go after the market shares of declining firms. The cases included here involved both strategies.

Firms could take advantage of union weakness in one of two ways. They could drive down labor standards and try to regain whatever control over the production process they had conceded in previous union contracts, and perhaps even establish union-free operations. Or they could encourage a cooperative, institutionally equal relationship with unions as part of a larger strategy of strengthening their product market positions. The companies discussed in this study chose the former approach.

3. Firms also adapted their community relations to suit their strategies. They exploited the fears and insecurities associated with deindustrialization by auctioning manufacturing jobs to those communities willing to bid the highest. The incentive packages the firms obtained included direct and indirect financial subsidies, and the firms were promised favorable business climates. In this way, corporations relocated production from one place to another. It is uncertain how many of them would have relocated in the absence of community subsidies, but the effect in any event was to sever the relationship between businesses and communities that existed under the grand designs of the postwar period.

4. The postwar system was disrupted by production relocations from high-wage union to low-wage nonunion plants; contract concession demands on unions and hourly workers under the threat of job and revenue losses; and pressure on communities to offer business subsidies in return for job retention or creation, to lower the "social wage" in the community, and to support firms in confrontations with unions and community activists over corporate policies and actions. Workers, unions, and communities were totally unpre-

pared for these corporate initiatives against them. Instead, they responded in the conventional ways associated with postwar business-union and business-community systems.

5. Union leaders initially tried without success to maintain the old standards and systems through direct job actions and limited, strategic contract concessions. Union members during this time often denied employers' threats and demands until it was too late—on the grounds that even though both plant and equipment were aging, and their contracts called for high wages and benefits, they could not be replaced because of their skills and experience. By the second half of the 1980s, however, neither unions nor workers were skeptical in the face of such threats. They now tried to devise more innovative (if not always successful) strategies, and by the late 1980s and early 1990s, as evident in some of the case studies, organized labor sometimes was able to adjust to the new environment.

6. Initially, communities responded by extending almost indiscriminately tax abatements, tax-exempt development bonds, and other direct and indirect business subsidies to manufacturers in hopes of retaining and creating jobs. In the Midwest and throughout the nation, communities accepted the wisdom of establishing a good business climate of maximum subsidies and minimum social costs to convince firms to locate in their communities instead of others.

Like the experiences of unions and union workers, however, those of communities did not always match their expectations, and by the second half of the 1980s, cities were suing companies on grounds of noncompliance to recover monies they had given them. Nonetheless, community leaders still seemed prepared to engage in bidding wars for the industrial jobs they desperately needed to replace those they had lost or were in danger of losing. Thus, when local unions decided to join or cooperate with community coalitions, they often found themselves allied primarily with community activists rather than with city officials.

The pattern that follows from these themes is that changes in the manufacturing environment have left local unions and governments uninformed, inessential, and unarmed and therefore defenseless against pragmatic employer strategies to make them bear the brunt of the costs of adjustment to the new productive system.

Explanations for Decline of Unions

Explanations for the recent decline of unions divide into those that view unions essentially as sellers of labor in competitive markets and those that view them in the context of power struggles over income distribution and workplace control. As indicated in chapter 1, the first explanation focuses on the adverse effects of high union wages on the costs of production and, hence, on employer competitiveness. Therefore, the argument goes, if employers try to weaken and defeat unions, or to avoid them altogether, it must be because the high costs of union labor are jeopardizing the employers' continued survival. If union members are losing jobs and unions generally are in decline, it must be because they have priced their employers (i.e., themselves) out of product markets.

The contrasting view holds that other forces determine the market success of firms and that employers resist and threaten unions because they want uncontested power over their workers and production processes and over the allocation of revenues and earnings. Although these cases contain elements that support both explanations, on balance, the findings support the relative power model.

CONVENTIONAL EXPLANATION

None of the firms discussed in these cases got into trouble in its product market because unions and collective bargaining forced its labor costs to be high relative to those of its competition. Some negotiated with strong unions and had high direct labor costs, but there is no evidence that either reason was the major reason for market problems. It is therefore unlikely that firms having operating difficulties could solve them simply by reducing their labor costs through contract concessions or by relocating production to nonunion, low-wage locations. Indeed, Jeszeck notes that the bulk of the union concessions Goodyear demanded at Akron during 1971–76, by its own estimates, would have saved the company some $2.4 million per year, at a time when foreign-made radial tires were threatening traditional markets and other companies were spending $75 to $100 million to build or expand a single tire-building facility.

At most, union labor was one factor among many in the competition equation and not the most important by any means. Most of the market difficulties the firms faced could be traced either to mistakes the firms made in product design and marketing or to long-term neglect of manufacturing plants and equipment—or to some combination of these conditions. When the firms finally responded to product market problems, however, they did so in ways that included either union concessions or union avoidance. More revealing, no firm discussed in this volume offered to join with its local union in a cooperative effort to improve product quality and design, to develop new product lines, or to lower production costs. They chose to weaken or escape unions; they were not forced to do so by competitive forces.

The new corporate strategies the firms employed were defensive in nature to the extent they were forced on the firms by the similar strategies of competitors and offensive to the extent they were initiated by (often new) firms that saw opportunities for profitable expansion in the changing industrial environment. I-R/Torrington, American Crane (Amhoist), and IBP saw opportunities in the changed labor market—that is, gains to be made from relocating operations from union to nonunion locations. IBP, for example, adopted a deliberate policy of nonunion, low-wage production as part of its larger strategy to displace old-line beef packers that had both unions and higher wages. IBP's policy included taking advantage of increasing unemployment levels and the availability of large pools of disadvantaged labor. The company hired hundreds of displaced factory workers and Asian immigrants as replacement workers in the Dakota City lockout/strike. Torrington and Amhoist simply relocated production to nonunion southern plants.

An implicit assumption of the conventional analysis is that market competition forces firms to be efficient and that this efficiency results in new products, new methods of production, and optimal organization of human resources within firms. The collective effect is dynamic, prosperous growth. A striking feature of the firms in these cases, however, was that all of them, to one degree or another, achieved short-term gains as a result of industrial decline, not economic growth and industrial innovation. In other words, they were "rent-seeking" rather than "entrepreneurial" capitalists, in the business of running down and disposing of capital assets, eroding labor standards, and diverting public monies to themselves, instead of in the business of creating new products and production methods and progressive labor relations and human resource systems. As a group, they took more out of the nation's productive system than they put in. To that extent they were far from being the agents of Joseph Schumpeter's "gale of creative destruction."[1] The unamity of their behavior suggests that rent seeking has been an important element in the decline of midwestern manufacturing unions and communities and has introduced destructive corporate objectives and behavior in place of creative pursuits.

An extreme example of such behavior and its adverse effects occurred after International Harvester sold Wisconsin Steel to EDC. The owners of Envirodyne organized EDC in such a way as to absolve Harvester of its financial obligations to veteran production workers when the mill was closed and to allow Envirodyne to escape pension and other costs associated with the closing. At the same time, EDC made windfall profits on Wisconsin Steel's back orders—without regard for quality, customer satisfaction, future orders, or new product development. Envirodyne had little to gain in the way of economic rent by ousting the union in that the independent local at Wisconsin Steel was so traditionally dependent on management and internally divided along racial and ethnic lines that it posed no threat to Envirodyne's rent-seeking strategy.

Two alternatives to the conventional explanation are strategic choice and corporate hegemony. Kochan, Katz, and McKersie (1986) explain the transformation of American industrial relations in the 1980s as the interaction between "deep-seated environmental pressures" of an evolutionary nature and "organizational strategies" in response to these pressures. The outcome reflects "strategic choices and values of American managers, union leaders, workers and public policy decision makers," although management strategies currently dominate industrial and labor relations (4–5). When all the parties understand these interactions and the consequences of their choices, they are better able to shape events to their mutual benefit and that of the society generally. In practice, this requires some form of worker participation and union cooperation.

Critics contend that the strategic choice model confuses choice with reactive behavior. Firms currently have less control over product markets than in the past; they therefore must adopt cost-cutting measures, including cutting labor costs. In other words, strategic choice theory adds little to neoclassical micro theories of price, output, and employment under competitive market conditions (Lewin 1987).

Others argue that the model does not lend itself to conventional scientific confirmation or rejection. Using domestic airlines as the test case, Leslie Nay (1991) evaluated three alternative explanations of collective bargaining outcomes: economic environment, strategic choice, and institutional factors. She concluded that strategic choice and institutions alone have little explanatory power but that when they are combined with economic variables they explain airline union concessions in the early 1980s.

Paradoxically, both the Kochan, Katz, and McKersie model and Nay's empirical findings are consistent with the conclusions in this book. The firms discussed here did have choices and did dominate labor relations. At the same time, no single variable fully explains the process that leads to this outcome. It is the *interaction* of economic, strategic, and institutional variables that determines who gains and who loses in the new industrial relations. Outcomes reflect the contours of power among affected groups. At one level the interaction involves uneven struggles between labor and management over distributional and industrial rights issues; at another level the struggle forces them to cooperate to maximize product output and quality. It is within this context that firms, unions, and communities choose their responsive strategies. Employers have more leverage against labor and local governments than they do against their customers and other businesses. That they can be expected to use this power does not bode well for the labor participation and cooperation that Kochan, Katz, and McKersie and others advocate. A critical prerequisite of a successful union-management partnership is a strong, independent union (Kochan, Katz, and McKersie 1986: 179–82: Marshall 1992; Kelley and Harrison 1992), but it is less likely to be realized in a time of union decline.

STRATEGIC CHOICE AND CORPORATE HEGEMONY

Another alternative explanation to the conventional analysis is that with the changed environment of the 1970s and 1980s, large corporations have regained their historic hegemony over local industry and have used that power to try to reestablish control over labor standards and economic development. The new approach to doing business with local unions and governments is so unlike the postwar approach that it represents nothing less than a grand design for dominance in labor and community relations. This does not require state-corporation conspiracy; it simply represents a culmination of individual corporate strategies in response to changing environments and the new opportunities they offer.

Four conditions were paramount in shaping the changed environment and helping firms reestablish dominance: (1) The production overcapacity that resulted from new forms of product competition gave firms—whether or not they were directly responsible for the additional capacity—the power to deny jobs, payrolls, and tax revenues to workers and communities, while diverting and defusing real and potential opposition by identifying the interests of the firm with those of others having stakes in the enterprises. (2) The economic stability and prosperity of the postwar decades, combined with the institutional successes of unions during those years, left union workers and industrial communities unprepared for and therefore unable to respond effectively to corporate mobility and demands for concessions and subsidies. (3) Corporate secrecy and centralized authority made firms unaccountable to local unions and communities and allowed them to withhold information at critical junctures. (4) A rightward shift occurred in the political climate, which made public policy indifferent or hostile to unions and collective bargaining.

The unfavorable political trends and public policies that undercut the labor movement in the 1980s are documented and analyzed elsewhere (Clark 1989; Goldfield 1987; Amott 1984; Moody 1988; Nissen 1990b).

Overcapacity. Production overcapacity plays a key role in these outcomes. It is a natural consequence of technological change and capital investment. It is also, ironically, a source of power for corporations in dealing with unions and communities because it turns an apparent source of weakness into a source of power—the power to deny jobs to workers who negotiate high wages and to deny revenue to governments that permit high social wages. Overcapacity drives traditional producers either to upgrade or to close existing plants, which in turn gives the companies enormous leverage in bargaining with unions and governments by legitimizing the companies' threats of what will happen if they do not get what they want.[2]

New plants are constantly coming on line with state-of-the-art production methods, making plants of older vintage relatively inefficient and, unless they are retrofitted, eventually obsolete. The result is that oligopolistic employers, such as the Akron tire producers, Torrington, the old-line meatpackers threatened by IBP, the industrial sweetener subsidiary of Standard Brands, International Harvester, and Amhoist, experienced intensified competition in their production processes. This prompted them to consider investing in new and refurbished plants and equipment so that they could restore their previous market shares and meet their target rates of return on owners' equity. But renovation and expansion produce industry overcapacity, which in turn holds down prices, so firms cannot achieve target profits through capital restructuring alone. They therefore choose to confront organized labor in order to reduce unit labor costs even further and in that way increase their per-unit profit margins. This is one reason many firms simultaneously build new plants *and* try to weaken or eliminate unions and collective bargaining.[3]

Existing production facilities become "disadvantaged" because firms choose to upgrade or maintain the competitive efficiency of their capital stock by investing elsewhere. Disadvantaged plants are abandoned as new product lines and production technologies become available and as the gains from low-cost labor pools and government deregulation and direct subsidies outweigh the costs of relocation. And, as the Akron and Torrington cases show, union concessions and improvements in productivity are ineffective in situations in which an individual plant no longer fits into the larger scheme of things.

Mobility in the context of changing technology and strategic investment gives firms the opportunity to implement product changes and relocation strategies without interference. The union and the community are powerless to reverse the process because the company already has taken steps to make the plant expendable, and, because corporate restructuring is done in confidence, in most instances workers, union officials, and community authorities do not know that the plant is doomed.[4] Absent sufficient information, unions and communities easily fall into a false sense of security, either because they believe they are in no danger, or, like several of the local unions in the cases, because they know they are in danger but think they have the power to prevail. In the cases here, union workers believed that labor relations was on a business-as-usual basis and that any union-management differences were limited and immediate in nature and could be handled through the customary bargaining compromises.

Common good. The firms in these cases succeeded in part because they were able to identify their own interests with those of the common good, no doubt aided by community acceptance of the business climate approach to economic development. Everyone favors more manufacturing jobs in a community; everyone is therefore under political pressure to do whatever the firm says is necessary to create or retain such jobs. It does not matter whether the concessions demanded actually are necessary from the operational perspective of the firm. The effect is to equate its objectives with those of the larger community. Workers and unions are depicted as being self-interested at the expense of the common good. This divides union and community stakeholders. It also isolates groups and organizations that might want to oppose corporate demands, insofar as the risks they take in questioning or challenging the businesses are too great.

Labor and community groups that tried to pressure the Akron tire companies, GM, I-R/Torrington, and Standard Brands into disclosing corporate strategies, reversing plant-closing decisions, or making financial settlements to compensate those who were adversely affected by their decisions received scant and only temporary support from their communities. Their actions were seen as threatening future job-creation and retention efforts. A striking example was the unwillingness of economic development officials and public officials to question or pressure the owners of the Blaw-Knox foundry into revealing their plans.

The effect of such intransigence is that unions and communities become divided from within and from one another. Workers become disillusioned because local unions are powerless in the face of corporate mobility and unaccountability and international unions either appear disinterested in the workers' predicament or become involved after it is too late to save jobs. Usually all that remains is litigation over pensions, severance pay, and other termination issues. Community members feel resentful and perhaps betrayed by the departing firm and in some instances blame organized labor and high wages for the closing. The example of the successful labor-community coalition built by the Calumet Project for Industrial Jobs shows that this is not inevitable. It is important to note, however, that labor-community coalitions of this order are the exception rather than the rule at this stage of industrial restructuring.

Misplaced union confidence. In these cases, especially those that occurred before the late 1980s, the unions and union workers had a misplaced confidence in their ability to negotiate solutions to their labor-management disputes and in their employers' dependence on the existing plant and labor force. This was based on their experiences from the postwar Golden Age of industrial job expansion and rising living standards, when unions and collective bargaining played central roles in basic industry. The clearest example of this misplaced confidence was the independent local union at Wisconsin Steel, which was unprepared because it had never had to fight to get what it wanted. By contrast, union members at Clinton Corn were accustomed to calling and winning strikes over improved terms and conditions. Thus, when a new group of top executives adopted a new market strategy for Standard Brands, the workers were not paying attention. Later, when the consequences of this change became apparent, they remained convinced they still could win in a showdown with the company.

It is revealing that the first person other than a manager or investment specialist to know that White Consolidated planned to divest the Blaw-Knox foundry was neither a local nor an international union official but a Calumet Project researcher who had read about the plan in the business press. Union workers at the Akron tire plants, American Crane, and I-R/Torrington were equally unprepared to respond to their firms' new strategies. For years they had been able to protect their labor standards and working conditions through routine negotiations with accommodating employers or, if not that way, through the use and threat of strikes.

None of the unions was prepared at the outset to broaden its range of activities beyond traditional collective bargaining. When the new realities became undeniable, the locals began to consider alternatives, but by then it was too late for most. The locals at IBP and LaSalle Steel were the exceptions. At IBP, the local had no choice but to construct a counterstrategy because all of its experiences with the firm had been hostile. The independent union at LaSalle had the benefit of an experienced and strategic partner in the Calumet Project.

Secrecy and centralization. Secrecy is a source of considerable strength and opportunity for companies undergoing restructuring. They do not knowingly share market strategies with other groups that have a stake in the enterprises and, as the Torrington, Amhoist, GM, and Blaw-Knox cases suggest, they go to great lengths to maintain confidentiality. This puts labor and the community at considerable disadvantage in protecting their own interests because they do not know which combination of product and labor strategies the firm is pursuing and therefore what their responses should be.[5]

As the Clinton Corn and Amhoist cases show, events overtake local unions that are ignorant of corporate reorganizations in progress. No union knowingly strikes a plant that has become superfluous to the company. To do so is to invite confrontational defeat at best and institutional destruction and job displacement at worst. Yet the workers at Clinton struck under such conditions. Workers at Torrington and Amhoist also struck at times, according to subsequent company statements, when the parent corporations were deciding whether or not to put those plants in the endangered category.

Likewise, communities do not knowingly give costly financial subsidies to firms that are prepared to abandon projects long before community benefits outweigh costs. Yet they do so, as the Playskool and Diamond cases demonstrate, because they have no way of knowing the long-term intentions of the firms. Responses to decisions involving industrial restructuring require a level of judgment and discretion that community officials do not have from the limited amount of information given to them, as, for example, the city of Detroit found out in the GM Poletown case.

Union and Community Responses

These cases show that there has been an erosion of traditional industrial and labor relations systems and a corresponding shift away from the "hard" or "arm's-length" bargaining that dominated the postwar decades (Healy 1965). Instead, employers effectively have overcome union attempts to resolve differences through collective bargaining by negotiating to stalemate and eventual crisis or by constantly escalating the price of settlement to the union. Bargaining has thus become ineffective as a dispute resolution mechanism.

Decline of the Post–World War II Industrial and Labor Relations System

As employers developed strategic responses consisting of both operating constraints and opportunities, they greatly weakened and in many instances destroyed what were presumed to be firmly established industrial and labor relations systems. The effect often was to discard bargaining or make it ineffective. The major tire companies, for example, began leaving Akron in the 1970s, and by the early 1980s none still made passenger-car tires there. In the process, postwar union organization and bargaining structures in tires were dismantled and replaced with partial unionization and selected pattern bargaining (which occurred also in meatpacking).

Standard Brands made it a practical impossibility for the local union at Clinton Corn to settle a strike undertaken in a blunder. The firm progressively raised the cost of settlement to the union and in that way drove the dispute toward its inexorable conclusion. In retrospect, once Standard Brand's consumer-branded products strategy was in place, the company clearly had no long-term stake in the plant or the city and no further need for union or community goodwill. From then on it threatened both the union and the community with plant closure and eventually eliminated the union altogether before leasing the plant to a rival producer.

Once White Consolidated decided to concentrate on household appliances, Blaw-Knox's function as a cash cow was assured, but the union and the community did not know that. Nor did they know that when White Consolidated sold the facility to a small group of investors, the latter was interested only in the remaining tank contracts and had no intention of upgrading either the machine shop or the foundry. Instead, the new owners tried to widen their short-term profit margins by getting the union to make contract concessions. When that failed, they tried to extend operations at Blaw-Knox a bit longer by making patriotic appeals to community leaders to petition the Pentagon to make additional purchases of the obsolete tank Blaw-Knox produced. Thus, when the last military contract was completed, the new owners simply shut the doors and walked away.

The pattern in these cases is toward polarized, no-compromise, institutional confrontation. Collective bargaining at Torrington, Akron tires, Clinton Corn, and Amhoist moved from traditional to hostile (union-avoidance) labor relations as part of wider company strategies. Elsewhere, IBP precipitated successive lockouts and strikes at its Dakota City plant but had to moderate its behavior when it ran afoul of Congress over alleged administrative law violations.

An important variable in determining the employer's labor strategy was whether the company could relocate production. If it could, as in the cases of the Akron tire makers, Torrington, and American Crane, it asked for concessions and held out the false promise that they might save jobs. The

Akron case is instructive on this point because it demonstrates the interactions among industry failure in the product market, union failure to organize the industry's relevant labor force, and the subsequent shift of production away from a high-wage location.

The competition originally confronting the domestic tire producers involved product lines and quality, not wages and labor costs. But the producers' responses and the subsequent industry shakeout revolved around comparative labor costs and the relocation of operations from Akron. Union labor therefore paid a high price for the industry's failure to respond in a timely manner to the threat from radial production. It and the community suffered not because they were the source of the problem but because they were the most vulnerable stakeholders in the competitive struggle over market shares between the old and new firms. The United Rubber Workers of America was unable to organize Michelin's new radial plants in North America and the plants that had been built by U.S. companies in the South and Southwest. This made Akron's labor standards and plants uncompetitive with those in the new facilities and therefore untenable. Goodyear shifted operations to nonunion plants outside Akron, other domestic producers phased down or got out of tire production altogether, and Michelin, Bridgestone, and Continental added domestic production capability in other locations.

By contrast, when firms could not or would not relocate operations, as at IBP and CCPC, they stayed and fought the unions. In those cases direct labor costs (as well as institutional union security) became key issues, although not in the conventional sense of labor-management relations in which compromise solutions are possible. The Clinton Corn local, for example, assumed that it was "business as usual" at the bargaining table and, as a consequence, miscalculated the context within which the 1977–78 round of contract negotiations occurred. It assumed that the company's improved profit performance justified and facilitated a substantial economic settlement for the workers. The union failed to understand that Standard Brands had no long-term interest in either the product or the Clinton facility but instead was interested in minimizing current production costs and the expenses of a shutdown, including negotiated severance pay and other labor costs that employers normally incur when they close plants covered by labor contracts.

CURRENT AND FUTURE INDUSTRIAL AND LABOR RELATIONS

The outcomes of cases involving industrial restructuring are not generally positive. They end mainly in closed plants, broken unions, deserted communities, and bitter labor relations. But what about those experiences of the 1980s in which employers agreed to continue operating and to make capital investments in their plants and equipment in exchange for substantial union concessions, the adoption of labor-management cooperation programs, and visible support from the community? What do they tell us to expect in the 1990s?

From the cases presented here, we would expect that the widespread industrial dislocations of the 1980s would embolden opportunist firms to make heavy demands on unions and communities in the 1990s and for the latter to accept them. Unions will accept such demands in view of the threat of plant shutdowns and to preserve jobs that still pay comparatively well in a period of overall decline in real wages and of a proliferation of low-wage service-producing jobs. In addition, communities can be expected to pressure unions and workers to make contract concessions and to accept the new labor relations; as these and other (Portz 1990) cases show, community leaders believe that retaining and creating any manufacturing jobs at all takes priority over challenging the terms and conditions of employment.

Union-management bargaining during 1991–92 at the Evansville, Indiana, refrigerator plant of the Whirlpool Corporation illustrates the new scenario.[6] Along with the other White appliance firms, Whirlpool was consolidating its U.S. manufacturing activities in the face of mature product markets and subsantial production overcapacity.[7] GE and White Consolidated, Whirlpool's two major rivals, had relocated refrigerator production to nonunion plants in the South and by 1989 were paying average wages as much as $4.75 an hour below those in the Evansville plant, although industry analysts noted that White Consolidated was experiencing production and quality problems at its South Carolina facility.

In contract negotiations in 1991, Whirlpool therefore asked the union local at Evansville for substantial wage and benefit concessions. The bargaining committee urged members to turn down the proposal, although the company threatened to cancel some $55 million in planned investment and perhaps to phase out the plant altogether if the union did not accept the concessions. Tempers flared when the mayor of Evansville publicly urged union members to approve Whirlpool's offer in the interest of "the economic future of the community." Some local officers vowed to retaliate against him in the next election. The members narrowly voted to accept the contract, however, and the incumbent union president and his running slate barely survived challenges from anticoncession candidates in the next election.

By mid-1991, Whirlpool had invested an estimated $115 million in the

Evansville plant (instead of the anticipated $55 million) and employment was at twenty-four hundred, the highest level in thirteen years. Whirlpool had also closed a Canadian refrigerator plant and moved additional production from its (unionized) Fort Smith, Arkansas, plant to Evansville. At this point the company asked to renegotiate the contract, which was not due to expire until February 1993. In return for the restoration of previous wage cuts and an improved pension plan, it wanted greater production flexibility, reduced pay grades and job classifications, union-management committees, pay-for-performance provisions, larger employee contributions to health-care premiums, and a long-term contract. These changes would make the plant competitive, company officials said, and justify making the additional investments and locating Whirlpool's new refrigerator lines in Evansville.

After initially voting down the offer, against strong recommendations to accept from the local Chamber of Commerce and public officials, members ratified a similar proposal a few months later when Whirlpool announced that the Evansville plant was uncompetitive and might have to be closed. The new four-year contract included a two-tier wage system and restorative wage increases; eliminated 60 percent of the existing wage classifications and half the pay grades; and established cooperative committees in the plant and improved pensions and early retirement benefits but higher payments by workers for health-care coverage. Whirlpool officials said they were pleased with the results for three reasons:

- The new labor-management committee would, among other things, establish employee-involvement programs to try to resolve shop-floor issues, such as how to make job security compatible with production flexibility and how to encourage voluntary layoffs in the event of production downturns.
- The increased wage differentials as a result of having fewer job classification and pay grades, combined with "equity raises" for jobs having higher skill requirements, would make it easier for Whirlpool to attract employees into high-paying, high-tech jobs.
- The bonus payments to employees for improved quality and output, instead of formula-based and deferred wage increases, would link worker effort to earnings.

Thus, to the extent that these negotiations accurately reflect the trends in labor and industrial relations in midwestern manufacturing towns, the future scenario in cases in which employers choose to invest in existing plants is likely to be one in which union members (even in traditionally militant locals) agree to significant changes in contract terms and language under considerable pressure from the community and realistic threats that they will lose their jobs if they do not do so. The changes unions accept will involve (1) a greater emphasis on the informal rather than the formal (i.e., contract) resolution of problems and differences; (2) greater use of internal labor market systems and individual worker motivation to advance within the system through skill and experience; and (3) more payments for performance than payments based on formula bargaining (comparability with workers in similar firms and industries and anual cost-of-living and productivity pay increases).

UNION-MANAGEMENT COOPERATION

The most frequent advice outside specialists give unions is to abandon their adversarial relationships with management in favor of cooperation. This, it is argued, lowers production costs and improves product quality, both of which make firms more competitive in domestic and global markets and therefore better able (and perhaps more willing) to provide secure jobs and improved terms and conditions of employment. Firms and entire industries are now experimenting with various cooperative programs, employee-involvement systems, and employee ownership schemes.

It is questionable whether this advice is generally applicable. David Brody (1971) and Ronald Filippelli (1990) argue persuasively that American employers historically have opposed unionized labor relations so powerfully and successfully that unions have been unable to shape the industrial environment that determines their fate. Unions have been widely recognized only during those few and fleeting moments when the alternative was even worse for capital, and even then the recognition was given grudgingly and reluctantly. It appears today that employers in the English-speaking economies generally oppose independent participatory roles for organized labor in any matters but those involving the lowest-level corporate decisions (i.e., specific work tasks on the shop floor).

In practice, most cooperative programs initiated by employers are designed to undermine and circumvent existing unions or to discourage their formation, while also reducing unit labor costs (see, for example, Rinehart 1984; Parker 1985; Alexander 1987; Bradley and Hill 1987; Grenier 1988; Lever-Tracy 1990). The cases in this book reinforce the view that regardless of its merits or shortcomings, institutional cooperation is not a panacea for manufacturing inefficiency and labor conflict because employers rather than unions are unwilling to enter into genuinely cooperative arrangements.

Unless employers take the initiative, such programs will not materialize. Where employers in these cases had both market and bargaining advantage over unions, they attacked and pressed their full advantage against them. They did not ask for cooperation.

Torrington, CCPC, and the Akron tire companies, for example, do not appear to have forgotten the postwar union power that made them observe certain labor standards in pay and working conditions and a certain degree of accountability to their workers in day-to-day production operations. Thus, they shied away from such constraints and accountability when the circumstances might have encouraged them to invite union and worker involvement in response to their changing fortunes in product markets. At the same time, new competitors such as IBP are unlikely to lose sight of why they fought to keep unions out of their plants in the first place or of the role that operating nonunion played in the success of their original strategy to achieve market share.

In an overall atmosphere in which intensified foreign and domestic product market competition encourages low-cost labor strategies by employers, unions are likely to face disagreeable options when they consider labor-management cooperation programs. Where employer power is so great that the firm can either break or avoid the union through capital mobility, union cooperation is necessarily reduced to equally unacceptable choices: to help employers carry out confidential operating strategies that often include job and pay reductions (and could lead to the elimination of the union itself) or to reject cooperation and risk being held responsible for the employer's operating difficulties and perhaps also the subsequent job losses. Local unions at Torrington, the Akron tire companies, and Blaw-Knox may have believed they had the option of cooperation available to them, but it proved to be an untenable option for them.

In situations in which companies or industries cannot easily avoid unions, as in auto and basic steel, cooperative programs are likely to offer unions expanded roles. Even then, however, such programs can lead to labor cost cutting and permanent downsizing of the unionized labor force if these are important corporate goals and if the unions have no agendas of their own in the changed relationship.

For labor-management cooperation to further union objectives, the employer has to give the union sufficient information on pending decisions that affect the firm's short-term production operations and processes and on management thinking about the firm's long-term options and prospects regarding industry and market trends. In none of these cases did the employer show much commitment to unions and collective bargaining as power-sharing, problem-solving institutions.[8]

COMMUNITY DEPENDENCY

These case studies generally support the community dependency thesis (see, for example, Lindblom 1982; Mollenkopf 1983; Portz 1990; Nash 1989). This thesis states that conventional norms and established power structures in industrial communities are such that economic, social, and political institutions and organizations are limited in their ability to control or influence the direction of economic change. Private corporations command the community's productive base and have more or less exclusive authority under law and custom to make critical decisions on capital investments, production locations, and employment structures. They determine the level and nature of industrial activity and therefore shape political and institutional behavior (as well as the choices made by affected individuals and households) without having to participate directly in controversial political and organizational processes. City councils, trade unions, and activist groups have to respond to the situations created and the choices dictated by the business initiatives, but their options are restricted and, consequently, so is their effectiveness. Such dependency is neither total nor unalterable, but it does give business a decided advantage.

In a study of critical plant closings in three industrial communities, John Portz found that in each instance local government "policymakers recognized the importance of the private economy and adjusted their needs and actions accordingly" (1990:141) regardless of whether the area economy was strong or weak at the time.

> In the course of supporting a private economy, government officials were also constrained in the types of policies they could initiate. More specifically, urban economic policies had to conform to the basic nature of a private enterprise economy, particularly the private control of investment. Without such conformity, local officials faced the possibility of further disinvestment.

Opposition to corporate hegemony in investment decisions or to special demands made by firms was depicted in the community as threatening the common good. When conditions changed for the worse, workers and residents alike were inclined to blame government for not giving the firm enough and organized labor for demanding too much.

In the event of plant closings or threatened closings during labor disputes, community leaders and groups can respond by (1) being passive (or neutral) bystanders, playing no role in the decision-making and adjustment processes;

(2) avoiding direct involvement in decisions but working with business to offset the adverse effects; or (3) becoming active participants in both decision making and adjustment (Portz 1990, chap. 1). The third response represents the only direct challenge to corporate hegemony, but even it is remedial in nature because the firm ultimately has a right to withhold investments and to close production facilities.

The cases discussed by Fasenfest illustrate the range of community responses when local governments try to retain or create manufacturing jobs. When firms close plants, governments either avoid any involvement they think might offend business and therefore jeopardize future jobs, or they join with union and activist organizations in efforts to force the departing firms to make financial compensation or restitution. Detroit cooperated fully with GM even though the company had closed plants in the city. Then the company unveiled plans to build a highly automated plant and made substantial demands on financial resources available to the city for economic development. But it neither shared information with city officials nor allowed them to participate in decision making involving the new plant.

Several years later the township of Ypsilanti, Michigan, challenged GM's decision to close its historic Willow Run plant and relocate production to a sister plant in Arlington, Texas. Internal company documents revealed during the proceedings indicated that GM estimated it could save money by closing either of the plants, but that it would save $74 million more by closing the Texas facility. The Willow Run plant would cost less to upgrade and its labor force had a lower absentee rate than Arlington's. GM officials anticipated difficulty securing a satisfactory work force in Texas. In support of Arlington's bid for the work, the documents indicated the plant had a better quality record, smoother labor relations, and greater operating flexibility than Willow Run. Ypsilanti sued GM for breach of an agreement in which it accepted $13.5 million in tax abatements in return for promises to retain some four thousand jobs there. The company denied there was such an agreement (*Detroit Free Press,* Dec. 17, 1992).

In February 1993, a Washtenaw County circuit court judge enjoined GM from closing the Ypsilanti facility on grounds that there was a promise to keep the plant open and, therefore, it would be unjust to allow the company "to simply decide that it will desert 4,500 workers and their families because it thinks it can make these cars a little cheaper somewhere else." The judge criticized Michigan's law on tax abatements as imprecise and ineffective. Government and industry need to cooperate to make American industry competitive, he wrote, but the effort should be national rather than local in scope, "not one in which industry simply views government as a part of its 'business climate' and another opportunity to increase profits." A university law professor who counseled Ypsilanti Township conceded that the decision probably would be overturned upon appeal, but added that the suit was not a useless exercise. "Henceforth, everybody dealing with the abatement process is going to be a little clearer and a little more explicit on what they're doing, what they're promising, what they're committing themselves to," he said (*Detroit Free Press,* Feb. 10, 1993).

Chicago and Duluth, in contrast, exercised their authority to force errant firms to repay monies they had obtained on promises to bring or retain manufacturing jobs into these cities. Of the other communities in the cases that occurred in the 1980s, most chose a corporatist response: they pressured unions to accept concession demands by employers (Akron; Clinton, Iowa; and initially Dakota City, Nebraska) or to abandon their efforts to require the firms to continue producing locally (South Bend and East Chicago). City governments at best were neutral, as in the case of Minneapolis–St. Paul.

Often, firms do not even ask communities to play an active role one way or the other, apparently preferring that they simply act as bystanders. In any event, during the 1980s, most local governments lacked either the will or the resources to play the role of the populist advocate.

New Forms of Institutional Power

Beyond the issue of cooperation is the more fundamental question of power. The standard prescription for the loss of union power is to organize the unorganized, penetrate predominantly nonunion sectors, grow as a percentage of the labor force, and obtain favorable changes in government regulation and labor law. These are obvious measures if organized labor is to represent workers effectively at national and local bargaining tables. But the experiences described here indicate that they are not enough. Unions also must recognize the common predicament they share with deindustrialized communities and with nonunion groups and individuals who are adversely affected by new corporate strategies. Unions have to consider accepting fundamental redefinitions of property rights in productive systems and of the social organization of work and production. Radical changes in industrial power and outcomes require nothing less.

A promising concept for unions trying to regain power is that diverse multiple stakeholders share the effects of corporate performance and strategies. These stakeholders include the firm's stockholders and directors, of course, but also its employees and the communities in which it does business. Most of these stakeholders typically have far deeper and longer relationships with the enterprise than do the shareowners and directors or, in the age of corporate mobility and diversification, the managers themselves. It is logical, therefore, that unions change their own grand design from one that depends exclusively on sustaining a postwar relationship with management, which may sever that relationship at any time, to one that focuses on creating strategic alliances with other stakeholders who stand to lose from corporate reorganizations and relocations. Three ways in which some unions have sought new allies to challenge business hegemony are by establishing control over mergers and acquisitions, undertaking corporate campaigns, and building labor-community coalitions.

ROLE OF 'STAKEHOLDERS' IN CORPORATE RESTRUCTURING

An emerging issue is who controls the corporation and in whose interest it should function (Greenfield and Graham forthcoming). Most of the cases presented here involved corporate mergers and acquisitions. The results were generally disastrous for the unions and the communities, both of which had no meaningful voice in the restructuring. All they could do was make various concessions and subsidies, in the mistaken expectation that doing so would save or create manufacturing jobs, and continue to pursue traditional labor relations and business climate strategies, despite their repeated failure to prevent job and revenue losses.

U.S. policy in the 1980s regarding industrial mergers and the corollary issues of corporate control and purpose resembled a financial free-for-all. Ownership was put up for grabs on the abstract principle that stock markets were the best and surest way to guarantee the efficient use of corporate assets and to ensure disciplinary control of corporate managers by shareholders, who, it was believed, could punish unproductive managers by selling their shares to corporate raiders. The objective, both theoretical and practical, was to maximize shareholders' monetary gains and corporate productive efficiency. Questions of income distribution among various groups of stakeholders and of the impact of such behavior on plants and communities were ignored (Singh forthcoming).

There are critical questions, however, involving both performance and equity. Empirical studies using postmerger profit data (the only criterion for corporate "performance" that is readily available) show slightly negative or, at best, neutral results following mergers.[9] But other empirical studies show that mergers do affect the distribution of income within corporations and that the major beneficiaries are shareholders and the main losers are employees (Shleifer and Summers 1988).[10]

If we are to avoid the lackluster industrial performance and distributional inequities and inefficiencies described in these cases, we need new concepts of corporate control and purpose. A promising avenue is the notion of stakeholder rights in business enterprises, whereby unions and communities are given a recognized stake, or vested right, in existing industrial operations and properties as a result of their lengthy, well-established relations with the corporations managing the properties. This concept runs counter to the social norms and legal language embedded in conventional thinking about rights, performance, and distribution. It emphasizes the cooperative dimensions of productive enterprises and efforts rather than their adversarial, exclusionary aspects.

Stakeholder rights arise naturally as an alternative approach when the stakeholders perceive there to be corporate violations of presumed social contracts between the community and its inhabitants on one side and the firm and its managers and owners on the other. These rights rest on perceptions and experiences that the interests of the shareholders are inconsistent with those of the stakeholders and that the latter need (and are entitled to have) independent rights of property to protect their own interests as well as to promote social well-being.[11] Unions are logical institutions to become involved in redefining and redesigning traditional rules and perceptions of property rights, insofar as the prevailing definition works against rather than for their members in the new industrial environment. Communities, of course, are their natural allies in this movement.

CORPORATE CAMPAIGNS

Linked to the stakeholder concept is the corporate campaign. During corporate campaigns, unions identify and try to influence other stakeholders to bring pressure directly on management to change its labor policies or, indirectly through government regulation, to convince managers that it is in their best interests to settle outstanding labor disputes. Shareholders, directors, and firms doing business with target corporations may be approached, but unions have not had much success in such efforts. They are more likely to find sympathetic allies among environmental groups, members of endangered communities, consumer advocates, religious organizations, and small businesses—anyone sharing the union's resentment about particular corporate practices. In this way, labor links its grievances with those of various social groups and seeks to resolve both grievances simultaneously. The object is to attack antiunion employers where they are most vulnerable to nonworkplace actions.

Corporate campaigns have resulted in varying successes for unions, but they represent an attractive alternative to direct job actions, formal organizing drives, and other traditional union tactics that are far less successful in today's hostile environment than they were in the past. The IBP case is an example. Others include the J. P. Stevens campaign, which jeopardized the company's financial and corporate links; the Litton campaign, which threatened the conglomerate's defense contracts on the grounds that its numerous subsidiaries were repeat violators of federal labor law; and the Beverly campaign, which challenged the nursing home chain's operating licenses with state regulatory boards (Mishel 1985).

So far unions have had both short-term and apparent long-term successes with corporate campaigns. They have gotten managers to soften or abandon their resistance to union organizing efforts or to settle ongoing labor disputes (Jarley and Maranto 1990). More important to this discussion, unions appear to have improved their long-term position by impressing government regulators, environmental activists, and other stakeholders, as well as their own members, with the legitimacy of their claims and the social significance of their actions (Jarley and Maranto 1991).

In 1991–92, the United Steelworkers and the AFL-CIO waged a successful campaign to get management back to the bargaining table in a dispute involving Ravenswood Aluminum Corporation in West Virginia. Management locked out seventeen hundred bargaining unit members in November 1990 after union negotiators rejected the company's final demands for contract concessions. Ravenswood continued operations with eleven hundred replacement workers. It then claimed the union had turned the dispute into a strike, thus making the new workers permanent replacements. The union brought unfair labor practice charges against Ravenswood and began a campaign to publicize alleged ownership and control of the company by Marc Rich, an international businessman wanted in the United States on felony charges related to various financial deals. The campaign also focused on the economic plight of displaced union workers and their families and cited the dispute as an example of how American workers have become vulnerable to the low-wage strategies of absentee-owned corporations.

In April 1992, after eighteen months of lockout and a great deal of anti-Ravenswood publicity, including a Bill Moyers public television documentary on the conflict, an expanded board of directors removed Ravenswood's chairman and chief officer, citing "a basic disagreement as to the future direction" of the firm. The board also appointed a special committee under the direction of former NLRB general counsel Peter Nash to arrange for a resumption of contract talks with the union. Negotiations resumed the following month (BNA 1992a:398). An agreement was reached shortly afterward.

UNION-COMMUNITY COALITIONS

The cases in this book suggest that unions are most effective when they have close alliances with and assistance from government regulatory agencies and concerned congresspersons (IBP and American Crane), there are economic development officials willing to enforce corporate compliance with commitments made in return for public subsidies (Playskool, Diamond Tool), there are supportive local politicians (Blaw-Knox, LaSalle Steel), there is a press willing to report stories critical of the corporation (IBP, Blaw-Knox, LaSalle Steel), and there is an aroused local community (Blaw-Knox, LaSalle Steel).

Although such alliances usually are long-term undertakings, unions can begin moving toward establishing them by (1) systematically cultivating relationships with local news media, (2) working with local economic development officials to alter exclusive business climate orientations and to ensure accountability in exchange for any public subsidies to corporations, (3) pursuing congressional oversight and federal agency enforcement of federal government regulations still in existence, and (4) developing ties with local clergy, academics, civic leaders, and others who share organized labor's concern for stable, safe, well-paying jobs in the community. It may be difficult for local union officials to expand in these nontraditional areas, but it is essential in the long run. Wider changes in national politics and public regulation are not likely to occur until innumerable "small changes" occur locally so that unions are integrated more solidly in their communities.

The modern economic environment puts unions and communities in common predicaments. Employers in these cases did not take community officials into their confidence when making decisions any more than they did union officials; nor did they allow standard agents and conventions of democratic pluralism to determine economic decisions and outcomes. Instead, the employers concealed their objectives and intentions from local public officials and tried to extract as much subsidy and support from the community as possible, while demonstrating minimal responsibility and providing minimal payment in return. To protect their interests, communities have to increase their control over economic decisions vital to local stability and well-being.

First, local economic development officials and public officials should attach conditions to public assistance given to corporations in the name of economic development. As the Playskool, Diamond Tool, American Crane, and Gary tax-abatement cases illustrate, such "strings" can give communities considerable leverage with corporations in the event they choose to relocate or terminate operations.

Second, state and local officials need to develop mutual "no-raiding" pacts that prohibit governments from using public incentives to lure businesses from other localities. Or, as the outcome of the Blaw-Knox case suggests, they should get directly involved in the sale and transfer of ownership of local productive assets. Because changes in ownership are a prime "early warning" that plant shutdown may be imminent, local economic development officials should interview prospective buyers to determine whether their intention is to maintain and upgrade the facility or to extract economic rent and shut down what remains. At the same time, they can try to persuade sellers to look for buyers committed to local production.[12]

The subsequent experiences of communities that have broken the business climate taboo—Chicago with Playskool, Duluth with Diamond Tool, and the Iowa communities with IBP—should encourage public officials willing to take a more proactive, less subservient stance toward employers. In no instance did the more demanding position by government produce an apparent "capital strike" or boycott by the business community in retaliation. Nor does it appear that Gary, Indiana, is being singled out in this regard as a result of its pioneering tax-abatement legislation. A more independent community policy may not be completely risk-free, but it does appear to involve minimal risk. More daring measures to redefine the relationship entirely would require an overall movement in the political and public opinion arenas away from the pro-business, antiunion policies of the 1980s.[13]

In conclusion, if they are to counter the negative effects of the grand designs developed and implemented by corporations in the 1980s, workers, unions, and communities will have to devise their own. The changes they confront are massive and fundamental. To be successful, the approach must be bold, wide ranging, and imaginative. Detroit, for example, boasted as many as two dozen auto and truck assembly plants after World War II; today it has two: GM's Poletown and Chrysler's Jefferson North, both of which assemble high-quality expensive vehicles, are automated, and employ a fraction of the production workers employed by the old assembly plants.

Membership in the United Auto Workers meanwhile dropped from 1.5 million in the mid-1970s to a reported 1.1 million in 1992, and the latter figure includes large numbers of retirees.

If the American Midwest is to retain a manufacturing presence, it is up to the workers and inhabitants of the region to see that it does, for the corporations have demonstrated that they have no obligation or commitment to continue producing in traditional factory towns. There is, after all, nothing inherent in the market economy to guarantee good jobs and prosperous communities as a right of passage for successive generations of workers and residents. Quite the opposite. Every time a profound change occurs in the industrial structure and in the social and political environment, previously secure livelihoods and stable institutions are disrupted. That is happening to midwestern workers, unions, and communities now just as it happened to New York artisans before the Civil War (Wilentz 1984) and to London's manufacturing workers during the late Victorian era (Jones 1971). In New York and London, it was decades before new movements, institutions, and struggles restored adequate living standards for blue-collar labor. Whether or not such standards will be restored in the American Midwest remains to be seen.

NOTES

CHAPTER 1

1. Real wages in the U.S. economy fell on average by 9 percent during the 1980s. Lawrence R. Mishel and David Frankel (1991:105–19) estimate that two-thirds of this decline is explained by industrial restructuring from goods-producing to non–goods-producing industries and most of the remainder by deunionization of the work force, foreign competition, and falling real minimum wages.

2. During 1960–73, Japan's annual increase in goods and services produced per person (adjusted for inflation) grew four times faster than that of the United States, and Germany's grew more than twice as fast; during 1973–88, however, Japan's grew five times and Germany's four times faster than ours.

3. Chicago, one of the region's historically great manufacturing towns, experienced comparable losses of 181 manufacturers in 1991 and 125 in 1990 (*Chicago Sun-Times*, Feb. 15, 1992, 30).

4. For a discussion of productive systems in this regard, see Wilkinson 1983a.

5. Jeszeck notes in this volume that they were encouraged to do this by the Big Three auto producers, which did not want to build cars requiring radial tires.

CHAPTER 2

1. In 1936, however, Goodrich threatened to displace five thousand Akron jobs if newly organized URW workers did not accept a wage reduction; the workers refused, but the jobs were not eliminated (Roberts 1944:161).

2. Wages were higher and working conditions better in the nontire plants of tire companies than in the rubber products plants of nontire companies. Nontire jobs had been leaving Akron since the 1950s, initially in the absence of union concessions but also after concessions were made in the early 1970s.

3. Firestone operated Seiberling as a separate division before closing the Akron plant in 1980. Unlike labor relations elsewhere during this time, no concession bargaining occurred at Seiberling.

4. Goodrich managers knew the domestic tire market eventually would be mainly radial but believed this would not occur for many years. Thus, they put the bulk of

the company's new investment into bias-belted tire production, a hybrid, which they saw as the transitional tire to radials. They were wrong in their time estimate. Smaller companies such as Cooper and Mansfield did not go into radial production initially but instead chose to stay with bias-ply tires as long as possible (Jeszeck 1982:62–66).

5. In 1965, Goodrich did agree to minor changes in the work rules favored by the union and to a vague promise to preserve jobs; in exchange, the company introduced the five-day, forty-hour workweek.

6. Goodyear, like most Akron tire companies, had been on the six-hour, six-day workweek, a schedule introduced by management in the 1930s in order to distribute the available work among more workers. Except for a Uniroyal plant in Detroit and some of the smaller Ohio tire companies, this schedule was unique to Akron. Workers preferred it to the regular workweek because it enabled them to take second jobs; over time management disliked six-hour shifts because they necessitated four shifts and increased supervisory, training, and fringe benefit costs. The URW locals nevertheless fought to keep four shifts in the Akron plants (Jeszeck 1986).

7. Goodyear wanted twenty-five specific contract rule changes in the new mold plant, the most important being the following: (1) to shift from a piece-work to a day-work compensation system and for the company to determine the level of output that constituted a "fair day's work" (this represented a significant surrender of bargaining power by the local); (2) to put the department on an eight-hour, forty-hour workweek instead of the previous six-hour, six-day schedule; (3) to consolidate craft and production job classifications; and (4) to test the new rules for ninety days in the old plant before implementing them at the new facility.

8. The 1979 pattern agreement for the first time required tire companies to give local unions and workers six months' notification of an impending plant shutdown and to bargain over decisions concerning closings. Before this agreement, companies did not have to notify the union of a pending reduction in operations.

9. "Tirebuilder" is the most highly skilled and strategic job classification in the industry's production process and wage structure. This is because employers have not been able to automate the process fully and radial tires require greater care in construction than traditional bias-ply tires.

10. Because the Akron concessions affected master contract provisions, approval also was obtained from other Goodrich locals and the international URW.

11. Goodrich also established a profit-sharing plan, but the plant continued to lose money, so two additional wage cuts became effective instead.

12. Some of these negotiations may have been initiated by the O'Neil family. GenCorp labor relations officials stated that civic-minded CEO Jerry O'Neil wanted to keep as much tire manufacturing in Akron as possible (interview, Hank Smith, vice president for labor relations, General Tire Company [now GenCorp], Akron, April 1980).

13. This conclusion is based on discussions with Local 9 members. The local leadership, however, appeared confident that concessions would result in a new Akron plant (interview, Nate Trachsel, president, Local 9, Akron, Dec. 1979).

14. Foreign tire companies do not necessarily have positive labor relations in their U.S. plants. In 1992, the URW filed suit against Michelin's Uniroyal-Goodrich division under the Racketeer Influenced and Corrupt Organizations (RICO) Act on

the grounds that the firm fradulently promised to keep open its Eau Claire, Wisconsin, tire plant in return for union contract concessions in 1975, 1983, and 1988. Michelin had acquired Uniroyal-Goodrich in 1989 and four months later announced it would close the Wisconsin facility by mid-1992 (BNA 1992b).

15. Interview with an industrial relations officer who wished to remain anonymous, Goodyear, Akron, Dec. 1978.

Chapter 3

1. This included an examination of the product's competitive environment—its potential for industry growth, demographic changes, market structure, and public policy—and its market profile—sales, share, quality, and cost of production.

2. Far from being unique to SBI, the zero-based strategy was state-of-the-art financial management at the time. Barry Bluestone and Bennett Harrison (1982:150–51) identified it as the optimal diversification strategy "in terms of a matrix arraying the market share of each of the corporation's product or service lines against the sales growth rate of each activity."

3. Company officials denied it, but industry analysts claimed the outgoing president of SBI objected to CCPC's role in the new strategy (*Wall Street Journal*, Oct. 2, 1978, 20).

4. Notable was a local DuPont plant that typically followed CCPC's wage and benefit patterns and sometimes matched specific changes within days. CCPC nonunion employees expected and received increases comparable to those negotiated for bargaining unit members (Judge interview).

5. CCPC also initiated hostilities with area building trades during this time. Before 1975 contract negotiations, it had asked for union concessions involving in-plant skilled trades. That year, however, CCPC approached the trades with long-term "project" agreements. These contained a variety of reductions in established labor standards in return for the company using union labor on specific building projects. When the locals refused to comply, CCPC canceled existing and planned projects and replaced some 250 craft workers with nonunion labor (Judge interview).

6. Twenty-two union grievances were arbitrated during 1975–79, compared with fifteen from 1939 to 1975. The union won 82 percent of those occurring after 1975 (*Des Moines Register*, Aug. 19, 1979).

7. Mike Krajnevich (interview, 1981) later claimed that the twelve-day strike was intended to demonstrate to SBI and the community the local's dissatisfaction with deteriorating labor relations at CCPC. In contrast, AFGM's district vice president (Frielinger interview) recalled that the strike was purely a bargaining tactic to get CCPC to negotiate a satisfactory settlement.

8. Their mishandling of the ratification process was a decisive error by local union officials. According to an officer of the international (Frielinger interview), the second vote was improper because local by-laws required the votes of at least two-thirds of the members present to reconsider committee votes and the dissidents did not have such a majority.

9. St. Mark's Methodist Church in nearby Camanche, Iowa, was especially supportive of the strikers and their families. For further discussion of the extent and

nature of this and other community involvement and of relations between the union and local government, see Fantasia 1988:193–214.

10. An area newspaper reported that 89 union members retired, 37 quit, 150 returned to work, and an unknown number left the area (*Quad-City Times,* April 21, 1980).

11. Employers often make such promises during labor disputes but then dismiss the replacement workers after reaching agreement with the union; apparently they prefer regular, experienced workers to temporary replacements. Management action following the 1984 Greyhound Bus strike is a case in point.

12. Even if all of the 414 challenged voters favored the union, it would have lost the election 567 to 462. To survive, Local 6 needed the 48 votes it actually got, those of all of its 510 striking members—many of whom had left the area—and several more from replacement workers and former union members who had gone back to work (*Clinton Herald,* June 14, 1980).

13. Rick Fantasia (1988:186) suggests that many of the experiences of the older union members at CCPC "had been drawn from the period when the social contract [between labor and management] seemed solid, and any suggestion that it could or would be broken would most likely have been given little consideration."

14. Fantasia (1988:213) hypothesizes that, although it was evident by 1980 that corporate aggression in labor relations was increasing, with a Democratic administration and Congress, "the leadership of a national union would not necessarily have seen it as a period in which union survival was at stake."

Chapter 4

1. Unless otherwise identified, quotations are from interviews conducted in the spring of 1984 with twelve Wisconsin Steel workers who were guaranteed confidentiality.

2. Adrienne Birecree has a similar analysis of Standard Brands Industries in her study of a 1979 strike against one of its subsidiaries, Clinton Corn Processing. See chapter 3 in this volume.

Chapter 5

1. The early organizing and bargaining experiences of Torrington's South Bend workers are from *South Bend Tribune's* Torrington Company clippings file; its UAW Local 590 file; the Michiana Oral Labor History Project in South Bend; and an interview with Don Gard, a longtime Local 590 official, by Keith Knauss in South Bend on July 16, 1984.

2. Information on wages, plants, and activities in the bearings industry is based on Torrington–Local 590 labor contracts and the minutes of the UAW National Bearings Wage-Hour Council, 1969–90, made available to the authors by the council; also see Craypo 1981:48.

3. Discussion of the 1975 strike is based on Gard interview; "UAW 590, Strike History, 1975," Local 590 document; *South Bend Tribune,* July 11, 12, and 14; and company proposals to the union, May 1, June 5, and July 18. Discussion of the 1978 negotiations is based on Gard interview; 1978 Local 590 pension proposal; "Local

UAW 590 Strike History, 1978"; memo from C. J. McNerney, manager, labor relations, to Don Gard, March 2, 1978; company proposal, June 15; and the 1978–81 labor agreement.

4. This account is based on company and union documents: "A Policy Statement on Quality Circles," n.d.; *Quality Circle Update,* April 7, 1980; and "Union Notice," April 18, 1980.

5. Deposition of Thomas E. Bennett, Oct. 10, 1986, Torrington, Conn., in Civil Action no. S85-00483, *Winard Anderson et al.* v. *The Torrington Company, Inc.*, U.S. District Court, Northern District of Indiana, South Bend Division, hereafter cited as Bennett deposition 1986; Paterson study 1–24.

6. This information is based on a comparison of the task force report and the reconstructed shred versions of drafts of the task force report.

Chapter 6

1. Another view of the political economy of place can be found in Harvey 1985.

2. In the 1989 Indiana gubernatorial race, a major issue was subsidies the incumbent administration gave Subaru-Isuzu to build an automobile assembly plant in Lafayette and whether enough jobs would be created to justify the subsidy. The 1990 Illinois gubernatorial election generated strong debate over whether or not the current administration had gotten the most jobs for its development dollars.

3. David Birch (1980) started the debate over the role of small businesses in job creation. Glenn Yago et al. (1984) argued that even though most new jobs appear to be created by small businesses, the large numbers of jobs lost because of plant closings require industrial job retention rather than small business incentives to be the focus of urban development efforts.

4. Thomas Moore (1985:121) has said, for example, "The most effective way for the government to carry out its constitutional mandate to promote commerce. . . . is to pursue economic policies that improve the business climate."

5. The winning community, Spring Hill, Tennessee, offered no incentive package to GM.

6. It is notable that Chrysler demanded and got subsidies from Wisconsin for its Kenosha plant (formerly an American Motors operation) and then closed the plant and moved operations elsewhere. Complaints from labor, community, and public officials forced Chrysler to fund worker retraining and relocation efforts.

7. Recall that this was part of the land-transfer agreement signed between the city of Detroit's CEDD and GM.

8. The site plan replicated a plant built earlier in what had been a remote cornfield in Oklahoma. Duplication of the design was part of a move toward increased standardization and rationalization in the automotive industry during the latter part of the 1970s.

9. A U.S. General Accounting Office study ("Urban Action Grants Information on Resident and Business Relocation from Poletown Project: GAO/RCED-48FS, Nov. 1989), found that residents and businesses were in better neighborhoods (as defined by crime, number of boarded-up structures, wild dogs, rundown buildings, and poorly maintained yards) following their relocation. Such studies do not,

however, take into account the emotional and economic hardships of the people being forced out of their homes and neighborhoods. The study also reports that few of the Poletown residents found employment in the new plant.

10. Although this program was phased out by the federal government in 1988, in one form or another financing subsidized by local and state governments is still a program of choice among local planners (see n. 17 below). The purpose of this section, therefore, is to consider when and if public-sector financial subsidies to ensure private-sector profitability are in the interest of the public sector.

11. The Milton Bradley Company owned Playskool, Inc., at the time the IRB was approved. Subsequently, Milton Bradley was purchased by Hasbro Industries, Inc., and it was a corporate restructuring and consolidation plan that included Hasbro closing the Playskool plant (Giloth and Rosenblum 1987:21).

12. In fact, the total savings to Hasbro Industries over the life of the IRB would have been $500,000 (Chicago Department of Economic Development, Playskool Briefing memo, n.d.).

13. Sales rose from $60 million in 1982 to $80 million in 1983 and were expected to reach $125 million by 1984 (Giloth and Rosenblum 1987:22).

14. Ironically, Hasbro Industries had to fly some of the Chicago employees to Boston to train workers there on the new machine.

15. This was not the only time a Minnesota company used an IRB and other forms of public subsidies to relocate a plant; see Chapter 8 in this volume.

16. Correspondence from Thomas Geoghegan, an attorney with the law offices of Leon M. Despres. In his letter (Sept. 17, 1986) he stated that the issue was not fraudulent intent (and therefore why the city did not sue) but rather whether there was a breach of a relationship of trust between Combustion Engineering and the city of East Chicago and the public based on the terms of the IRB. If so, then the company acted improperly by neglecting to inform the community of its change of plans and is consequently vulnerable to legal remedies brought by the community.

17. *Area Development* (Jan. 1990), a monthly magazine targeted at state development officials and corporate site planners, provides a complete guide to state business investment programs. The list shows that although IRBs are no longer available, states still rely heavily on low-interest loan programs to subsidize plant relocations and startups.

CHAPTER 7

1. Information on the history of the Blaw-Knox foundry is from Little 1985:II-1 and II-2.

2. In addition to the Blaw-Knox Foundry and Mill Machinery Company, which included the East Chicago foundry and three other facilities in West Virginia and Pittsburgh, White Consolidated was selling Blaw-Knox Food & Chemical Equipment, Blaw-Knox Equipment (steel mill equipment), Aetna-Standard (steel mill equipment), ATF-Davidson (printing equipment), Bullard Castings (foundry), Duraloy (castings and tubing), and R-P&C Valve (valves and controls). Together these companies accounted for about $200 million in yearly sales, approximately 9.5 percent of WCI's total sales.

3. The ex-managers I interviewed requested anonymity. Local union officials did not. All of the interviews occurred during the fall, 1989.

4. I am indebted to Lynn Feekin, director of the Calumet Project, East Chicago, for providing me with the Lehman Brothers prospectus.

5. Discussion of the feasibility study is based on Little 1985; *Gary Post-Tribune,* July 20, 1985; *Hammond Times,* July 21, 1985; *American Metal Markets/Metalworking News,* Aug. 5, 1985, 13; *Crain's Chicago Business,* Aug. 19, 1985, 2.

6. These estimates are similar to those in the Lehman Brothers prospectus: "With the end of the armor contract, the division will be faced with the task of building commercial casting sales to a profitable level. . . . In order to do so, the division estimates initial capital expenditures of $8 million to $11 million over 5 years are required to transform the #2 foundry into a state-of-the-art small castings operation."

7. The threat of eminent domain had been successfully employed by New Bedford, Massachusetts, in a widely publicized case involving the Morse Cutting Tool plant, owned by Gulf and Western. See Doherty, n.d.

8. Army Undersecretary James Ambrose replied to an inquiry from Congressman Peter Visclosky (D-Ind.) by noting that any further work would be "intended, in any case, to give Blaw Knox 'running room', if possible. Thus, I do not understand why Blaw Knox would advise commercial customers that their needs cannot be met. The proposal we are considering does not match, nor can it, the total capacity Blaw Knox has" (letter, Ambrose to Visclosky, June 26, 1986). Ambrose appeared puzzled by Blaw-Knox's claim to Congressman Visclosky; he had assumed the company was being truthful to Visclosky in representing its conversion efforts, specifically that the conversion was being hindered by uncertainty over the government's intentions. In reality, the company never intended to convert but had to conceal this fact from the congressman to get his help in obtaining more tank orders.

The Army Material Command had responded to the pressure from Visclosky by recommending that the government order 210 more tanks, even though the need for them was questionable. Army Undersecretary Ambrose refused to carry this recommendation to Congress, however (letter, Robert J. Tomsich, CEO of Blaw-Knox, to Visclosky).

9. This was true of the state's two Republican senators and the city's Democratic mayor. It was less true of Democratic congressman Peter Visclosky, who, although he held a conventional business climate perspective, was willing to support an independent worker-community viewpoint. He urged corporate officials in writing to make themselves more accountable to the workers and community. No other politician did this.

CHAPTER 8

1. Data on the St. Paul bargaining unit are from Amhoist computer printout material, as of June 6, 1985. The number of workers effectively displaced by the St. Paul plant and foundry closings is higher than the 700 to 750 who were directly affected insofar as many plant workers and molders were phased out in the days and weeks before the closings; fully one-half of the 127 foundry workers were released

between December 1984 and June 1985, when the foundry closed (interview, John Kaufman, representative, Molders, Aug. 11, 1985).

Chapter 9

1. Meatpacking includes beef, pork, lamb, veal, and poultry products. This discussion involves beef-packing unless otherwise noted.

2. What began as competition among many small packers in the 1840s ended in dominance by a few large ones in the 1880s. Lewis Corey (1950), David Brody (1964), and Jimmy M. Skaggs (1986) attribute the industry's early consolidation and subsequent oligopoly to the commitment of old-line packers to horizontal consolidation and vertical integration of ownership and production and to the support they received in this regard from banks and railroads. Another interpretation (Yeager 1981; Perry and Kegley 1989) is that technical advances such as refrigerated rail cars and economies of large-scale production forced the largest and most efficient packers to become even larger and more efficient and prompted them to form cartels and eventually merge their companies to stabilize the industry.

3. A Federal Trade Commission report described the beef trust cartel that functioned around the turn of the century. Representatives of the Big Five packers "met regularly" in Chicago under the auspices of Henry Veeder, an attorney and the son of a Swift executive: "At these meetings the territory was divided and the volume of business to be done by each packer was apportioned upon the basis of statistics compiled by Veeder, penalties being levied when one of them exceeded his allotment in any territory" (cited in Skaggs 1986:100).

As with producer cartels generally, the success of this one fluctuated with the times. On balance, however, it held together until the major firms accepted a 1920 antitrust consent decree that curtailed its organizational power. Meatpacking nevertheless continued to be dominated by an oligopoly (few sellers) vis-à-vis prices and production and an oligopsony (few buyers) vis-à-vis livestock purchases, thus squeezing consumers at one end and cattlemen at the other.

4. IBP vigorously resisted union organizing drives, for example, when it intimidated witnesses in NLRB proceedings following a union campaign at its Emporia, Kansas, plant (Iowa Beef Processors, Inc., and Local 222, 1976).

5. In settling a 1970s dispute at the Dakota City plant, an arbitrator accepted this argument in principle and cut the wage differential between it and the rest of the industry "by nearly half," rather than eliminate it entirely as the union had wanted. The reason for narrowing the wage gap, said the arbitrator, was to avoid giving IBP an unfair advantage over old-line packers or vice versa (BNA 1974:A16).

6. Industry productivity, which had been rising steadily since 1967 (Carnes 1984), rose even faster with the shutdown of these older plants. Closing outdated facilities during 1980–83 reduced the average wage-labor cost in a pound of meat from $.05 to $.04. According to figures compiled by the U.S. Department of Agriculture, labor costs at packinghouses as a share of retail prices declined from $.067 per $1.00 of sales in 1956 to $.041 in 1976 (Prosten 1977:20).

7. IBP regularly calculated the weighted average base wage being paid in rival beef plants (both union and nonunion) that slaughtered a thousand or more head of cattle

daily. This calculation is called the Beef Industry Wage Index. IBP has consistently claimed it cannot pay more than the index and remain competitive (Perry and Kegley 1989:174–77).

8. About five hundred Asians were employed at the plant when the lockout occurred. Later, most joined the strike and refused to cross picket lines despite direct company appeals to do so. IBP recruited at least an equal number of Asians as replacement workers when the union struck.

9. As a result of criticism raised by such blanket exemptions, OSHA began random comprehensive inspections in 1986 of every tenth manufacturing employer. With no more than a thousand OSHA inspectors available nationwide, however, it is questionable how effectively the new policy could have been implemented.

10. IBP threatened to give the Dakota City replacement workers permanent jobs, but after the strike it reinstated experienced strikers to the exclusion of the replacements.

11. IBP's vice president in charge of human resources was asked whether in fact he had asked

> Q. anybody who was in a position to know first hand, are there any other records. Did you ever ask?
>
> A. Congressman, I never went down and talked to the individuals involved.
>
> Q. [The medical examiner] or anybody? Did you ever ask anybody the direct question, are there any records that they [the union, OSHA, and the committee] could be talking about that aren't covered?
>
> A. I don't recall asking that specific question. (U.S. Congress, 1987, pt. 3: 83).

12. The UFCW-IBP-OSHA agreement was signed a month after OSHA levied a fine of $4.3 million, the agency's largest single penalty to date, for safety violations at Morrell's Sioux Falls, South Dakota, packing plant, where three of every four workers suffered OSHA recordable injuries in 1987. In April 1985, OSHA inspectors had exempted the Sioux Falls plant from a full-scale inspection because the numbers on its OSHA 200 form were below the national average; in April 1987, OSHA proposed a $690,000 fine against Morrell for illegally underreporting injuries at the plant (U.S. Congress 1987, pt. 2:2).

13. An IBP shareholders' report articulates this belief: "Since its homegrown start in Iowa, the Corporation has done better than average in handling its normal *internal* business problems. Yet, there are three *external* relationships that have tended to become more problematic as the Company has grown in size. These are relations with organized labor, governmental bodies, and the press." The report then itemized IBP's grievances against each of the three (*IBP Annual Report* 1976:9; emphasis in original).

14. Opponents were aware that in 1981 a citizens group had made similar charges against IBP and discouraged it from building a major pork plant in Stanwood, Iowa. A woman identified as the principal organizer of the Stanwood group was a popular speaker and media figure in the Manchester effort.

15. Two small Kansas towns used state and county subsidies to outbid a Colorado community for a new IBP beef plant employing up to eighteen hundred. IBP got substantial reductions in county taxes and exempted itself from paying local taxes by locating the plant near but not inside either town. Local residents reportedly refused

to work in the plant for any length of time, but the citizens of one town (population 1,200) had to tax themselves an additional $350,000 yearly to provide for the influx of IBP workers living in trailer parks (*Kansas City Times,* May 12, 1982, A1, A12).

16. This discussion is taken from material prepared by Jerry Paar, Division of Labor Studies, Indiana University, Indianapolis. The UFCW also considered calling a nationwide consumer boycott against IBP but decided against it in the absence of brand-name IBP products and because of the union's ongoing organizing campaigns at other IBP plants, where a boycott would have been viewed as contrary to worker as well as company interests.

17. In 1988, one month after being fined a second time for plant safety violations, IBP agreed voluntarily to let the UFCW represent production workers at its Joslin, Illinois, pork-packing plant. It recognized the union on the basis of signed authorization cards, something it had not done for the UFCW before then. A year later it recognized the union on similar grounds at an Iowa plant acquired from Oscar Mayer (Bernstein 1988).

Chapter 11

1. Schumpeter (1962:83) distinguished between the dead hand of predatory rent-seeking activity in capitalist economies and the invigorating force of creative entrepreneurial activity: "The fundamental impulse that sets and keeps the capitalist engine in motion comes from the new consumers' goods, the new methods of production or transportation, the new markets, the new forms of industrial organization that capitalist enterprise creates."

2. For discussion and analysis of this power to deny, see Ralph Nader and William Taylor's (1986) report on interviews with a former U.S. Steel president on his decision to close the company's South Works steel complex in Chicago.

3. Adrienne Birecree (1991) develops this analysis in her explanation of International Paper's lockout and eventual decertification of union locals during the late 1980s. For further discussion of the interaction among technology, production overcapacity, and firm profits, see W.E.G. Salter 1960.

4. This was the complaint of California assemblywoman Maxine Waters in her 1984 confrontation with GM president F. James McDonald over the corporation's unwillingness to confirm whether or not it intended to continue operating the Los Angeles–area Camaro plant: "Several years ago the management of the [Los Angeles] Goodyear Rubber plant convinced the workers that if they only worked harder and turned out more tires per hour, they might save their jobs. People worked sick and worked injured and raised production—and Goodyear closed the plant anyway. We found out later that the central office had already decided to close the plant well over a year before it was announced" (cited in Mann 1987:207).

5. Gordon L. Clark (1991) considers the implications of corporate "secret keeping" in three cases of plant closings that resulted in lost pensions: Continental Can, the LTV Corporation, and International Harvester–Wisconsin Steel. Traditional social science explanations, based on utilitarian models, dismiss the normative, ethical dimensions of such behavior as being inadmissibly subjective and in that way also dismiss labor and community outrage and retribution against these actions as being irrelevant and irrational. Clark argues, however, that the utilitarian approach

misses both the social and the institutional significance of corporations keeping "unethical secrets" from their unions and employees as well as from the Pension Benefit Guarantee Corporation. These actions violate conventional notions of social obligation and trust and of fair treatment of dependent parties; they also undermine the stability of key social institutions, in this case of the nation's private pension system.

6. This discussion is based on newspaper articles by Doug Sword, business writer for the *Evansville Courier,* published during December 1989–February 1992, which he kindly made available to us.

7. Whirlpool also expanded rapidly into Western Europe in anticipation of a unified European economy. It acquired the home appliance business of Philips N.V., one of Europe's largest manufacturers. Whereas 5.5 percent of Whirlpool's revenues came from Europe before the merger, 37.5 percent did afterward; Whirlpool's operating profits from Europe went from a $3 million loss in 1988 to an $83 million profit in 1991 (*South Bend Tribune,* March 15, 1992).

8. The effect is to further erode institutional trust between U.S. labor and management. This is an important disadvantage because institutional trust may undergird successful worker-management cooperation in Germany and Japan but, by contrast, be absent in France and Britain, where constructive labor-management cooperation has never materialized (Lorenz 1992). The implications for U.S. labor relations is that the more employers try to manipulate and exploit workers under the guise of labor-management cooperation, or through direct attacks on unions and bargaining units, the lower will be the level of trust. Ironically, the lower the level, the less likely employers are to get the worker effort and production flexibility they say they need to be competitive.

9. The typical U.S. (and British) firm is under considerable pressure to focus on short-term profit performance because of the threat of takeover and the preoccupation of institutional investors (e.g., pension fund trustees) with achieving short-term results on managed investments: "This is particularly harmful of the real economy as it discourages long-term investment, innovation and product development. All this puts the U.S. and the U.K. industry . . . at a competitive disadvantage in relation to economies where such stock market induced pressures do not prevail" (Singh 1992:11).

10. A body of literature using the "event study" methodology concludes that industrial relations and labor policy events generally affect share values and hence shareholder wealth. Adverse events to unions, such as lost strikes and certification elections, two-tier wage systems, and contract concessions, result in higher share value and therefore in transfers of wealth from workers to owners, to the extent that labor's gains from collective bargaining come out of profits rather than through higher prices (Thomas and Kleiner 1992; Olson and Becker 1990; Abowd 1989; Becker 1987; Becker and Olson 1986; Ruback and Zimmerman 1984). This method assumes that stock markets process event information accurately and efficiently so that the subsequent prices of shares reflect true asset values, an assumption that has not gone unchallenged (e.g., Camerer 1989).

11. These arguments and the efforts of the "stakeholders movement" to implement them at state and local levels (antitakeover laws, eminent domain, intervention in judicial procedures) are reviewed and analyzed in Greenfield and Graham forthcoming.

12. Better "early warnings" of the impending change in ownership, plant closing, product relocation, or change in labor relations practices linked to a change in product market strategy would have helped most of the unions involved in the cases discussed in this book. With longer lead times, they might have formulated alternative strategies of their own. Mandatory disclosure of company conditions or plans, such as the "Vredling" proposals, which were considered but eventually abandoned in Europe, would be a step in this direction (Feekin and Nissen 1991; Ranney 1988; LeRoy, Swinney, and Charpentier 1986).

13. Discussion of new forms of institutional power necessarily focuses on the domestic scene. But in this age of global interaction it is imperative for U.S. unions to forge protective alliances with labor movements in other countries and trade blocs. Such initiatives are essential if workers hope to promote their mutual interest when dealing with employers whose activities cross national boundaries and diverse labor markets.

References

Abowd, John M. 1989. "The Effect of Wage Bargains on the Stock Market Value of the Firm." *American Economic Review* 79 (Sept.): 774–800.

Alcaly, Roger E., and David Mermelstein. 1977. *The Fiscal Crisis of American Cities: Essays on the Political Economy of Urban America with Special Reference to New York.* New York: Vintage Books.

Alexander, Kenneth D. 1987. "The Worker, the Union and the Democratic Workplace." *American Journal of Economics and Sociology* 46 (Oct.): 387–97.

Amott, Teresa L. 1984. "The Politics of Reaganomics." In *Free Market Conservatism: A Critique of Theory and Practice,* ed. Edward J. Nell, 164–83. London: Allen & Unwin.

Barrett, James R. 1987. *Work and Community in the Jungle: Chicago's Packinghouse Workers, 1894–1922.* Urbana: University of Illinois Press.

Becker, Brian. 1987. "Concession Bargaining: The Impact on Shareholder Equity." *Industrial and Labor Relations Review* 40 (Jan.): 268–79.

Becker, Brian, and Craig Olson. 1986. "The Impact of Strikes on Shareholder Equity." *Industrial and Labor Relations Review* 39 (April): 425–38.

———. 1987. "Labor Relations and Firm Performance." In *Human Resources and the Performance of the Firm,* ed. Morris M. Kleiner et al., 43–85. Madison, Wisc.: Industrial Relations Research Association.

Bensman, David, and Roberta Lynch. 1987. *Rusted Dreams: Hard Times in a Steel Community.* New York: McGraw-Hill.

Bernstein, Aaron. 1988. "How OSHA Helped Organize the Meatpackers." *Business Week,* Aug. 29, 82.

Birch, David. 1980. *Job Creation in Cities.* Cambridge: MIT Program on Neighborhoods and Regional Change.

Birecree, Adrienne. 1984. "Decertification: A Case in Point." Ph.D. diss., University of Notre Dame.

———. 1991. "Capital Restructuring and Labour Relations: The International Paper Company Strike." *International Contributions to Labour Studies* 1: 59–86.

Bluestone, Barry, and Bennett Harrison. 1982. *The Deindustrialization of America:*

Plant Closings, Community Abandonment, and the Dismantling of Basic Industry. New York: Basic Books.

BNA. *See* Bureau of National Affairs.

Bradley, Keith, and Stephen Hill. 1987. "Quality Circles and Managerial Interests." *Industrial Relations* 26 (Winter): 68–82.

Brody, David. 1964. *The Butcher Workmen: A Study of Unionization.* Cambridge: Harvard University Press.

———. 1971. "The Expansion of the American Labor Movement: Institutional Sources of Stimulus and Restraint." In *The American Labor Movement,* ed. David Brody, 119–37. New York: Harper & Row.

Bureau of National Affairs. 1974. "Arbitrator Rules on Iowa Beef Dispute." *Daily Labor Report,* May 9, A-16.

———. 1987a. "UFCW Charges Major Meatpacker with Records Deception; Seeks OSHA Probe." *Labor Relations Week,* Jan. 28, 73.

———. 1987b. "Union Seeks Inspection at IBP Plant, Charges Hazards from Productivity Drive." *Labor Relations Week,* March 18, 253.

———. 1991. "URW Reaches Tentative Pact with Bridgestone/Firestone." *Labor Relations Week,* April 24, 380–81.

———. 1992a. "Ravenswood Board Removes Boyle as Chief Executive." *Labor Relations Week,* April 22, 398.

———. 1992b. "Rubber Workers Union Files RICO Suit Seeking $145 Million over Plant Closing." *Labor Relations Week,* Jan. 15, 58–59.

Camerer, C. 1989. "Bubbles and Fads in Asset Prices." *Journal of Economic Surveys* 3 (1): 3–41.

Carnes, Richard. 1984. "Meatpacking and Prepared Meats Industry: Above-Average Productivity Gains." *Monthly Labor Review* 107 (April): 37–42.

Clark, Gordon L. 1989. *Unions and Communities under Siege: American Communities and the Crisis of Organized Labor.* New York: Cambridge University Press.

———. 1990. "Unethical Secrets, Lies and Legal Retaliation in the Context of Corporate Restructuring in the United States." *Transactions, Institute of British Geographers* 15: 403–20.

Concerned Citizens. 1983. *An Injury to One Is an Injury to All, One Year of Our Lives: The Clinton Corn Strike, 1979–1980.* Clinton, Iowa.

Corey, Lewis. 1950. *Meat and Man: A Study of Monopoly, Unionism, and Food Policy.* New York: Viking Press.

Corporate Data Exchange. 1980. *CDE Stock Ownership Directory: Agribusiness.* New York: CDE.

Craypo, Charles. 1981. "The Decline of Union Bargaining Power." In *New Directions in Labor Economics and Industrial Relations,* ed. Michael J. Carter and William H. Leahy, 107–66. Notre Dame, Ind.: University of Notre Dame Press.

———. 1984. "The Deindustrialization of a Factory Town: Plant Closings and Phasedowns in South Bend, Indiana, 1954–1983." In *Labor and Reindustrialization: Workers and Corporate Change,* ed. Donald Kennedy, 27–67. University Park: Department of Labor Studies, Pennsylvania State University.

———. 1986. *The Economics of Collective Bargaining: Case Studies in the Private Sector.* Washington, D.C.: BNA Books.

———. 1992. "Changes in Labor Relations and the New Labor Force in U.S. Productive Systems." In *Labor Relations in a Changing Environment,* ed. Alan Gladstone et al., 297–307. New York: Walter DeGruyter.

Crouch, Mark. 1986. "Job Wars at Ft. Wayne." *Labor Research Review* 9 (Fall): 46–65.

Cumbler, John. 1989. *A Social History of Economic Decline: Business, Politics, and Work in Trenton.* New Brunswick, N.J.: Rutgers University Press.

Cummings, Scott, ed. 1988. *Business Elites and Urban Development.* Albany: State University of New York Press.

Detroit, City of. 1980. *Environmental Impact Statement: Central Industrial Park, and Cities of Detroit and Hamtramck, Michigan.* Detroit Community Economic Development Department. December.

Detroit Community Economic Development Department. 1981a. "Standard Federal Assistance Report." Submitted to the Federal Highway Administration, Department of Transportation. October.

———. 1981b. "Request for and Reservation of Program Funds: Application to the Economic Development Agency of the Department of Commerce." September.

Diesing, Paul. 1971. *Patterns of Discovery in the Social Sciences.* Chicago: Aldine-Atherton.

Doherty, Barbara. n.d. "The Struggle to Save Morse Cutting Tool." Southeastern Massachusetts University Labor Education Center, North Dartmouth. Typescript.

Eaton, Adrienne, and Paula Voos. 1991. "Unions and Contemporary Innovations in Work Organizations, Compensation, and Employee Participation." In *Unions and Economic Competitiveness,* ed. Lawrence R. Mishel and Paula Voos, 173–215. Armonk, N.Y.: M. E. Sharpe.

Fantasia, Rick. 1988. *Cultures of Solidarity.* Berkeley: University of California Press.

Fasenfest, David. 1986. "Community Politics and Urban Redevelopment." *Urban Affairs Quarterly* 22(1): 101–23.

———. 1988. "Urban Policies, Social Goals and Producer Incentives: Are Market Mechanisms and Policy Objectives Compatible?" In *Market-Based Public Policies,* ed. Richard C. Hula, 137–57. London: Macmillan.

Feekin, Lynn, and Bruce Nissen. 1991. "Early Warning against Plant Closings: Issues and Prospect." *Labor Studies Journal* 16(4): 21–33.

Filippelli, Ronald. 1990. "The Historical Context of Postwar Industrial Relations." In *U.S. Labor Relations, 1945–1989: Accommodation and Conflict,* ed. Bruce Nissen, 137–71. New York: Garland.

Fink, Gary M. 1977. "Grain Millers International Union." In *Labor Unions,* ed. Gary M. Fink, 134–35. Westport, Conn.: Greenwood Press.

Freeman, Richard B. 1986. "The Effect of the Union Wage-Differential on Management Opposition and Union Organizing Success." In *American Economic Review, Proceedings* 26 (May): 92–102.

Galbraith, John Kenneth. 1981. *A Life in Our Times: Memoirs.* Boston: Houghton Mifflin.

General Accounting Office. 1986. "HUD Review of Urban Development Action Grant to Wilmington, North Carolina." Feb.

General Motors Corporation. 1981. "Central Industrial Park Project Development Agreement between General Motors Corporation as Developer and the Central Industrial Park Project Joint Venture." April 30.

Geoghegan, Thomas. 1991. *Which Side Are You On? Trying to Be for Labor When It's Flat on Its Back.* New York: Farrar, Strauss and Giroux.

Giloth, Robert, and Robert Mier. 1986. "Democratic Populism in the USA: The Case of Playskool and Chicago." *Cities: An International Quarterly on Urban Policy,* Feb., 72–74.

Giloth, Robert, and Susan Rosenblum. 1987. "How to Fight Plant Closings." *Social Policy* 17 (Winter): 20–26.

Glickman, Norman, and Douglas Woodward. 1989. *The New Competitors.* New York: Basic Books.

Glyn, Andrew, Alan Hughes, Alain Lipietz, and Ajit Singh. 1990. "The Rise and Fall of the Golden Age." In *The Golden Age of Capitalism: Reinterpreting the Postwar Experience,* ed. Stephen A. Marglin and Juliet B. Schor, 39–125. Oxford: Clarendon Press.

Goldfield, Michael. 1987. *The Decline of Organized Labor in the United States.* Chicago: University of Chicago Press.

Goodfellow, Matthew. 1968. "Three Management Errors That Lead to Unionization." *Boxboard Containers,* Dec., 56–59.

Goodman, Robert. 1979. *The Last Entrepreneurs: America's Regional Wars for Jobs and Dollars.* New York: Simon and Schuster.

Grayson, J. Paul. 1985. *Corporate Strategy and Plant Closures: The SKF Experience.* Toronto: Our Times Publishing.

Green, Hardy. 1990. *On Strike at Hormel: The Struggle for a Democratic Labor Movement.* Philadelphia: Temple University Press.

Greenfield, Patricia A., and Julie Graham. Forthcoming. "Workers, Communities and Industrial Prosperity: An Emerging Language of Rights." *Employee Responsibilities and Rights Journal.*

Grenier, Guillermo J. 1988. "Quality Circles in a Corporate Anti-union Strategy: A Case Study." *Labor Studies Journal* 13 (Summer): 5–27.

Harrison, Bennett, and Barry Bluestone. 1988. *The Great U-Turn: Corporate Restructuring and the Polarizing of America.* New York: Basic Books.

Harrison, Bennett, and Sandra Kanter. 1978. "The Political Economy of States' Job Creation Incentives." *Journal of the American Institute of Planners* 44 (October): 424–35.

Harvey, David. 1985. *The Urbanization of Capital.* Baltimore: Johns Hopkins University Press.

Hatsopoulos, G. N., P. R. Krugman, and L. H. Summers. 1988. "U.S. Competitiveness: Beyond the Trade Deficit." *Science,* July 15, 299–307.

Hayes, Robert H., and William J. Abernathy. 1980. "Managing Our Way to Economic Decline." *Harvard Business Review* 58 (July–Aug.): 67–77.

Healy, James J., ed. 1965. *Creative Collective Bargaining: Meeting Today's Challenges to Labor-Management Relations.* Englewood Cliffs, N.J.: Prentice-Hall.

Hilke, John C., and Philip Nelson. 1987. *International Competitiveness and the Trade Deficit.* Washington, D.C.: U.S. Federal Trade Commission.

Hill, Richard Child. 1978. "At the Crossroads: The Political Economy of Postwar Detroit." *Urbanism Past and Present* 6: 2–21.

———. 1981. "Economic Crisis and Political Response in Motor City." Paper presented at the Conference on Economic Crisis and Political Response in the Auto City: Detroit and Turin, Dec. 10–13, Detroit.

Hirsh, Barry T. 1991. *Labor Unions and the Economic Performance of Firms.* Kalamazoo, Mich.: W. E. Upjohn Institute for Employment Research.

Hotz-Holt, Beat. 1988. "Comparative Research and New Technology: Modernization in Three Industrial Relations Systems." In *New Technology and Industrial Relations,* ed. Richard Hyman and Wolfgang Streeck, 61–75. London: Basil Blackwell.

Howland, Marie. 1988. *Plant Closings and Worker Displacement: The Regional Issues.* Kalamazoo, Mich.: W. E. Upjohn Institute for Employment Research.

International Management. 1979. "Zero Base Helps Rationalize Product Strategy." Feb., 38–41.

Iowa Beef Processors, Inc., and Local 222, Meat Cutters, AFL-CIO. 1976. 226 NLRB No. 210.

Jarley, Paul, and Cheryl Maranto. 1990. "Union Corporate Campaigns: An Assessment." *Industrial and Labor Relations Review* 43 (July): 505–24.

———. 1991. "Strategic Implications of Union Corporate Campaigns." In *Proceedings of the Forty-third Annual Meetings of the Industrial Relations Research Association,* 85–95. Madison: Industrial Relations Research Association.

Jeszeck, Charles. 1982. "Plant Dispersion and Collective Bargaining in the Rubber Tire Industry." Ph.D. diss., University of California, Berkeley.

———. 1986. "Structural Changes in Collective Bargaining: The U.S. Tire Industry." *Industrial Relations* 25 (Fall): 229–47.

Jones, Gareth Stedman. 1971. *Outcast London: A Study in the Relationship between Classes in Victorian Society.* New York: Pantheon.

Karier, Thomas. 1992. "Trade Deficits and Labor Unions: Myths and Realities." In *Unions and Economic Competitiveness,* ed. Lawrence R. Mishel and Paula Voos, 15–39. Armonk, N.Y.: M. E. Sharpe.

Kelley, Maryellen R., and Bennett Harrison. 1992. "Unions, Technology, and Labor-Management Cooperation." In *Unions and Economic Competitiveness,* ed. Lawrence R. Mishel and Paula Voos, 247–86. Armonk, N.Y.: M. E. Sharpe.

Knoke, William, and William Albrecht. 1970. "Economics of the Sweetener Industry." *MSU Business Topics* 18 (Winter): 43–48.

Kochan, Thomas A., Harry C. Katz, and Robert B. McKersie. 1986. *The Transformation of American Industrial Relations.* New York: Basic Books.

Kuhn, James W. 1961. *Bargaining in Grievance Settlement: The Power of Industrial Work Groups.* New York: Columbia University Press.

Lawrence, Robert Z. 1984. *Can America Compete?* Washington, D.C.: Brookings Institution.

LeRoy, Greg, Dan Swinney, and Elaine Charpentier. 1986. "Early Warning Manual against Plant Closings." Working Paper no. 2. Chicago: Midwest Center for Labor Research.

Lever-Tracy, C. 1990. "Fordism Transformed? Employee Involvement and Workplace Industrial Relations at Ford." *Journal of Industrial Relations* 32 (June): 179–96.

Lewin, D. 1987. "Industrial Relations as a Strategic Variable." In *Human Resources and the Performance of the Firm,* ed. Morris M. Kleiner et al., 1–41. Madison: Industrial Relations Research Association.

Lindblom, Charles E. 1982. "The Market as a Prison," *Journal of Politics* 44 (May): 324–36.

Linneman, Peter D., and Michael L. Wachter. 1986. "Rising Union Premiums and the Declining Boundaries among Noncompeting Groups." *American Economic Review, Proceedings* 76 (May): 103–8.

Little, Arthur D., 1985. "Reuse of the Blaw-Knox Castings and Machining Mill." Unpublished report. June.

Logan, John R., and Harvey L. Molotch. 1987. *Urban Fortunes: The Political Economy of Place.* Berkeley: University of California Press.

Lorenz, Edward H. 1992. "Trust, Cooperation and Flexibility: A Framework for International Comparisons." *Industrial Relations* 31 (Fall): 455–72.

Magaziner, Ira C., and Robert B. Reich. 1982. *Minding America's Business: The Decline and Rise of the American Economy.* New York: Vintage Books.

Mann, Eric. 1987. *Taking on General Motors: A Case Study of the Campaign to Keep GM Van Nuys Open.* Los Angeles: Institute of Industrial Relations, University of California.

Markusen, Ann R. 1985. *Profit Cycles, Oligopoly, and Regional Development.* Cambridge: MIT Press.

———. 1987. *Regions: The Economics and Politics of Territory.* Totowa, N.J.: Roman & Littlefield.

Markusen, Ann R., and Virginia Carlson. 1989. "Deindustrialization in the American Midwest: Causes and Responses." In *Deindustrialization and Regional Economic Transformation: The Experience of the United States,* ed. Lloyd Rodwin and Hidehiko Sazanami, 29–59. Boston: Unwin Hyman.

Marlin, Matthew. 1986. "Reevaluating the Benefits and Costs of Industrial Revenue Bonds." *Urban Affairs Quarterly* 21: 435–41.

Marshall, F. Ray. 1987. *Unheard Voices: Labor and Economic Policy in a Competitive World.* New York: Basic Books.

———. 1992. "Work Organization, Unions, and Economic Performance." In *Unions and Economic Competitiveness,* ed. Lawrence R. Mishel and Paula Voos, 287–315. Armonk, N.Y.: M. E. Sharpe.

Midwest Center for Labor Research. 1987. "Partial Shutdown of Diamond Tool and Horseshoe Company: Analysis, Outlook, and Options for Public Intervention." Report prepared for Directly Affiliated Local Union 18650. June.

Milling and Baking News. 1974. "Standard Brands Up to New Records in 1973 for 18th Year." Feb. 5.

Mishel, Lawrence R. 1985. "Strengths and Limits of Non-Workplace Strategies." *Labor Research Review* 7 (Fall): 69–70.

Mishel, Lawrence R., and David M. Frankel. 1991. *The State of Working America.* Armonk, N.Y.: M. E. Sharpe.

Mishel, Lawrence R., and Paula Voos. 1992. *Unions and Economic Competitiveness.* Armonk, N.Y.: M. E. Sharpe.

Moberg, David. 1986. "Hooked on Tanks." *Progressive,* Sept., 30–32.

Mollenkopf, John H. 1983. *The Contested City.* Princeton: Princeton University Press.

Moody, Kim. 1988. *An Injury to All: The Decline of American Unionism.* New York: Verso Press.

Moody's Industrial Manual. 1979. "SBI: Profile." New York: Moody's Investors Services, Inc. 4060–61.

Moore, Thomas. 1985. "Let's Get Stingy with Business and City Halls." *Fortune,* April 1, 120–24.

Moore, Thomas, and Gregory Squires. 1988. "Public Policy and Private Benefits: The Case of Industrial Revenue Bonds." In *Business Elites and Urban Development,* ed. Scott Cummings, 97–117. Albany: State University of New York Press.

Moskowitz, Milton, Michael Katz, and Robert Levering, eds. 1980. *Everybody's Business: The Irreverent Guide to Corporate America.* San Francisco: Harper & Row.

Nader, Ralph, and William Taylor. 1986. *The Big Boys: Power and Position in American Business.* New York: Pantheon.

Nash, June C. 1989. *From Tank Town to High Tech: The Clash of Community and Industrial Cycles.* Albany: State University of New York Press.

Nay, Leslie. 1991. "The Determinants of Concession Bargaining in the Airline Industry." *Industrial and Labor Relations Review* 44 (Jan.): 307–23.

Nissen, Bruce. 1990a. "Union Battles against Plant Closings: Case Study Evidence and Policy Implications." *Policy Studies Journal* 18 (Winter): 382–95.

———, ed. 1990b. *U.S. Labor Relations, 1945–1989: Accommodation and Conflict.* New York: Garland.

Nissen, Bruce, and Lynn Feekin. 1992. "For the Public Good: Calumet Project Organizes for Labor and Community–Based Economic Development." *Labor Research Review* 19 (Fall): 15–29.

Northrup, Herbert. 1989. "From Union Hegemony to Union Disintegration: Collective Bargaining in Cement and Related Industries." *Journal of Labor Research* 10 (Fall): 337–76.

O'Connor, James. 1973. *The Fiscal Crisis of the State.* New York: St. Martin's Press.

Olson, Craig, and Brian Becker. 1990. "The Effects of the NLRA on Stockholder Wealth in the 1930s." *Industrial and Labor Relations Review* 44 (Oct.): 116–29.

Ozanne, Robert W. 1967. *A Century of Labor-Management Relations at McCormick and International Harvester.* Madison: University of Wisconsin Press.

Parker, Mike. 1985. *Inside the Circle: A Union Guide to QWL.* Boston: South End Press.

Pascarella, Thomas A. 1986. "Rejoinder to Matthew Marlin." *Urban Affairs Quarterly* 21: 443–47.

Pascarella, Thomas A., and Richard D. Raymond. 1982. "Buying Bonds for Business: An Evaluation of the Industrial Revenue Bond Program." *Urban Affairs Quarterly* 18: 73–89.

Perrucci, Carolyn C., Robert Perrucci, Dena B. Targ, and Harry R. Targ. 1988. *Plant Closings: International Context and Social Costs.* New York: Aldine de Gruyter.

Perry, Charles R., and Delwyn H. Kegley. 1989. *Disintegration and Change: Labor Relations in the Meat Packing Industry.* Philadelphia: Industrial Relations Unit, Wharton School, University of Pennsylvania.

Peterson, Paul E., ed. 1985. *The New Urban Reality.* Washington, D.C.: Brookings Institution.

Piore, Michael J., and Charles F. Sabel. 1984. *The Second Industrial Divide: Possibilities for Prosperity.* New York: Basic Books.

Portz, John. 1990. *The Politics of Plant Closings.* Lawrence: University Press of Kansas.

Prosten, Jesse. 1977. "IBP in Poor Position to Defend Its Actions." *Butcher Workman* 63 (April): 20.

Ragin, Charles C. 1987. *The Comparative Method: Moving Beyond Qualitative and Quantitative Strategies.* Berkeley: University of California Press.

Ranney, David. 1988. "Manufacturing Job Loss and Early Warning Indicators." *Journal of Planning Literature* 3 (Winter): 22–35.

Rinehart, James. 1984. "Appropriating Workers' Knowledge: Quality Control Circles at a General Motors Plant." *Studies in Political Economy* 14 (Summer): 75–97.

Roberts, Harold S. 1944. *The Rubber Workers: Labor Organization and Collective Bargaining in the Rubber Industry.* New York: Harper.

Ruback, Richard S., and Martin B. Zimmerman. 1984. "Unionization and Profitability: Evidence from the Capital Market." *Journal of Political Economy* 92 (Dec.): 1134–57.

Rubin, George. 1988. "A Review of Collective Bargaining in 1987." *Monthly Labor Review* 111 (Jan.): 24–37.

Russo, John. 1986. "Saturn's Rings: What GM's Saturn Project Is Really About." *Labor Research Review* 9 (Fall): 67–77.

Salter, W.E.G. 1960. *Productivity and Technical Change.* Cambridge: Cambridge University Press.

Sawers, Larry, and William K. Tabb. 1984. *Sunbelt/Snowbelt: Urban Redevelopment and Regional Restructuring.* New York: Oxford University Press.

Schleifer, Andre, and Lawrence W. Summers. 1988. "Breach of Trust in Hostile Takeovers." In *Corporate Takeovers: Causes and Consequences,* ed. Alan J. Auerbach, 33–56. Chicago: University of Chicago Press.

Schneirov, R. n.d. "Haymarket and the New Political History Reconsidered: Workers' Class Presence in Chicago's Municipal Politics, 1873–1894." Typescript.

Schumpeter, Joseph Alois. 1962. *Capitalism, Socialism, and Democracy.* 3d ed. New York: Harper & Row.

Sengenberger, Werner. 1990. "The Role of Labour Standards in Industrial Restructuring: Participation, Protection and Promotion." Discussion Papers in the New Industrial Organization Program. Geneva: International Institute for Labor Studies, International Labor Organization.

Singh, Ajit. Forthcoming. "Regulation of Mergers." In *Regulation as an Industrial Strategy,* ed. Roger Sugden. New York: Routledge.

Skaggs, Jimmy M. 1986. *Prime Cut: Livestock Raising and Meatpacking in the United States, 1607–1983.* College Station: Texas A&M University Press.

Swanstrom, Todd. 1985. *The Crisis of Growth Politics: Cleveland, Kucinich, and the Challenge of Urban Populism.* Philadelphia: Temple University Press.

Thomas, Steven L., and Morris M. Kleiner. 1992. "The Effects of Two-Tier Collective Bargaining Agreements on Shareholders Equity." *Industrial and Labor Relations Review* 45 (Jan.): 399–51.

Tinstman, Dale C., and Robert L. Peterson. 1981. *Iowa Beef Processors, Inc.: An Entire Industry Revolutionized!* New York: Newcomen Society.

U.S. Congress. House. 1986. *Hearing before the Subcommittee on Housing and Community Development, Committee on Banking, Finance and Urban Affairs.* 99th Cong., 2d sess.

———. House. Committee on Government Operations. 1987. *Underreporting of Occupational Injuries and Its Impact on Workers' Safety.* Pts. 1, 2, and 3. 100th Cong., 1st sess.

———. 1988. *Here's the Beef: Underreporting of Injuries. OSHA's Policy of Exempting*

Companies from Programmed Inspection Based on Injury Records and Unsafe Conditions in the Meatpacking Industry. 100th Cong., 2d sess.

U.S. Department of Commerce. 1971. *Industrial Outlook 1971.* Washington, D.C.: GPO. Jan.

U.S. Department of Labor. Bureau of Labor Statistics. 1982. *Technology and Labor in Four Industries.* Bulletin no. 2104. Jan.

———. 1988. *Industry Wage Survey: Iron and Steel Foundries, October 1986.* Bulletin no. 2291. Feb.

U.S. Securities and Exchange Commission. 1979. 10-K filing, SBI.

———. 1985. 10-K filing, Amhoist.

———. 1986. 10-K filing, B. F. Goodrich.

Viani, Laura. 1990. "Steelworker Union Seeks Info on LaSalle's Plans for Its Grinding Department." *American Metal Markets/Metalworking News,* Dec. 10, 2, 7.

Way, Philip. 1987. "American Enterprise in a Time of Change: Implications for Industrial Relations." In *Proceedings of the Thirty-ninth Annual Meetings of the Industrial Relations Research Association,* 183–90. Madison: Industrial Relations Research Association.

Wilber, Charles, and Robert S. Harrison. 1978. "The Methodological Basis of Institutional Economics: Pattern Model, Storytelling and Holism." *Journal of Economic Issues* 12 (March): 61–89.

Wilentz, Sean. 1984. *Chants Democratic: New York City and the Rise of the American Working Class, 1788–1850.* New York: Oxford University Press.

Wilkinson, Frank. 1983a. "Productive Systems." *Cambridge Journal of Economics* 7 (Sept.–Dec.): 413–29.

———. 1983b. *The Dynamics of Labour Market Segmentation.* New York: Academic Press.

Williams, Willard F., and Thomas T. Stout. 1964. *Economics of the Livestock-Meat Industry.* New York: Macmillan.

Wylie, Jeanie. 1989. *Poletown: Community Betrayed.* Champaign: University of Illinois Press.

Yago, Glenn, et al. 1984. "Investment and Divestment in New York, 1960–80." *Annals of the American Academy of Political and Social Science* (September): 28–38.

Yeager, Mary. 1981. *Competition and Regulation: The Development of Oligopoly in the Meat Packing Industry.* Greenwich, Conn.: JAI Press.

About the Contributors

Adrienne M. Birecree is an assistant professor of economics at Radford University. She received her Ph.D. in economics from the University of Notre Dame. Her publications include case studies on the effects of corporate restructuring on labor relations in the domestic paper industry in the 1980s. Currently she is studying the impact of restructuring in bituminous coal during the same period.

Charles Craypo is a professor in and the chair of the Department of Economics at the University of Notre Dame. He has also been on the faculties of Michigan State, Pennsylvania State, and Cornell universities. His graduate degrees, in economics, are from Michigan State University. His journal and book publications focus on unions and collective bargaining in the United States. Currently he is gathering empirical information on low-wage workers in South Bend, Indiana, and completing an institutional study of changing labor relations in the meatpacking industry.

Gene Daniels is the district environmental coordinator for the United Brotherhood of Carpenters and Joiners' Health and Safety Fund. He is the coauthor of two guides for union leaders. Daniels has an M.A. in industrial relations from the University of Minnesota.

David Fasenfest, who holds an M.A. in economics and an M.A. and Ph.D. in sociology from the University of Michigan, is on the faculty of the Department of Sociology and Anthropology at Purdue University. He has served as the director of urban and economic development research in the Urban Research Institute of the University of Louisville and has published articles in *Urban Affairs Quarterly*, the *Journal of Urban Affairs*, and *Economic*

Development Quarterly. He is the editor of *Community Economic Development: Policy Formation in the U.S. and U.K.* and the author of a forthcoming book, *Income Stories: A Decade of Rising Income Inequality*. His research projects include an analysis of the politics of community displacement and infrastructure development.

CHARLES JESZECK is a senior labor economist in the Human Resources Division of the U.S. General Accounting Office. He received his Ph.D. in economics from the University of California at Berkeley in 1982 and later served as research director for the California AFL-CIO and as assistant research director for the Service Employees' International Union. He has been a visiting faculty member at Barnard College and the University of Massachusetts, Amherst. Jeszeck is the author of journal articles and government reports on collective bargaining in the domestic tire industry, unemployment insurance, occupational safety and health, and enforcement of the Fair Labor Standards Act. Currently he is researching and writing on demographic changes in the U.S. school-age population.

KEITH KNAUSS is a professor of labor studies in the Division of Labor Studies in the School of Continuing Studies at Indiana University at South Bend. He has served as northern region coordinator for labor studies at the South Bend campus since 1972. Knauss holds an M.A. in industrial relations from the University of Minnesota. He and Michael Matuszak have co-authored articles on labor studies and labor education in the United States and on employers' use of cell-manufacturing processes in operating nonunion. Their ongoing work concerns the nature and impact of union avoidance strategies and the interaction between antiunion corporate culture and quality improvement programs.

MICHAEL MATUSZAK is a labor education specialist at the Center for Labor Education and Research at the University of Kentucky. Until 1983 he was a member of and held various offices in UAW 590 at the now-closed Torrington/Ingersoll Rand heavy bearings plant. He has an M.A. in general studies from Roosevelt University in Chicago and is completing a Ph.D. in sociology at the University of Kentucky.

BRUCE NISSEN is an associate professor of labor studies at Indiana University Northwest in Gary and a board member of the Calumet Project for Industrial Jobs. He is the editor of *U.S. Labor Relations, 1945–1989: Accommodation and Conflict* and co-editor of *Theories of the Labor Movement*. He has also written journal articles and chapters of books on employee involvement, labor education, enterprise zones, and labor-community coalitions. Currently he is completing a book on plant-closing experiences in northwest Indiana in the period from 1984 to 1992.

DAVID C. RANNEY is an associate professor in the School of Urban Planning and Policy and the Center for Urban Economic Development at the University of Illinois at Chicago. He received his M.A. and Ph.D. from Syracuse University. Currently he is doing research on the impact of transnational investments on the loss of manufacturing jobs in Chicago.

Index